HOLLYWOOD DIVAS, INDIE QUEENS, AND TV HEROINES

Hollywood Divas, Indie Queens, and TV Heroines

Contemporary Screen Images of Women

Susanne Kord and Elisabeth Krimmer

ROWMAN & LITTLEFIELD PUBLISHERS, INC.
Lanham • Boulder • New York • Toronto • Oxford

ROWMAN & LITTLEFIELD PUBLISHERS, INC.

Published in the United States of America
by Rowman & Littlefield Publishers, Inc.
A wholly owned subsidiary of The Rowman & Littlefield Publishing Group, Inc.
4501 Forbes Boulevard, Suite 200, Lanham, MD 20706
www.rowmanlittlefield.com

P.O. Box 317, Oxford OX2 9RU, UK

British Library Cataloguing in Publication Information Available

Library of Congress Cataloging-in-Publication Data

Kord, Susanne.
  Hollywood divas, indie queens, and tv heroines / Contemporary screen images of
women / Susanne Kord and Elisabeth Krimmer.
     p. cm.
  Includes bibliographical references and index.
  ISBN 0-7425-3708-0 (alk. paper) — ISBN 0-7425-3709-9 (pbk. : alk. paper)
  1. Women in motion pictures. 2. Motion pictures—United States. I. Krimmer,
Elisabeth, 1967– II. Title.

PN1995.9.W6K597 2005
791.43'6522'0973—dc22

2005012963

Printed in the United States of America

♾™ The paper used in this publication meets the minimum requirements of
American National Standard for Information Sciences—Permanence of Paper
for Printed Library Materials, ANSI/NISO Z39.48-1992.
Manufactured in the United States of America.

Contents

☆ 1 ☆

HOLLYWOOD

In 1988, Jodie Foster received an Academy Award for her portrayal of a victim of gang rape in *The Accused*. In 1997, Kim Basinger was awarded an Oscar for playing a prostitute in *L.A. Confidential*. In 1995, Mira Sorvino joined the list of hookers with a statue of gold for her portrayal of a prostitute in *Mighty Aphrodite*. *Pretty Woman* (1990), the story of an L.A. whore qua Cinderella, established Julia Roberts as a force to be reckoned with and earned a total U.S. gross of $178,406,268. In *Striptease* (1996), Demi Moore's character makes a living as a topless dancer in a sleazy nightclub. Julianne Moore appears as a porn star in *Boogie Nights* (1997) and as a kept woman in *Magnolia* (1999). Who says there are no roles for women in Hollywood?[1]

A survey of recently published books on women in Hollywood reveals an impressive list of studies on actresses of the 1930s and 1940s but hardly anything on the most recent crop of female heroes. Most discussions of the actresses who define femininity for the 1990s and early 2000s remain relegated to gossip columns and perfunctory movie reviews. It is the purpose of this book to fill this gap. Our readings of over thirty films with female stars take a critical look at the kinds of female role models that populate the most recent products of the Hollywood dream machine. Such an analysis is crucial because popular film holds sway over our collective imagination like no other cultural artifact. The female characters who illuminate the screens of our movie houses not only reflect and perpetuate the status and options of women in today's society but also play an active part in creating new female role models.[2] They show us what we are, what we were, and what we could, should, or (do not) want to be. When at their best, movies give birth to new visions of female strength and freedom. At their worst, movies ridicule, denigrate, deny what real women have long achieved, and re-place it with specters from the past. Most commonly, however, Hollywood movies present an uneven mixture of both. They take away with one hand what they give with the other. The commercial pressures that influence today's film industry mandate production for mass audiences and thus tend to favor films that offer a little something for everybody. In numerous movies, reactionary female stereotypes are paired with progressive and remarkable women characters.

The movies and actresses discussed in this book were selected according to a variety of criteria. For the most part, we focus on films whose substantial success at the box office proves that they strike a chord in the collective imagination. But we have also included some films and performers who, in our opinion, have not received the attention they deserve. There are numerous other actresses who merit mention but have been excluded largely due to confinements of space. A discussion of Penélope Cruz, Cameron Diaz, Catherine Zeta-Jones, Elisabeth Shue, Drew Barrymore, Cate Blanchett, Juliette Binoche, Alicia Silverstone, Charlize Theron, Christina Ricci, Kate Winslet, or Kate Beckinsale would have offered interesting insights but far exceeds the scope of this project. There are some other, even more apparent omissions, of great movies as well as great ac-tresses: where, the reader might ask, is our discussion of Susan Sarandon, Michelle Pfeiffer, Jodie Foster, Nicole Kidman, Meryl Streep, Jennifer Lopez, or Helen Hunt? Each of these actresses would seem deserving of her own chapter, and it could certainly be argued that each of them had a cultural impact as great as the four we chose to include. To us, the most important criterion was the question whether an actress was "in" at the moment and had been "in" through-out the 1990s. "In" and "out" in Hollywood are, of course, highly unstable cat-egories: nothing changes more quickly than the status of a Hollywood actor—particularly if the actor in question is female. Were we to begin planning this book today, in 2004, Nicole Kidman would surely have been a "chapter woman." As it was, all four of the women we selected had higher status and vis-ibility than Kidman when we began to conceptualize this book in the 1990s. For this very reason, it was important to us to include only women who had more than one or two hits during that decade but who had a steady career of block-busters throughout the 1990s—a criterion that would apply to all of our four fi-nalists but not, for example, to great actresses like Sarandon, Streep, Foster, or Hunt.[3] Assessments of an actress's talent, the quality of her acting, or her im-portance in the "high" cultural sense (such as continued critical success in venues like the *New York Times*) also had no influence on our decision to include or omit her. In each case, we are interested in types and characters and what they mean for us as viewers, not in the lives and personalities of individual stars. Although we know that the star personality offscreen may be as much a performance as the on-screen persona, we do not concern ourselves with the actresses' biographies or gossip about their lives.[4] Thus our ultimate selection was determined to a far greater extent by the actress's *screen persona* than by her offscreen personality, cultural importance, or assessments of her achievements.[5]

Past literature on women and Hollywood film has tended to either glorify or condemn specific eras in movie history. The pre-Code era of the 1920s, for example, is frequently hailed as the decade of socially and sexually liberated women in the movies.[6] The screwball heroines of the 1930s are considered to be feisty, fun-loving, and headstrong models of femininity. Even the female victims of the 1940s and 1950s melodramas, although subjugated in the end, are often seen as images of emancipation. The films of the Hollywood Renaissance of the 1960s and 1970s have been interpreted as icons of social experimentation influenced by the civil rights movement, 1970s feminism, and flower-power culture or, alternately, as fantasies that insult us with "the worst—the most abused, neglected, and dehumanized—screen heroines in film history."[7] Women of the 1980s were given a choice between the demonic and hysterical wife-murdering, bunny-cooking mistress of *Fatal Attraction* and the high-powered business woman turned provincial mom of *Baby Boom*.[8] So what were the 1990s all about? Had we finally overcome the eras of celluloid stereotyping, victimization, or demonization, or were female moviegoers of the 1990s facing another cultural backlash?[9]

Our answer is as resolutely noncommittal as the movies themselves. Unlike much of the existing film literature, which frequently reviles recent film as conservative, reactionary, or apolitical, we believe that these movies offer a ragbag of contradictory messages.[10] The current conditions of movie production and distribution do not favor a specific political stance but result in films that try to incorporate the progressive as well as the conventional. Always seeking "a point of comfort" for as many viewers as possible, entertainment holds steady in the middle of the road.[11]

PRODUCTION AND DISTRIBUTION SINCE 1990

If anything can be claimed about Hollywood films since the 1990s, it is this: Hollywood movies have become *big*—big budgets, big spectacles, big stars, big releases, big corporations, and big mergers.[12] The numbers speak a clear language: the average advertising budget for a feature film increased from $3.54 million in 1980 to $24 million in 2000.[13] Production costs have skyrocketed from an average of $2 million in 1972 to between $80–100 million, at an average of $90 million.[14] It stands to reason that films of this scale need to recoup costs and that, in order to do so, they must appeal to as large an audience as possible. Although individual artistic visions still play a part in the making of Hollywood movies, they are undoubtedly trumped by the bottom line—making good on initial investments, and if possible making a profit, is the Hollywood film's main job. Instead of producing different films for various target groups, each Hollywood film has to cater to different audiences simultaneously, offering something for everyone. Hence the recent trend toward genre benders, such as horror-comedies or action-romances; hence the inclination to avoid explicit political commitment.[15] This has an effect on the portrayal of women in movies, as well: Hollywood heroines are designed to appeal to both the stay-at-home mom and the high-powered female executive, to the traditionalist and feminist alike. When transferred from the real world to celluloid, neither type rules the screen; rather, both appear in curiously watered-down form.

Moreover, the distinction between traditional Hollywood, often seen as "conservative," and independent film production, often interpreted as taking a more progressive stance, is blurring. Having realized that nonmainstream films can turn a significant profit, major studios have begun to acquire indie films. Thus it is not correct to claim that mainstream Hollywood products are necessarily conservative: whenever "it becomes commercial to take an unconventional viewpoint or to verge into experimental forms," studios are happy to do so.[16]

Agency, when applied to individual actors, is equally ambivalent. On the one hand, major stars wield far more power than they did in the studio system of the 1930s where actors, as employees under contract, had to conform to studio expectations. The trend toward packaging, that is, presenting a ready-made package consisting of director, actor(s), and script that the studio then finances, increases the power of individual players vis-à-vis the studio.[17] As the performance of a movie on the opening weekend has a determining influence on the financial take through secondary markets such as video and franchising, a star's ability to open a movie has become crucial. But although these factors augment a star's clout, other trends have a limiting impact. Studios lower their financial risk by backing presold products, that is, "adaptations of products known in other forms," such as sequels, series, remakes, and films based on video games or blockbuster books.[18] One form of preselling is typecasting: stars who have once been successful tend to reappear as the same character in a different movie. Meg Ryan, for example, has played a drug addict and a helicopter pilot but will forever be known as the Queen of Romantic Comedy.

To say that Hollywood films are not inherently conservative is not to say that there is no sexism in the industry. The highest-grossing film of all time, *Titanic*, with a smashing profit of $600 million, owes its overwhelming success to repeat visits by young women.[19] Thus one might expect that more blockbusters would attempt to target women viewers. This, however, is not the case: the average blockbuster caters to a predominantly male audience. Given this contradiction, one could reasonably wonder whether the economic calculations of studio bosses are taking a backseat to unquestioned gender expectations.

The decisive importance of income from secondary sources, such as videos, video games, franchising, and distribution to overseas markets, is also an established fact in film literature. But there is no research on the gender-specific implications of this fact. Film genres are gender specific, and because some genres, such as romantic comedies, do not lend themselves to franchising in the same way action films do, women's films are likely to be less profitable and therefore also likely to receive less financial backing. There is a theme park for *Waterworld*, but there is no *Pretty Woman* theme park where interested fans can go shopping on Rodeo Drive or drive Edward's luxury sports car; there is a video game for *Terminator*, but there is no corresponding product for *Runaway Bride* where players could try their own skills at hair-dyeing. Lara Croft holds her own as the sole female action figure, but can we imagine a similar figurine of Kathleen Kelly, proud owner of an independent bookstore in *You've Got Mail*?

WE, THE AUDIENCE, OR, WHO WATCHES THIS STUFF?

In writing this book, we have made the following assumptions: Hollywood movies, like all manifestations of culture, are ideological—not in the sense that they force people to see things in a certain way but, rather, in the sense that they produce in people the tendency to do so.[20] Hollywood movies, like all cultural artifacts, offer to "constitute not only the sense of the world for us, but also our sense of ourselves, our sense of identity, and our sense of our relations to other people and to society in general."[21] But that does not necessarily mean that the ideological offer implied in a movie will be accepted by all (or even most) viewers, or by all viewers at all times, or by all viewers in the same way. A prime example for this would be the many different ways in which Madonna's image has been seen.[22] The traditional media and religious fundamentalists have condemned her as advocating promiscuity—as Madonna, the tart. Feminists have objected to her sexually submissive postures in videos—Madonna, the agent of patriarchy. Madonna's fans see her as flouting patriarchy and taking charge of her own sexuality—Madonna, the liberator. Cultural studies writers have seen her as parodying conventional representations of women and liberating cultural artifacts, from lipstick to crucifixes, from their original and ossified contexts—Madonna, the cultural critic and strategic resister. All of these interpretations are perfectly defensible, depending on who is watching.

The second assumption that guides our analysis follows logically from the first: although Hollywood is ideological, there are many ways in which viewers may respond to the ideologies packaged in the movies. According to Stuart Hall, there are three general ways in which people can "read" cultural (which is to say, ideological) texts: the dominant, the negotiated, and the oppositional reading.[23] A dominant reader will simply agree; an oppositional reader will completely oppose. Negotiating readers accept a part of whatever ideology is on offer and adapt it to their own situations; they take what is there and try to make sense of it for themselves. It is reasonable to assume that most movie audiences consist largely of "negotiating" viewers and that both "dominant" and "oppositional" viewers are comparatively rare. It goes without saying that the Hollywood movie machine has a stake in creating a largely "dominant" audience. This is not a conspiracy theory: Hollywood is not a sinister conglomerate *intending* to coerce audiences into agreement with backward views of women. Rather, the production and marketing of Hollywood films are guided by the notion of an implicit audience. Hollywood has a rather specific view of Joe and Jane Moviegoer. All major studios spend millions of dollars each year on market research trying to predict what Joe and Jane want to see. Thus, whenever we use the majestic plural, the "We" of the audience, in our analyses, we are referencing the concept of an implied audience—well aware that the actual audiences of Hollywood productions are both more diverse and less predictable than marketing research may assume.

The many different ways in which the audience may read a movie create a continuous need for the Hollywood movie machine to "woo" the audience, to convince the skeptics, to win and rewin their consent to the images it presents.[24] This, in turn, means that Hollywood must strive to present "mixed messages," that is, ideologies flexible enough to appeal to a large audience consisting mostly of "negotiating" viewers. A blockbuster must allow for a lot of mental wiggling room, and of course it cannot *look* like ideology. It is this inherent contradiction that makes women's roles in Hollywood movies such a fascinating topic. The portrayal of gender in film is a cultural offer to real-live women in the audience, and the way gender is packaged reflects both Hollywood's desire to have women respond as "dominant" viewers and its awareness that most will "negotiate" the messages they are given into something else.

THE INVISIBLE WOMAN? WOMEN IN THE 1990s

Because this book is concerned with the representation of women in film from 1990 to 2003, it is only natural that our analysis would be informed by our knowledge of the actual political, economic, educational, and familial status of women in U.S. society from 1990 to 2003. Of course, we are acutely aware that Hollywood movies do not and are not intended to provide an accurate picture of society. Nevertheless, let us imagine, for a few crazy minutes, a Hollywood that is both socially and politically conscious.[25] Let us further fantasize that Hollywood movies, intent on changing women's lives for the better, strive to present the challenges and problems of today's women. If such a cinema were reality, what could we expect to see?

The first blockbuster in this New Hollywood would be a melodrama entitled *Born to Be Poor*. It would star Nicole Kidman as Laura Clary, a single mother of two who works in the garden tools department at Wal-Mart. Laura, a typical example of woman's economically disadvantaged status in the U.S. economy—according to the Census of 2000, women in the United States are still more likely to be poor and families headed by a woman with no husband are in a particularly precarious position—is barely getting by.[26] When the epileptic spasms of her handicapped daughter Hope (Christina Ricci) get worse, Laura, who has no medical insurance, appeals to the mercy of Dr. Brad Leitberger (Matthew McConaughey). Brad, a well-meaning but not particularly talented surgeon, approaches his ex-wife Lindsay (Jodie Foster), the only female brain surgeon in the United States, who, in spite of twenty years of professional experience, still makes considerably less than Brad. To be precise, Lindsay, like the average American woman working full time, makes 27 percent less than a man with comparable degrees and training.[27] Moreover, Lindsay, whose first and only child, Nathan, was born when she was thirty-eight, still resents Brad. Although Lindsay cannot forgive Brad for his consistent refusal to share child care and household responsibilities, which led not only to their divorce but to Lindsay's decision not to remarry, she makes an effort to overcome their differences when she hears of Laura's desperate situation. So as to be able to operate immediately, Lindsay calls her Cuban nanny Luz (Salma Hayek), who has been taking care of Nathan for the past six months. Unfortunately, Luz's recent visa application was denied, and she is being repatriated to Havana. Both Laura and Lindsay use all their combined charm to work on Brad to take care of his son while Lindsay operates on Hope. Brad relents, the surgery is successful, and a grateful Laura marries Brad to the sound of Bryan Adams's "Everything I Do, I Do It for You."

The only movie able to top the triumphant box office success of *Born to Be Poor* would be a political thriller entitled *Terms of Estrangement*. It stars Whoopi Goldberg as Penelope Walker. Penelope grew up in the Brooklyn projects. Penelope's younger sister Marilyn is a single mother of two who works as a maid at a downscale motel for $5.15 per hour; her older brother Jake is in prison for a narcotics violation; only Penelope herself managed to go to college. With a newly minted degree in law and a healthy share of idealism, Penelope decides to enter the field of politics. Because of her firsthand experience with the living conditions in the projects, which might best be described as Third World pockets in the United States, Penelope feels particularly passionate about health care for all Americans and decides to work for Thelma Spence (Susan Sarandon), wife of President Dick Spence (Richard Gere). Penelope wants to help Thelma minimize the health disparities between white and black Americans (for white males, the life expectancy is 73.8 years, as opposed to 66.4 for black males). Unfortunately, Thelma's plans soon meet with the disapproval of the Republican members of Congress. A fatal combination of character flaws—Thelma is both intelligent and outspoken—leads to the downfall of the First Lady and all her reform plans. Although Thelma was soon to garner public sympathy en masse for standing by her man during Dick's affair with Kimberly Sparks (Cameron Diaz), the overhaul of the American health care system was abandoned.

Disappointed with her political experience, Penelope accepts a job at an elite university on the West Coast, where she meets Allegra Corn (Oprah Winfrey). Penelope is vastly impressed with Allegra, and the two women become friends. Penelope attends Allegra's piano concerts and accompanies Allegra, formerly the head of a large oil company, to the christening of a supertanker in her honor.[28] They get along wonderfully until Penelope asks Allegra to help her improve the situation of black students and scholars. Allegra, who believes that talented individuals do not need the crutch of affirmative action, refuses flat out. The day Penelope is denied tenure, Allegra, who has chosen to throw in her lot with that of the Republican candidate, Wyne Port (Jack Nicholson), leaves for Washington. The last scene shows Penelope on a ship bound for Sweden to the sounds of Barbra Streisand's "A Piece of Sky."

It is pretty obvious that scripts such as these would not be turned into Hollywood movies. Poverty and racial discrimination are not exactly blockbuster material. Health care and affirmative action are too controversial and complex to form the subject of a glitzy film. Moreover, though Hollywood movies do not often occupy themselves with political issues, the rare examples that do depict larger social and political topics tend to bypass "women's" issues. For example, *The Insider* (1999) paints a picture of corporate corruption in the tobacco industry, but there are no comparable films that deal with the difficulties of finding suitable child care. There are many movies that offer glimpses into the periphery of society, ranging from drug dealing to petty crime, but the fringe world of the working poor, most of whom are women, remains invisible in mainstream Hollywood film. In fact, what is absent in these movies is often more telling than what we do see. Consequently, any analysis of the portrayal of women in Hollywood film faces a dual challenge: it must be as concerned with that which is not represented as it is with interpreting individual films. In order to understand what we are watching, we have to learn to see what is not there. It is only when we fill in the gaps that we begin to see the bigger picture.

SO WHAT DO WE GET FROM HOLLYWOOD?

Our interpretations are not simply based on the assumption that women viewers are not just cultural dupes tricked by a cynical industry to swallow female stereotypes. Rather, we assume that these movies also have something to give that women want to have. Mixed in with the expected fare of gendered stereotyping are images of empowerment, confirmation, and comfort. Women's films are designed to function as father confessor, psychiatrist, and female support group rolled into one. They aim to provide the answer to our identity crises, relieve us of our bad conscience, reconcile our differences with the world, and provide comfort for our inadequacies. Well aware of gender-specific soft spots, films for women pay particular attention to questions of self-esteem, self-assertion, and identity formation. You feel bad because you dumped your fiancé? Don't! Julia Roberts did it several times in *Runaway Bride*, and they were all fine! Your boyfriend left you, and you think it's your fault? Don't! It happened to Meg Ryan in *French Kiss*, and there was nothing wrong with her! Do you sometimes feel like nobody really knows who you are, that you don't even exist? Well, Sandra Bullock in *The Net* felt the same way, but in the end, she made her presence felt! Do you feel overweight, undesirable, and stupid? So did Renée Zellweger in *Bridget Jones's Diary*, and look at those two gorgeous men battling for her affections! Do you sometimes want to kick the shit out of your guy, some guy, or any guy at all? Watch *Charlie's Angels*, they do it for you! Films make our daydreams come true; they act out our omnipotence fantasies, boost our confidence, and make us feel okay just as we are. They may do so for entirely cynical reasons, but it is still nice to hear it every once in a while.

It is more difficult to view the kind of pseudoreconciliation that characterizes these movies as positively. Although many of these films depict conflicts and problems that make up our everyday world, they offer solutions that work only in the realm of the imaginary.[29] Grave dysfunctions that would be recognized, in the real world, as painful and problematic are smoothed into slightly amusing personal quirks on celluloid. The alcoholism of Maggie Carpenter's father in *Runaway Bride*, for example, gives rise to countless comical scenes but merits only one fleeting serious confrontation. The union of the romantic protagonists often serves to obscure irreconcilable differences of a political, economic, or ideological nature. When Joe Fox and Kathleen Kelly finally end up together in *You've Got Mail*, they represent a happy union of corporate America and independent family entrepreneurship that glosses over the fact that he drove her out of business. In the world of Hollywood, conflict does not exist; if it does, it does not hurt. Just as we are encouraged to make light of Mr. Carpenter's alcoholism or Kathleen's loss of her business, we never get a sense that Lara Croft or Charlie's Angels are in any real danger, even as they are assaulted by heavily armed villains or hang from the edge of a cliff. Many of these films tread a fine line between comforting fantasy and mendacious ideology. Marisa's miraculous rise from maid to manager (and senatorial wife) in *Maid in Manhattan*, for instance, can be seen both as an empowering fantasy and as a pernicious lie—the one that claims that anyone has a chance to move from the log cabin to the White House and deflects our attention away from racial discrimination and the real plight of low-wage workers in America.

So why do we swallow this? Is it because it is easier to take an interest in the happy denouement of personal conflicts than in the resolution of social or economic ones? Why does the final kiss in *You've Got Mail* erase all memory, both Kathleen's and ours, of the sordid business practices that Joe Fox used to ruin her? Certainly, the aura of the individual star has a lot to do with it. The integrity and sweetness that we associate with the Meg Ryan character make the ruthlessness of corporate America palatable. Similarly, Julia Roberts's playfulness in *Pretty Woman* makes prostitution look like a party. Thus, star power and viewing pleasure serve "as the bait for swallowing ideological assumptions that are repressive and demeaning."[30] This effect is heightened by the fact that lighter forms of entertainment, such as romantic comedies, resist analysis. Because of "their implicit 'don't take it too seriously'" stance, romantic comedies make "particularly effective vehicles for ideology."[31]

So are we cultural dupes after all? Well, if we are, we should know: the movies themselves tell us so in no uncertain terms. Interestingly, many recent Hollywood productions are highly self-conscious and make fun of the stereotypes and formulas they employ so blithely. *Pretty Woman*, for example, first presents its heroine Vivian, and us, with a fairy-tale ending, uniting the hooker with the business mogul, and then admits to what we timidly suspected all along: "This is Hollywood. . . . Keep on dreaming!" In *Sleepless in Seattle*, we support Annie's longing for love as destiny even as we are told by Annie's friend and confidante that Annie does not want to be in love: she wants to be "in love in a movie." Again, self-referentiality of this kind is somewhat ambivalent. On the one hand, it shows a refreshing honesty that flatters our sense of sophistication: the film offers the usual wish fulfillment, but it does so with a wink and a smile. On the other hand, self-referentiality can also be little more than an excuse to indulge in ancient stereotypes and get away with it once again. Irony and parody have the power to freshen up traditional formulas that have long gone stale; spiced up with this new twist, the same old fare can be served up again for our consumption.

FEMINISM LITE, OR, PSYCHOLOGY IS CHEAP

Even though the portrayal of women in today's Hollywood films is neither strictly conservative nor clearly progressive, certain trends reappear with great regularity. Almost every film pays lip service to some form of feminism, but it is feminism lite. Whereas gender-specific emotional needs are taken very seriously, social, political, and economic conditions that disadvantage women in the real world fade from view. If such concerns do appear, we have left the realm of lite entertainment and entered that of drama, even tragedy. The average romantic comedy encourages women's self-assertion and self-acceptance, but societal change and social justice are beyond its capacity for wish fulfillment. In *You've Got Mail*, for example, Kathleen Kelly learns how to be assertive but is defeated in the fight to save her independent bookstore. More often than not, social or economic issues as they affect women in American society are eluded altogether. There are almost no romantic comedies in which women struggle to combine family and career; biological clocks do not tick; glass ceilings present no obstacle; if faced with sexism, women are not victimized but, rather, meet it head-on with a witty repartee. Most astonishingly, there are hardly any poor women: even low-paid maid and single mom Marisa in *Maid in Manhattan* does not inhabit a single room or a weekly rental but, in fact, lives in a fairly spacious Manhattan apartment and in the end moves up into the ranks of the ultrarich via marriage to Chris. Similarly, there are no middle-aged women trying to gain access to continuing education or additional training: the women in these films are already overqualified. Romantic comedies and particularly action films are peopled with computer geniuses, multilingualists, and Ivy League graduates. Among the few women who learn anything at all are Gracie in *Miss Congeniality*, who acquires the fine arts of putting on makeup and eating with her mouth shut, and Vivian in *Pretty Woman*, who receives a crash course in social etiquette and shopping. It is small wonder that even the most high-powered women professionals in romantic comedies exhibit no ambition of any kind. Professional ambition, for women, is relegated to the realm of drama and even in this context easily constitutes a death warrant: Karen Emma Walden's drive and achievements as a fighter pilot in *Courage under Fire* are rewarded with the Congressional Medal of Honor—but only posthumously.

It would appear that lite entertainment is far more comfortable portraying personal growth than societal change. Psychology is cheap; social fairness costs dearly. Stories portraying a woman's search for her own identity are therefore the stock-in-trade of romantic comedies. Whether you suffer from low self-esteem or feel ignored and invisible, whether you are the object of abuse and neglect or simply the victim of an inferiority complex, films will administer a sugarcoated pill for your every ailment. If you feel isolated, have no friends, and wish desperately to be part of the human family, films will provide you with confidants, relatives, neighbors, lovers, and friends. In *While You Were Sleeping*, Miss Lonely Heart Lucy, orphaned and abandoned, marries not just her sweetheart but his entire family. In *French Kiss*, Kate, abandoned by her fiancé and expatriated by her country, finds true love in Paris and grows new roots in a French vineyard. Indeed, being embedded in a functional community is central to the happy ending of a romantic comedy. In almost every final kissing scene, the happy couple is surrounded by an enthusiastically applauding crowd. In addition to love, the romantic comedy provides us with the pleasing spectacle of community approval, in which we as viewers happily join.

WHAT WE ARE DOING AND WHY

The following chapters discuss the representation of women in Hollywood movies since 1990. Chapters 1 through 4 are devoted to individual actresses whose success at the box office attests to their popularity throughout the 1990s: Julia Roberts, Sandra Bullock, Meg Ryan, and Renée Zellweger. In each of these chapters, we sketch the actress's recurring screen persona, the "type" with which she is most frequently identified, and provide close readings of four of her films. Chapter 5 singles out several movies that mark the high and low points of 1990s filmmaking, focusing on the politics of romantic comedy and on the newly emerging genre type of the female action hero. Chapter 6 investigates "hidden alternatives," actresses with nontraditional body and personality types who have frequently been banished to nonmainstream films or supporting roles: Judi Dench, Kathy Bates, Parker Posey, Whoopi Goldberg, and Frances Mc-Dormand. Our last chapter moves to the small screen. Characters such as Buffy the Vampire Slayer and Dana Scully in *The X Files* prove that television offers more room for innovative gender roles than is possible on the big screen.

All our readings are based on the assumption that these films are political but do not express their politics explicitly. They convey distinct messages, whether we are aware of them or not. Unfortunately, the more successful and omnipresent a movie is, the less likely it is to receive serious scrutiny. The products of the Hollywood dream machine are universal subjects of conversation at dinner parties; we watch them on the big screen in the cinema, on a small screen at home, and on tiny screens on airplanes and in fitness studios. Movies reach us whether we are three or ninety-three years old, and they reach a far larger audience than any other medium. And all these movies present us with images of femininity that have the power to strengthen, discourage, or simply annoy us. It is high time we became more aware of the messages behind these images. It is high time we started to ask if this is as good as it gets.

NOTES

1. Mick Lasalle (*Complicated Women: Sex and Power in Pre-Code Hollywood* [New York: St. Martin's Press, 2000], 88) makes a similar point.

2. See Molly Haskell, *From Reverence to Rape: The Treatment of Women in the Movies* (New York: Holt, Rinehart and Winston, 1974), 12.

3. This is the main reason why we are not discussing *Thelma and Louise*, which surely must be counted as one of the most significant representations of women in the 1990s. For the differentiation between star and actor, see Richard Dyer, who claims that "you don't have to be a good actor to be a star. Stars are performers whose presence fascinates, who interest us intensely for what we take them to be" (*Only Entertainment* [New York: Routledge, 1992], 112).

4. See Geoff King, *New Hollywood Cinema: An Introduction* (New York: Columbia University Press, 2002), 150.

5. One reason we did not include a chapter on Jennifer Lopez, for example, is that the press coverage she receives usually focuses much more on her person than on her films.

6. A sizable segment of film literature claims that more women were in decision-making positions in film before and during the 1920s than at any other time in history (Marc Wanamaker, "Afterword," in *Reel Women: Pioneers of the Cinema, 1896 to the Present*, Ally Acker [New York: Continuum, 1991], 335–36) or that women dominated in

early and middle ages of film (Haskell, *From Reverence to Rape*, 11–12; Laura Mulvey, *Fetishism and Curiosity* [Bloomington: Indiana University Press, 1996], 41; Dawn B. Sova, *Women in Hollywood: From Vamp to Studio Head* [New York: Fromm International, 1998], ii; Hans J. Wollstein, *Vixens, Floozies and Molls: 28 Actresses of Late 1920s and 1930s Hollywood* [Jefferson, N.C.: MacFarland and Co., 1999], 1).

7. Haskell, *From Reverence to Rape*, 30. See also King, *New Hollywood Cinema*, 14.

8. Much film literature considers the film heroines of the 1980s highly dangerous; see, for example, Alan Nadel's (*Flatlining on the Field of Dreams: Cultural Narratives in the Films of President Reagan's America* [New Brunswick, N.J.: Rutgers University Press, 1997], 9) theories about the implied AIDS discussion in *Dangerous Liaisons*.

9. Cf. the literature that claims that in the 1990s, women moved into network relationships that had theretofore been held only by men and assumed power positions and decision-making roles at major studios (statement and data in Sova, *Women in Hollywood*, 181–84; and Christina Lane, *Feminist Hollywood: From* Born in Flames *to* Point Break [Detroit: Wayne State University Press, 2000], 37). Lane (*Feminist Hollywood*, 38–39) sees a decline in women's roles in Hollywood films simultaneous with the increase in women's presence as producers and directors and concludes that women's greater presence in Hollywood coincides with increasingly distorted and disturbing representations of women in film.

10. See, for example, Krin Gabbard, "Saving Private Ryan Too Late," in *The End of Cinema as We Know It: American Film in the Nineties*, ed. Jon Lewis (New York: New York University Press, 2001), 131–38; Philip Green, *Cracks in the Pedestal: Ideology and Gender in Hollywood* (Amherst: University of Massachusetts Press, 1998), 35–36; Haskell, *From Reverence to Rape*, 2; Alexandra Juhasz, "The Phallus Unfetishized: The End of Masculinity as We Know It in Late-1990s 'Feminist' Cinema," in *The End of Cinema as We Know It: American Film in the Nineties*, ed. Jon Lewis (New York: New York University Press, 2001), 215–17; Jon Lewis, "The End of Cinema as We Know It and I Feel. . . : An Introduction to a Book on Nineties American Film," in *The End of Cinema as We Know It: American Film in the Nineties*, ed. Jon Lewis (New York: New York University Press, 2001), 5; Marita Sturken, "*Affliction*: When Paranoid Male Narratives Fail," in *The End of Cinema as We Know It: American Film in the Nineties*, ed. Jon Lewis (New York: New York University Press, 2001), 203; Frank P. Tomasulo, "Empire of the Gun: Steven Spielberg's *Saving Private Ryan* and American Chauvinism," in *The End of Cinema as We Know It: American Film in the Nineties*, ed. Jon Lewis (New York: New York University Press, 2001), 115. See also Yvonne Tasker, who points out that "thriving on ambiguity, Hollywood cinema performs that most utopian of exercises—it has its cake and eats it too" (*Spectacular Bodies: Gender, Genre and the Action Cinema* [London: Routledge, 1993], 91).

11. See Dyer, *Only Entertainment*, 46.

12. See Wheeler Winston Dixon, who writes: "The 1990s genre film is everywhere a creature of excess" ("Introduction: The New Genre Cinema," in *Film Genre 2000: New*

Critical Essays, ed. Wheeler Winston Dixon [Albany: State University of New York Press, 2000], 4). The big mergers during the 1990s include Time and Warner Communications, Paramount Communications and Viacom, Universal and Seagram Vivendi, the Disney Corporation and Capital Cities/ABC, and Time Warner and Turner Broadcasting, a deal complicated by an end-of-the-century merger with AOL, as well as the acquisition of Twentieth Century Fox by the Rupert Murdoch's News Corporation. See King, *New Hollywood Cinema*, 67; Lane, *Feminist Hollywood*, 33; Lewis, "The End of Cinema as We Know It and I Feel. . . ," 2.

13. King, *New Hollywood Cinema*, 58.

14. Thomas Elsaesser, "The Blockbuster: Everything Connects, but Not Everything Goes," in *The End of Cinema as We Know It: American Film in the Nineties*, ed. Jon Lewis (New York: New York University Press, 2001), 17; Christina Klein, "The Hollowing-Out of Hollywood: 'Runaway Productions' Boost Profits but Also Take Jobs Abroad," *YaleGlobal*, April 30, 2004, available at www.yaleglobal.yale.edu; "US Cinema Chronology," available at http://homepages.unl.ac.uk/~westwelg/fm323/resources/chrono.html (July 15, 2003).

15. King, *New Hollywood Cinema*, 136–39.

16. Lane, *Feminist Hollywood*, 33.

17. See Lane, *Feminist Hollywood*, 29–30.

18. King, *New Hollywood Cinema*, 50.

19. King, *New Hollywood Cinema*, 138–39.

20. See John Fiske's ("British Cultural Studies and Television," in *What Is Cultural Studies? A Reader*, ed. John Storey [London: St. Martin's Press, 1997], 116–17) general discussion about the ideological nature of the media.

21. Fiske, "British Cultural Studies and Television," 118.

22. All the following examples are taken from Fiske's Madonna discussion in "British Cultural Studies and Television," 131–41.

23. Stuart Hall's theory of the "preferred reading" is developed in his essay "Encoding/Decoding" (in *Culture, Media, Language*, ed. Stuart Hall, Dorothy Hobson, Andrew Lowe, and Paul Willis [London: Hutchinson, 1980], 128–39).

24. This idea is based on Gramsci's theory of hegemony, interpreted by Fiske as describing "the process by which a dominant class wins the willing consent of the subordinate classes to the system that ensures their subordination" ("British Cultural Studies and Television," 120).

25. Tasker speaks of Hollywood's "reluctance to engage with underlying economic and political forces" (*Spectacular Bodies*, 103).

26. For more information, see U.S. Census Bureau, "Census Brief: Women in the United States, a Profile, 2000," available at www.census.gov/prod/2000pubs/cenbr001.pdf; and U.S. Census Bureau, "We, the American Women," available at www.usembassy.de/usa/etexts/soc/we-women.pdf.

27. See U.S. Census Bureau, "Census Brief."

28. Condoleezza Rice was on the board of Chevron, and there is indeed a supertanker named in her honor. For more information on Rice, see Laura Flanders, *Bushwomen: Tales of a Cynical Species* (London: Verso, 2004), 29–72.

29. King, *New Hollywood Cinema*, 109.

30. Martha P. Nochimson, *Screen Couple Chemistry: The Power of 2* (Austin: University of Texas Press, 2002), 34.

31. Geoff King, *Film Comedy* (London: Wallflower Press, 2002), 55.

☆ 1 ☆

The Newborn Identity
Julia Roberts

"What's your name?"
"What would you like it to be?"

—*Pretty Woman* (1990)

Who is Julia Roberts for us? Is she a hard-core prostitute or an innocent child? Is she a "best friend" or a harpy trying to steal someone else's fiancé? Is she a superstar or just a girl? Does she like her eggs scrambled or poached? Julia Roberts's most popular movies very often do not present us with a fully formed character but, rather, show a woman in search of her own identity, a search on which we get to accompany her. Naturally, for a heroine in a romantic comedy, the quest for identity entails finding the right partner, a task made formidably difficult by the indeterminacy of her identity and even her gender.

In many movies, the Julia Roberts character is portrayed as a woman who does not yet know who she is and what she wants. Her lack of identity is usually linked to her desire to accommodate the expectations of other characters or of society at large. She tries on many different identities, many of them ill-fitting and many of them, as in the above quotation, defined by others. In *Pretty Woman* (1990) she encourages first Edward and then the hotel manager to choose a name for her. In *Notting Hill* (1999), she goes by a plethora of pseudonyms, ranging from Bambi and Mrs. Flintstone to Pocahontas. Paradoxically, the less she knows herself, the easier it is for us to identify with her. The problem of asserting your own identity—as opposed to accommodating the wishes of others—is, of course, one with which many women are familiar; its universality and easy recognizability may be one reason for Julia Roberts's tremendous popular success. Also appealing, for us as women viewers, is her character's inability to find, or keep, the right man: she is often entangled in a series of dreadful relationships with men who are disastrously wrong for her. This enables us to feel slightly superior—after all, we wouldn't put up with some of these half-wits. But it also offers relief: if a woman as stunning as she is has trouble finding Mr. Right, no wonder we're struggling!

The Julia Roberts type is a hodgepodge of vulnerability and innocence on the one hand and omnipotence fantasies on the other. Despite her stunning looks, she is often portrayed as strangely unfeminine, either as a childlike creature who squeals with pleasure in her bubble bath or as a more mannish type who runs a hardware store and knows how to fix cars.[1] Thus, finding her femininity becomes an integral part of her search for identity: in *Runaway Bride* (1999), Maggie the mechanic metamorphoses into a designer; in *Notting Hill*, the action heroine matures into a genteel leading lady straight out of a Henry James novel. In each of these instances, her heightened femininity equals greater sophistication and societal status. Ironically, what appears as internal development and self-expression actually amounts to an act of conformity that results in a much more conventional character.

Before the Julia Roberts type is streamlined in this fashion, she presents an imp, a childish tease with a mean streak whose antics are made palatable to us through her sweet innocence and vulnerability. Like a child, she knows how to live in the moment; she takes a malicious pleasure in harmless acts of revenge. In *Runaway Bride*, for example, she conspires with her friend to dye Ike's hair in psychedelic colors; in *Pretty Woman*, she gets back at a store clerk who had earlier refused to serve her by gleefully showing off her many expensive purchases made elsewhere. At the same time, she is presented as vulnerable: "You hurt me," she reproaches Edward in *Pretty Woman*, "don't do it again." Because of her childlike quality and her vulnerability, she is granted all the license that we would afford a child. We forgive her when she abandons man after man at the altar (*Runaway Bride*) or when she exhibits an almost criminal ingenuity in pursuit of her man (including men who are engaged to other women, as in *My Best Friend's Wedding* [1997]), and even her sexual forwardness in *Pretty Woman* seems perky and cute rather than lustful and sinful, as one would expect from a professional prostitute.

Just as she combines innocence with sexual experience, she embodies both underdog existence and omnipotence fantasy. Initially disadvantaged—a prostitute in *Pretty Woman*, a country bumpkin in *Runaway Bride*, a hunted victim in *The Pelican Brief*, an abused wife in *Sleeping with the Enemy*—she always emerges triumphant. She fights the entire world and wins (*The Pelican Brief*);

she combines professional success as an industrial designer with marriage to Mr. Right (*Runaway Bride*); she marries the man of her dreams even as she is handed her next Oscar (*Notting Hill*)—in short, she is rewarded with a fairytale ending (*Pretty Woman*). This is part of what we, as moviegoers, crave, and the films deliver every time. But they also remind us that we are, indeed, watching a fairy tale: what makes Julia Roberts films so particularly charming is their self-referentiality. They do not pretend to depict reality but, rather, admit quite openly that they are selling dreams. The Julia Roberts vehicle gives us the happy ending we have come to see, but it also tells us in no uncertain terms that we will not encounter this ending outside of the movies. This implies a degree of cynical and capitalist hardheadedness: happiness is available to us for only nine dollars. But it is also an open acknowledgment of what movies can, or cannot, do for us.

Pretty Woman. Directed by Garry Marshall. Buena Vista. Release Date in the United States: March 23, 1990. Total U.S. Gross: $178,406,268

Can we ever see and not believe? When words contradict images, do we ever listen? *Pretty Woman* portrays a society in which every relationship is infected with and destroyed by money. Every scripted conversation demonstrates that there is no way out, but every image we see proves that true love will be redeemed in the end.

Edward Lewis (Richard Gere) is an excessively rich mergers and acquisitions shark who gets lost in a sleazy L.A. neighborhood. He picks up the prostitute Vivian Ward (Julia Roberts), who agrees to show him the way to his hotel. Edward ends up hiring Vivian for a week to serve as his escort. As they get to know each other, they fall in love. Because of Vivian's moralizing influence, Edward abandons his corrupt business practices; Vivian, in turn, is rescued from the streets, and the two of them live happily ever after.

Zooming in on fake gold coins that keep changing hands, the very first shot of *Pretty Woman* establishes money as the crucial agent that determines and dominates every human interaction.[2] The fact that it is a man who distributes coins to women and the comment "A penny for your ear; how much for the rest?" highlights that sexual relationships are not exempted from monetary circulation. The film insists that even romantic relationships cannot escape the corrupting influence of money.[3] Edward's relationships with his ex-wife and his ex-girlfriend revolve around financial transactions. The terms of the divorce settlement (his wife got the house) and the services his girlfriend owes him (she does not want to be at his beck and call) constitute the sole subject of all their conversations. When we finally meet Vivian, we are hardly surprised to learn that she is a prostitute. After all, so is everybody else in the world of *Pretty Woman.*

When Edward asks Vivian for directions, she immediately demands money for this small favor. This sets the tone for their entire relationship. Their honest and explicit negotiation of the financial underbelly of their romance makes intimacy between them possible. It is this openness that leads Edward to admit that he too screws people for money. Of course, as soon as Edward is willing to acknowledge this fact, he is transformed by this insight. He rejects his former cutthroat practices and commits to rescuing the company that he had planned to destroy.

Interestingly, Edward's journey toward emotional wholeness is portrayed as a story of sexual empowerment. In the beginning we are bombarded with images of Edward's impotence. He drives a car with a stick, but he sure doesn't know how to use it. Vivian, on the other hand, is very comfortable with sticks. When the two arrive at the door of his penthouse apartment in the hotel, Edward fails to slide the card key into the electronic lock. We need hardly wait for his first sexual encounter with Vivian (the precise nature of which is laid out through the juxtaposition with scenes from *I Love Lucy,* in which Lucy gets sprayed on the face) to understand that he just doesn't know how to slip it in. Needless to add that Edward is also afraid of heights. Moreover, Edward's impotence is given a homosocial context. The place of Edward's wife or mistress seems to have been occupied by his lawyer Stuckey (Jason Alexander). Like a neglected wife, Stuckey keeps asking Edward where he has been and whom he was with. When Edward finally leaves Stuckey for Vivian, the furious lawyer reproaches him with the stereotypical: "I gave you the ten best years of my life."

Although the theme of impotence is somewhat formulaic, and its execution is less than subtle, the movie gives it an interesting twist by linking it to the unproductive nature of Edward's professional activities. "We don't build anything, we don't make anything," Edward tells his partner Stuckey, and we begin to realize wherein lies the origin of his affliction. In *Pretty Woman,* economic problems are transformed into sexual dysfunction and can thus be solved in the bedroom.[4] With Vivian's help, Edward overcomes both his professional and his sexual sterility, as the audience takes comfort in the thought that Edward's excessive riches are bought at the price of sexual malfunction.[5] His moral reformation, on the other hand, leads to sexual bliss and to his reacceptance into the patriarchal fold. The fatherly owner of the company that Edward promises to save rewards him with a pat on the shoulder. Conveniently, this patriarch has a grandson but no son; thus Edward, estranged from his now-deceased biological father during the last fifteen years, has finally found a replacement.

Just as Edward's impotence is linked with his financial prowess, Vivian's innocence, which remains wholly unperturbed by her sexual competence, is established through her naïveté about money. Vivian keeps underselling herself when asked for her price and yet rejoices when Edward, to whom her highest demands must seem like spare change, consents to her bargain offers. Anything more than twenty dollars seems to exceed Vivian's horizon, and this ignorance functions as a sign that Vivian is far less corrupted than Edward. Her innocence is further underscored by her childlike behavior. Vivian avoids chairs, sitting down on tables or on the floor. Even scenes that are potentially sexually loaded reinforce her childlike purity. When she revels in foam in the luxurious penthouse bathtub, she resembles a kiddie in the tub, albeit without the rubber duckie, not a woman who makes a living by selling her body. As her last name indicates, Vivian is indeed Edward's ward. Whereas her influence on Edward is humanizing, the education he bestows on her is civilizing. Vivian learns how to use a napkin and cutlery, and she is introduced to opera music, polo, and chess. Fundamentally, however, she does not change. All that is required is some polish.

Although Edward's miraculous reformation in which he suddenly grows a heart might not strike us as the most realistic element of the movie, its fairy-tale quality pales in comparison with the portrayal of true love in the midst of *Pretty Woman*'s capitalist extravaganza.[6] Again, it is not the fact that Vivian is a prostitute that makes the happy ending hard to swallow. Rather, it is Vivian's gradual transition to the status of wife that precludes all hope that they might live happily ever after.[7]

As Vivian settles down in Edward's hotel room, she abandons her previous professional pursuits—as minimal and undefined as they are—and assumes the looks and behavior of "the little wife." She trades in her dominatrix boots for a polka-dotted cocktail dress. Her multicolored collection of condoms is replaced by lacy nightgowns in black and white, and her job description changes from selling herself to shopping. Bored but patient, she waits until Edward comes home from the office and happily watches TV as Edward continues to work until long after midnight. As we vividly remember the fate of Edward's ex-wife and are treated to insights into the marital disaster of Edward's partner Stuckey, we might be hard-pressed to think of marriage as a happy ending. Where marriage is defined as a different kind of prostitution, the role of the wife offers no viable alternative to that of the prostitute. Indeed, the movie itself shows some awareness of this when Vivian refuses Edward's offer of a nice apartment in exchange for a long-term relationship. Asked what kind of arrangement she would like instead, Vivian does not ask him to marry her but simply responds, "I want more." Pressed for details, she relates her dream of a knight in shining armor.

Paradoxically, it is this fairy-tale scenario that must be counted among the most realistic features of the movie. *Pretty Woman* admits quite frankly that there is no happy ending in a world like this.[8] As Vivian's friend Kit informs us, the only person for whom it ever worked out is "Cinde-fuckin'-rella." But even as the movie insists on the impossibility of romance, it proceeds to show it all the same. In the final scene, Edward Lewis, the knight in a white limo (and at this point we finally understand why he bears the names of no less than two princes!), rescues his princess with his umbrella-sword as the voice-over reminds us: "This is Hollywood. . . . Keep on dreaming!" We might be tempted to conclude that *Pretty Woman* enacts what it portrays. Like Edward and Vivian, who admit to screwing people for money, *Pretty Woman* admits to screwing us. We are the customer, the movie is the whore, we are paying to be fucked, and, like Edward, we are having the most wonderful time.

My Best Friend's Wedding. Directed by P. J. Hogan. Sony Pictures. Release Date in the United States: June 20, 1997. Total U.S. Gross: $126,813,153

After watching *My Best Friend's Wedding*, we might be inclined to define comedy as a genre that possesses all the essential structures, characters, and plot elements of tragedy—only it's fun.[9] *My Best Friend's Wedding*, a modern-day screwball comedy, presents us with two archetypes that haunt the modern woman: the female professional who cannot hang on to her man and the ditz who has given up everything so as not to lose said man.[10] By the end of the film, the career woman still has not found love and the girlie girl still does not know what to do with herself, but we have had the most wonderful time watching them progress from point A to point A.

My Best Friend's Wedding introduces us to the food critic Jules (Julia Roberts), whose most stable long-term relationship with a man is that with her gay editor George (Rupert Everett). Jules appears to be perfectly content with her life until she receives a call from her old friend and one-time flame Michael (Dermot Mulroney), who announces his upcoming marriage to Kimmy (Cameron Diaz), the daughter of a Chicago millionaire. Jules is hit with the realization that she loves Michael and hurries to the airport to break up the young couple as speedily as possible. But all her intrigues fail, and the final scene shows Jules dancing with George as the newlyweds leave for their honeymoon.

When viewers first meet Jules, they immediately suspect that she is a woman in dire need of feminization. In the first scene, a small army of male cooks and waiters strives frantically to please Jules's delicate taste buds. Jules is not in the

least perturbed by her power to make or break a restaurant. Her numerous professional accomplishments include a degree from an Ivy League institution and
a recently published book. However, her area of competency does not extend to
romance. Even George has stopped setting her up with men because she does
not "have the first idea what to do with them." This characterization continues
as Kimmy informs us that Jules "is not up for anything conventional, anything
that's a female priority." As though to underline her point, the bridesmaid's
dress that Jules is trying on as Kimmy offers insights into her character tears
apart, and Jules reverts to wearing men's suits, her hallmark outfit during the entire movie.[11] Later on, Michael refers to her as "practically his best man," and a
couple of adolescent boys respond to her commanding tone with a snappy,
"Yessir!" But "male" competence and independence are not all there is to Jules.
Jules's masculine demeanor barely hides the chain-smoking hysteric who cannot
contain her desperate longing for a husband and empties the entire contents of
her hotel minibar when she sees her hopes for marriage dwindling. If Jules were
not Julia, we might not be quite as willing to identify with her.

Kimmy, on the other hand, is not exactly a viable alternative. The child bride
whom Michael has chosen for himself is a caricature of a person. Her emotional
range begins with excessively hyperactive joyfulness, skips the realm of even-
handed normality, and ends with sobbing desperation. Kimmy's most memorable moment is her impressively untalented rendition of "I Just Don't Know
What to Do with Myself" in a karaoke bar—a song that incidentally also offers a
succinct description of Kimmy's outlook on life. She has left college without a
degree in order to follow Michael, whose job as a reporter of third-rate sports
events takes him around the country to numerous undistinguished small-town
localities. Kimmy's only demonstrable skill consists in her relentless dedication
to Michael. Brides like Kimmy make single women look good, and relationships
like that between Kimmy and Michael make spinsterhood seem appealing.[12]

Although Michael is committed to marrying Kim, he keeps flirting with Jules
as his neglected fiancée looks on in embarrassed humiliation. Though we never
quite understand why Kimmy is attracted to Michael, we do know that he is
drawn to her total commitment to prop up his fragile self-esteem. When Kimmy
pleads with Michael to give up his low-prestige, low-income job for profitable
employment in her father's corporation, a furious Michael yells out: "I'm not
good enough for you." Only Kimmy's prompt promise to sacrifice all her own
wishes and needs can restore the balance. If Kimmy and Michael were not redeemed by occasional moments of deep, mutual concern for each other's well-
being, there would be no hope for this union. Even as it is, we feel inclined to
congratulate Jules on her happy escape from marital misery. After all, whereas

Kimmy can look forward to a life dedicated to assuaging white male anger, Jules gets to enjoy the company of the dashingly handsome, highly educated, and fun-loving (but lamentably gay) George.

Jules's gay friend George functions as a catalyst who brings out the madness that Kimmy's family has defined as normality. During his first encounter with Kimmy and her relatives, George mimics the tone and gestures of everybody he is introduced to. Surprisingly, this behavior endears him to Kimmy's relatives, even as it ridicules their peculiar antics for the audience. Pretending to be Jules's fiancé, George tells his captivated audience that he met his beloved in a lunatic asylum, upon which all assembled relatives promptly identify him as one of their own. Whereas Jules has remained an outsider, George is easily accepted into the family fold because he acts out their own insanity. In spite of this, George does not lose the sympathies of the audience, who recognizes that he is only acting; in fact, he is presented as the most loving and stable person in the entire movie. When Jules is teamed up with George in the end, we feel that she got the better end of the deal.

There is yet another reason why Jules may have made out better than Kimmy in the end. Kimmy's self-sacrifice gets her a real but prosaic marriage, with all its compromises and disappointments. Jules's noble renunciation, on the other hand, is rewarded with the perfect happiness that only movies afford. Kimmy and Michael may be the "real" couple, but Jules and George are Doris Day and Rock Hudson, forever unreal and forever having fun. Jules may not have found the man of her dreams, but, hey, she can always, as George puts it, "Susan-Hay-ward-it-all." Thus, the unexpected happens after all. Although a romantic comedy, *My Best Friend's Wedding* celebrates having fun as a single person over being married to a bore.[13] And although it sets us up for another *Taming of the Shrew* destined to culminate in the feminization of the career woman, it ends up rewarding Jules with the highest of all prizes: a life in movie land.

Runaway Bride. Directed by Garry Marshall. Paramount Pictures. Release Date in the United States: July 30, 1999. Total U.S. Gross: $152,149,590

Runaway Bride, directed by Garry Marshall, offers two radically different story patterns effortlessly presented as one harmonious package.[14] Like a trompe l'oeil picture that changes from a representation of an old crone with a hunchback into that of a young beauty with a hat, depending on the viewer's focus, *Runaway Bride* is both a reenactment of *The Taming of the Shrew* and the portrait of a woman who emancipates herself in spite of numerous obstacles.

Runaway Bride tells the story of Ike Graham (Richard Gere), an initially cynical and misogynist reporter, who publishes a column about Maggie Carpenter (Julia Roberts), a man-eater from Hale, Maryland, who has already abandoned three grooms at the altar. When Maggie complains to Ike's editor about the numerous inaccuracies of fact in his story, Ike is fired. To restore his reputation through some hands-on investigative journalism, Ike sets out for Hale. Of course, the two antagonists fall in love, and Maggie, after one last dash from marital bliss, finally hands in her running shoes to Ike.

From the beginning, the movie establishes the theme of wanting and longing. The opening song, "I Still Haven't Found What I'm Looking For," performed by U2, invites us to share the characters' unfulfilled yearning, a task that we are all the more willing to engage in because the genre of romantic comedy offers a guarantee that our quest will not go unrewarded. If the promised happy ending does not provide sufficient comfort, the representation of Hale as a paradisical village where nobody's feelings are ever seriously hurt, assures us further that we have entered a realm in which desire comes with no risks or strings attached. It so happens that not a single one of Maggie's jilted fiancés holds a grudge against her. Fiancé number one, Gill, the hippie car mechanic, is too self-absorbed and quite possibly too addled by years of drug abuse to focus on any other person for an extended period of time. Fiancé number two, Brian, became Father Brian, found solace in God, and offers nothing but forgiveness to a tentatively remorseful Maggie. Even number three, who spilled the story to Ike and seems to have developed a slight alcohol problem in the wake of his experiences with the man-eater, is not seriously troubled and finds new romantic bliss in the very bar where he indulges his prematrimonial hangover. Finally, Maggie's last "victim," the football coach Bob, whom she leaves for Ike during their wedding rehearsal, ends up rooting for Ike some ten hours after Maggie has dumped him. Truly, Hale, Maryland, is a world in which actions have no consequences and nobody ever really gets hurt. Confrontations are tiny ripples in a sea of indestructible human connections. "I don't like that you're drunk all the time," says Maggie to her alcoholic father. He does not respond, she proceeds to eat her dinner, and the movie never revisits the topic of his alcoholism. Who wouldn't like to get a break like that?

The absence of conflict sets the stage for the movie's most beguiling sleight of hand: the union of female self-assertion with submission to male authority, the joining of lovers in a relationship that combines both emancipation and subordination. Ike has barely begun to apply his considerable analytical powers to the case of Maggie Carpenter when he realizes that the man-eater ends up (almost) hurting others because she does not know her true self. Finding her true self, developing her individuality, becomes the new goal for the confused femme fatale. However, lest the audience be frightened by too much woman power, individuality is quickly redefined as the ability to identify how you like your eggs. Maggie, who ate scrambled eggs with Brian and egg whites only with Bob, finally realizes that it is poached eggs that she has always been longing for. Such is the value of individuality in a movie that expresses its vision of small-town family harmony by bombarding us with multiple images of twins in strollers, twins walking hand in hand, triplets in strollers, and, last but not least, the family dog and its identical, albeit wooden, twin brother.

Although Maggie's self-discovery is the focus of attention, Ike is far more than a mere catalyst. He is the agent who initiates, guides, and controls her transformation. During their confrontation at the premarital luau, Ike lectures Maggie in no uncertain terms about her true needs and desires. The fact that he keeps telling her what she really likes in no way conflicts with her task of self-discovery because Ike has direct insights into her psyche. Ike's educational efforts are shown at great length, whereas the final, solitary, and somewhat undefined steps of Maggie's project of self-reform occur offscreen. Thus, we may rejoice in Maggie's emancipation as we rest assured that such emancipation is controlled by and performed in service of Mr. Right. Tellingly, the culmination of Maggie's progress toward self-determination is

Identity is just over the next hill. Julia Roberts in Runaway Bride *(1999). PARAMOUNT/THE KOBAL COLLECTION/BARRY WETCHER.*

her proposal of marriage to Ike. Although Maggie is ostensibly cast in the masculine role, forcing her way into his apartment and kneeling in front of Ike in the manner of a male suitor, the words she speaks are not her own but, rather, quote the romantic philosophy previously promoted by Ike.

It comes as no surprise that Mr. Right himself is a contradiction in terms. He is a misogynist who turns feminist agent while managing to remain firmly embedded in male society. One of the opening shots that establishes Ike's character for us shows a series of photographs of male luminaries that begins with Einstein and ends with Ike. Throughout the movie, scenes in which Ike defends Maggie against multiple forms of small-town humiliation alternate with images of Ike mingling and bonding with Maggie's father, her numerous ex-fiancés, and all available Hale dignitaries from the mayor to the police chief. It is certainly true that Ike too undergoes a process of transformation and reform, but although Maggie instigates his change, she does not direct it. Initially Ike is presented as a troubled individual whose emotional deficiency finds expression in his bitter diatribes against women. Very soon, however, our attention is redirected toward Maggie's problems and Ike's efforts to take care of her. If he too is reformed in the process of healing her, his betterment is entirely the result of his own doing.

Runaway Bride not only presents emancipation and subordination as easily compatible, it also equates true liberation with successful feminization. When we first meet Maggie, she wears an overall, runs a hardware store, and entertains her friends with illuminating remarks about the properties of hydraulic fluid. Unlike Ike, Maggie knows how to fix cars and is not afraid of snakes. When angered, she blows off steam through boxing. By the end of the movie, she wears a skirt and has managed to channel her mechanical interests into the much more gender-appropriate outlet of artistic design. Her belated female socialization, quite possibly delayed by the absence of her mother, is completed when she hands over her running shoes to Ike.

Runaway Bride teleports us to a Xanadu where actions have no consequences and where female self-determination, romantic bliss, and male bonding are presented as not only compatible but mutually reinforcing. Would we pay nine dollars to spend some time in this paradise? Of course we would!

Notting Hill. Directed by Roger Michell. Universal Studios. Release Date in the United States: May 28, 1999. Total U.S. Gross: $116,089,678

Notting Hill affords a glimpse into the lives of the rich and famous while reminding us of our own drab reality. It tells the love story of Anna Scott (Julia Roberts), introduced by the film as "Hollywood's biggest star," and William Thacker (Hugh Grant), whose name is more than evocative of British novelist William Makepeace Thackeray (1811–1863), most notably the author of *Vanity Fair, or, A Novel without a Hero* (1847). Like Thackeray's novel, this story seems to lack a hero: not only is William portrayed as the most patient, endearing, reticent, honest, long-suffering, and shy man ever to grace the silver screen, but he also functions as the story's first-person narrator. Coupled with his natural reticence and honesty, his role as the story's narrator practically mandates the portrayal of his own life as drab and unglamorous. Every aspect of William's life that could possibly hold any allure or excitement is diluted: rather than living in London, he lives in Notting Hill, a "village within London"; rather than traveling, he sells travel books. His shop is losing money, presumably because William is too honest to make much of a salesperson, and after his wife abandoned him "for someone who looks like Harrison Ford," he is in financial difficulties severe enough to force him to take in a roommate. Thus William leads a "half life" whose only glamour comes from watching Anna Scott films. Then along comes Anna, who from the very beginning controls the terms of their relationship: she initiates the first kiss, the first date, and the first sexual encounter and eventually ends up proposing to him. He rejects her proposal because he cannot believe that his drab normality could actually be transformed into a Hollywood movie. Only when he begins to believe in that possibility is he able to retract his rejection of her. The love story concludes with a happy ending combining aspects of each lover's reality. In one shot, they emerge from Anna's limousine on their way to the ceremony where Anna will receive her Oscar; the next portrays the bourgeois happiness of the highly pregnant Anna and William, no longer watching a movie but reading a book, on a park bench.

The very aspect of this film that is most incredible, a movie star's interest in a nonhero, a Mr. Normality, is also thematized most extensively. For Anna, as it turns out, is not only enamored of Mr. Normality; she is enamored of normality itself. Part of her unhappiness with her outwardly glamorous life as a highly successful, famous, rich, and beautiful actress is motivated by easily understandable aspects: she is hunted by reporters wherever she goes, supervised by her production manager, humiliated by the publication of nude photos she had taken when she was young and foolish—in short, she is denied privacy and all the things that are part of privacy, including love. Anna's pursuit of normality is easily recognizable as a pursuit of identity, as a search for the person behind the many pictures or images of her, the person who could lay claim to love and a "normal" life. In her life as a star, her identity is elusive, overlaid by images that almost always emphasize Anna's lack of reality. Images of her films are shown in black and white, so that the coloring distances her from the multicolored "normality." Throughout the movie, she is beleaguered by fans who, greedy for autographs, value the image rather than the person; she is mistaken for a different actress, indicating that this image is exchangeable with any other, or—worst of all—she is not recognized at all, implying that the image could be erased at any time. To protect her compromised "privacy" as a "person," she checks into hotels under pseudonyms that are taken from cartoon characters like Bambi, Mrs. Flintstone, and Pocahontas, names that themselves stand for film images. That this lack of a "real" existence, the reduction of the star to her image, is to be viewed as a fate that affects all famous people is established in the recurring discussion of actors reduced to various (usually sexualized) body parts: Mel Gibson's ass and Meatloaf's breasts feature prominently in pillow talk between the lovers. In these scenes, a further layer of irreality is added to the reduction of persons to parts: what we see on the screen may not even be Mel's *real* ass, it may be that of a body double. The ultimate reduction of Anna to her screen image is performed by a group of men in a restaurant who proclaim that Anna is a prostitute and generalize this statement to apply to actresses in general: "In over 50 percent of all languages, the word for 'actress' is the same as the word for 'prostitute,'" one of them informs us. We, the audience, are complicit in this reduction because we, too, watch her in the movies or watch the film audience watching her movies.

When William's life, devoid of glamour, and Anna's life, devoid of substance, intersect, Anna's question—"Who am I, really?"—becomes William's. In his quest for her love he has to establish first and foremost what is behind the image. At this point, he begins to share in her greatest fear: that there might be nothing there or that whatever person there is might never emerge from behind the image. "There are too many pictures of you, too many films," he tells her as a reason for his rejection, a sentence in which *pictures* can be read both as a British term ("movies") and as an American term ("image"). "Hollywood's biggest star" is ineligible as an identity because Anna herself views stardom as an illusion: "The fame thing isn't really real," she tells William. The star image is also ineligible for another reason, one the audience may identify with even more: it would give her the upper hand in the relationship and turn him into her subordinate.[15] We get a taste of this in the scene in which Jeff (Alec Baldwin), a self-styled "famous actor" and Anna's then-boyfriend, mistakes William for room service and orders him to take out the trash. If there is to be any kind of "normal" life for Anna, the film must find a way to create a "normal" male–female relationship. William must either be superior or, at the very least, exist on an even footing with her. Hence it is Anna who proposes to, and is initially rejected by, William, and hence there is also the necessity for the film to overturn the initial gender reversal in the portrayal of both characters. At the outset of the film, William is portrayed as patient, long-suffering, and above all understanding and supportive, the user of girlish words like *whoopsidaisies* and incompetent at boyish pursuits—he has great difficulty climbing a fence that Anna scales with ease. Toward the end, when William orders a customer to leave his store and mounts the courage to reject Anna, he has clearly gained in self-confidence and assertiveness. Anna, though perhaps not undergoing a significant change in character (and this makes sense, given that we are unsure what precisely her character is), does undergo a recognizable shift in *image*. At the outset, she is an action heroine (a female role rare to nonexistent in real Hollywood), performing daring feats in space capsules and submarines; at the end of the film, she stars in a Henry James adaptation. Her transformation from action hero to long-suffering and submissive aristocratic leading lady is prompted by William, for it is he who initially suggested Henry James to her. The love story is only possible because he becomes more of a "real man" and she *portrays* more of a "real woman" at the end of the film.[16] The question that remains at the end is: Is that sufficient? Is the acting, the image of a "real woman," enough to enter into a "normal" life?

It would seem initially that the film answers this question in the affirmative: when Anna proposes to William, in words that haunt him until he retracts his rejection of her, she does not portray herself as an individual but generically. "I'm just a girl," she says, "standing in front of a boy, asking him to love her." Thus normality is defined as commonality: what makes Anna special is precisely that she *is not* special, that she could be any girl asking any boy this most central of all questions. The success of this love story depends on William's ability to believe in her normality rather than her stardom, to believe that she is a "girl" rather than the unreachable "goddess," as William's friend Max (Tim McInnerny) describes her. William, and with him the audience, is fighting to believe this in the face of overwhelming evidence to the contrary: the many scenes we have seen in which she, as an image, is portrayed in a loving relationship and therefore she, as a person, is interpreted as out of reach for mere mortals. "Somewhere in the world there is someone who is allowed to kiss her," remarks William's roommate Spike (Rhys Ifans) dreamily as both watch Anna on-screen kissing a man. Consequently, when William first kisses Anna, he comments: "It's the sort of thing that happens in dreams, not in real life." After their first night together, he still considers it "surreal" that he is allowed to see her naked, but she dryly reminds him that he shares that privilege with everyone else in the world. There is, of course, a difference here: whereas the world possesses her mere image, he—at least—possesses her actual body. But body, or body parts, as we are constantly reminded in the list of sexualized body parts of famous people, is not a sufficient stand-in for personhood; it cannot constitute identity.

For Anna, the quest for identity is part and parcel of her quest for normality: identity can only be established in contrast to the dream world of Hollywood. She gets a taste of normality on her first date with William, where they—rather than going out to a five-star restaurant followed by an opera premiere—attend a birthday dinner for William's little sister Honey (Emma Chambers). William's friends at the dinner are, without exception, presented as underachievers who delight in telling their own hard-luck stories and vie with each other for the distinction of being the biggest loser. The normality that Anna longs for is here presented as consisting of drab little lives defined by failed business ventures, accidents that put people into wheelchairs, and financial difficulties but also—and this is the aspect of "normality" that appeals to Anna—by humorous self-flagellation, friendship, community support, and serious sharing. Anna's attempt to compete with them, to "normalize" her glamorous life, consists of pointing out the tragic truths that are erased by the screen image, among them the constant diets and operations that are the basis of her good looks and—most shockingly—an admission of her lack of talent and her fear that her career will end when her beauty wanes. (The film later negates this by awarding her an Oscar for her portrayal of the Henry James heroine, an award that, despite her disclaimer of it as "nonsense," is presumably to be understood as an acknowledgment of high-quality work.) This scene documents one of the central paradoxes of the film: while its audience dreams of riches, fame, and glory—all the things that Anna embodies—Anna desires the normal life lived by that audience. Thus the audience's act of moviegoing—the manifestation of its dream of fame and riches—is rewarded *both* by the portrayal of a rich and glamorous heroine *and* by that glamorous heroine's validation of the audience's own life.

On the other hand, the desirability of normality is starkly negated when it is stripped of its contact with glitz and glamour, that is, when William loses Anna and has to "face the facts," as his friend Max admonishes him. "Facing the facts" means going through a series of dates with awful women (nongoddesses, in other words); William's final disinterest in a perfectly nice and attractive woman informs the audience unequivocally that he is not available for anyone but Anna. Thus the film's dream world, initially defined as Hollywood glamour, is now redefined as true love: in a discussion between William and his friends, true love, such as the one between his friends Bella (Gina McKee) and Max, is so rare as to be virtually out of reach for mere mortals. It is a strangely ambiguous scene partly because it invites the audience to view Bella and Max's marriage as paradise, even though Bella is confined to a wheelchair and they cannot have children. But it also redefines the "dream" in a manner that makes it possible for

William and Anna to pursue it again, and that in turn enables the audience to identify with their quest. In the end, it is not up to William and Anna alone to realize their dream: both communities—Anna's community of admirers and reporters and William's community of friends—play an important part in bringing them together. In this manner, their principal desire, that a balance can be struck between illusion and reality, between the dream world and normality, is identified as our desire. The happy couple declares their love for each other in terms kept deliberately obscure in order to fool the audience. But of course the audience understands perfectly, and it applauds, it approves. At the end of the film, William and Anna get to have it all, glitz and normality, fame and privacy, only because their audience cooperates: it forms a satisfyingly enthusiastic backdrop for their red-carpet entrance at the Academy Awards. And it is strangely absent when our couple feels the need for an intimate moment, such as in the final scene when William and Anna relax on the park bench, undisturbed by autograph seekers or photographers.

Notting Hill leaves the audience with a bewildering mixture of statements about image and identity, illusion and reality. Clearly, the film has some highly self-referential moments. On the one hand, Anna's pursuit of William can easily be read as the love declaration of a star to her audience: Anna wants to be loved because of who she is, not for her image; after all, a star depends on her audience for affirmation and approval. The film offers fulfillment of the viewers' dreams of fame and glory in the standard way, by inviting them to identify with someone rich, famous, and glamorous, and *simultaneously* portrays the average life of the audience as more desirable. The satisfaction offered to viewers of *Notting Hill* is twofold: we are told that our lives are already better than those of the rich and famous—but then you might also, as does William, achieve riches and fame in addition to preserving your fantastic average life. But there are two instances that betray the film's disingenuousness in this paradoxical portrayal: the utter emptiness of William's life without Anna (also documented in the recurring song "She," which describes her as the entire purpose of William's life) and the fact that in the end, the "real" event that leads to the establishment of Anna's normal life is defined as a movie. William and Anna's mutual declaration of love is witnessed by thousands, but his own sister, who has throughout the film done her utmost to bring the two together and is, in fact, the first to suggest that they marry, misses the crucial moment. The audience's reaction alerts her that something significant has happened, and when she asks Spike, "What happened?" he responds with the generic formulation of the satisfied moviegoer: "It was good." Thus the very act on which Anna's claim to a normal life must rest, the declaration of love, takes place not in private but in front of a huge audience and is seen, indeed reviewed, as a movie.

Notting Hill leaves us with two directly contradictory messages: we, the audience, with our limited finances, job worries, and even serious physical limitations, lead much more desirable lives than the rich and famous, who either are utter snobs, like Anna's boyfriend Jeff, or if they are decent people like Anna, actually long for our lives. On the other hand, the happiness established for the couple who is our test case in the film is an unlikely mix of Hollywood glamour and bourgeois privacy: taken by themselves, both Anna's life in the Hollywood dream and William's life in everyday reality are depicted as utterly miserable existences. In the end, we are offered a deal: for a mere eight or nine dollars, we, the audience, are invited to partake in the lives of the rich and famous—by going to the movies—for two or three hours before we are sent back to our drab little lives. While we dream of stardom, the film validates our less-than-glamorous existence by portraying it as the star's dream. It is the least the film can do in return for our acknowledgment and approval of stardom. *Notting Hill* simultaneously supports and disappoints our dreams: we love the stars, and the stars . . . well, the stars at least pretend to love us back.[17] We enjoy the film because it admirably manages to show us what we want, but we leave the theater knowing that our love story with the stars, unlike that between Anna and William, will never be consummated.

Erin Brockovich. Directed by Steven Soderbergh. Universal Studios. Release Date in the United States: March 17, 2000. Total U.S. Gross: $125,548,685

Julia Roberts's performance of the underdog heroine Erin Brockovich in the eponymous movie was awarded an Oscar and has often been hailed as the star's departure from the frivolous fare of the *Pretty Woman*-variety and her entry into the ranks of serious character actors. However, in many ways, *Erin Brockovich* replays the same themes that characterize most other Julia Roberts vehicles.

Like most other Julia Roberts characters, Erin is on a quest for her true identity, in her case embodied by the right job, or rather, any job at all. "All I've ever done is bend my life around what men decide they need," Erin declares as she is about to change her life. If Erin differs from other Julia Roberts heroines, it is because her surroundings are a lot less glamorous than what we have come to expect. Where *Pretty Woman* contents itself with a brushed-up two-minute sketch of the milieu of dealers and prostitutes, *Erin Brockovich* contains a somewhat realistic portrait of the life of an unemployed single mother of three. Erin lives in a downscale home infested by cockroaches which she cannot afford to have fumigated. Unable to pay for decent childcare, she must rely on the services of a sour-mouthed babysitter who has no qualms to leave the kids unattended whenever she feels like it. Erin has no degree, no resume, no job, no insurance, and no money to pay her bills. What she does have is a sick baby, two useless ex-husbands, a neck injury incurred through no fault of her own in a car accident caused by the reckless driving of a posh doctor, and a tiara from her one-year reign as Miss Wichita. But while it is true that *Erin Brockovich* presents a nuanced and elaborate portrayal of the kind of underdog existence that remains invisible in most Hollywood movies, the movie also contains the same kind of vibrant omnipotence fantasy and full-fledged fairy tale ending that make most other Julia Roberts movies so successful. Although she has no legal degree or job experience of any kind, Erin proves to be superior to every lawyer she works with. When her firm wins its major lawsuit against PG&E, it is in large part because of Erin's intelligence, quick-wittedness, and people skills; finally, Erin herself ends up with a two-million dollar check for her hard work. *Erin Brockovich* is based on a true and inspiring story, but that is not to say that it has not been carefully reworked to fit the mold of the classic Julia Roberts vehicle: underdog overcomes all adversity and is rewarded with a fairy tale ending.

NOTES

1. See Anthony Lane, *Nobody's Perfect: Writings from the* New Yorker (New York: Alfred A. Knopf, 2002), 699.

2. According to Lane, *Pretty Woman* "delivered a bitter, all but unanswerable slap to the mantras of the sixties: money, contrary to what Paul McCartney had informed us, could buy you love" (*Nobody's Perfect*, 697). Catherine L. Preston points out that *Pretty Woman* is the only one of the 1990s romantic comedies that "makes class difference a part of the plot" ("Hanging on a Star: The Resurrection of the Romance Film in the 1990s," in *Film Genre 2000: New Critical Essays*, ed. Wheeler Winston Dixon [Albany: State University of New York Press, 2000], 234). See also Alan Nadel, who claims that *Pretty Woman* portrays "the pervasive commodification of all relationships" (*Flatlining on the Field of Dreams: Cultural Narratives in the Films of President Reagan's America* [New Brunswick, N.J.: Rutgers University Press, 1997], 107).

3. It is true, however, that the film, in particular the Rodeo Drive sequence, also celebrates the art of shopping and consumerism (Stella Bruzzi, *Undressing Cinema: Clothing and Identity in the Movies* [New York: Routledge, 1997], 15).

4. In this, *Pretty Woman* conforms to the rules of classic screwball comedy. See Kathleen Rowe, who points out that screwball comedy often shifted "one set of social contradictions—the slippery issue of class in Depression America—onto the more readily managed ones of gender and generation" (*The Unruly Woman: Gender and the Genres of Laughter* [Austin: University of Texas Press, 1995], 125).

5. Paradoxically, the prostitute Vivian is cast in the role of the virginal heroine of screwball comedy who restores the hero to sexual potency. For example, Ellie (Claudette Colbert) in *It Happened One Night* helps Peter (Clark Gable) to regain his trumpet, whereas David (Cary Grant) in *Bringing Up Baby* has lost his bone and relies on Susan (Katharine Hepburn) to help him find it (Rowe, *The Unruly Woman*, 128).

6. See Bruzzi, who points out that *Pretty Woman* "deliberately announces itself as a fairy tale" (*Undressing Cinema*, 14). The most egregious fairy-tale element in *Pretty Woman* is, of course, the suggestion "that anyone can be upper class, that is, be woken to a call to shop and spend enough money to demand 'sucking up'" (Nadel, *Flatlining on the Field of Dreams*, 109). Nadel points out that this is the perfect "fairy tale ending to the story of President Reagan's America" (*Flatlining on the Field of Dreams*, 109).

7. In this, too, *Pretty Woman* adheres to the conventions of screwball comedy: "The pedant's encounter with the unruly woman points him toward becoming the adventurous and virile Ideal Male. The unruly woman, her job done, can then settle into the domesticity of the Ideal Woman" (Rowe, *The Unruly Woman*, 147).

8. Nadel suggests a different reading of the repeated allusions to Hollywood: "Whereas Hollywood has more commonly been regarded as the producer of fantasies, of escapes from reality, in this construction, it is a place where dreams may really come true, where dreaming can be rewarded" (*Flatlining on the Field of Dreams*, 109).

9. According to Rowe, the transgressive woman finds her home in the genre of comedy (*The Unruly Woman*, 96), a claim that is certainly true for *My Best Friend's Wedding*. Note, P. J. Hogan also directed and wrote *Muriel's Wedding*, which, like *My Best Friend's Wedding*, privileges friendship and fun over the boredom of a conventional marriage.

10. For a discussion of *My Best Friend's Wedding* in the context of screwball comedy, see Robin Wood, *Hollywood from Vietnam to Reagan . . . and Beyond* (New York: Columbia University Press, 2003), 295–98.

11. Yvonne Tasker points out that Hollywood movies frequently portray successful women as masculine—"advancement is presented as a form of masculinization" (*Working Girls: Gender and Sexuality in Popular Cinema* [London: Routledge, 1998], 41).

12. See Wood, who claims that "our confidence in the Dermot Mulroney/Cameron Diaz marriage is subtly but thoroughly undermined" (*Hollywood from Vietnam to Reagan . . . and Beyond*, 300).

13. It is this trait that marks *My Best Friend's Wedding* as a true successor of the screwball comedy. As Wood points out, "The romantic comedy is primarily about the construction of the ideal romantic couple, while the screwball comedy is primarily about liberation" (*Hollywood from Vietnam to Reagan . . . and Beyond*, 296).

14. The title *Runaway Bride* claims a connection to the screwball comedy and its "runaway bride" heroines. See also Maria DiBattista, who maintains that "the runaway bride is in flight not so much from authority as from a real knowledge of her self" (*Fast-Talking Dames* [New Haven: Yale University Press, 2001], 24).

15. William is a descendant of the professor-hero of classic screwball comedy who must endure "an extraordinary series of humiliations. But at the same time, he has had the best day of his life" (Rowe, *The Unruly Woman*, 145).

16. *Notting Hill* is a perfect example of what Rowe has called "a benign male fantasy in which men surrender rational control only to have their social and sexual power restored" (*The Unruly Woman*, 118).

17. Anthony Lane describes *Notting Hill* as a film that manages "to meet and flatter our expectations without bruising our assumptions" (*Nobody's Perfect*, 287).

Running Woman
Sandra Bullock

"What did you think you were trying to do, save the world?"
"No, not the world, just myself."

—*The Net* (1995)

Of all blockbuster Hollywood heroines, Sandra Bullock is probably the most versatile in terms of genre. Unlike most of her equally successful colleagues, such as Julia Roberts or Meg Ryan, she is not predominantly identified with romantic comedy, although some of her biggest hits are in that genre (*While You Were Sleeping* [1995], *Practical Magic* [1998], *Forces of Nature* [1999], and most recently *Two Weeks Notice* [2002]). But elsewhere she appears as a lawyer (*A Time to Kill* [1996], *Two Weeks Notice*), a cop (*Miss Congeniality* [2000], *Murder by Numbers* [2002]), a computer analyst (*The Net* [1995]), a nurse (*Gun Shy* [2000]), or a screenwriter (*28 Days* [2000]), and her professional persona in most of these films takes precedence over getting her hitched at the end. Some of her films, such as *Murder by Numbers*, *The Net*, *Forces of Nature*, or *28 Days*, manage to do away with the girl-gets-boy at the end entirely. Her professional competence, always shown to be impressive, is counterbalanced by personal failings: she is a dysfunctional alcoholic (*28 Days*), the wallflower nextdoor (*The Net*, *While You Were Sleeping*), the ugly duckling (*Miss Congeniality*), the angrily shouting political activist (*Two Weeks Notice*), or not even perceived as female (*Miss Congeniality*, *Murder by Numbers*). She very often appears unfeminine as well, disheveled, gawky, and clad in frumpy sweaters; and as she clumsily runs into doors, falls on her rump, and knocks over plants, we become aware that she portrays someone fundamentally maladjusted, someone incapable of living in the world. Her point of departure at the beginning of the film is nearly always the same, at odds with the world, on the defensive. Sandra Bullock plays characters with an important piece missing: women deprived of any human contact (*While You Were Sleeping*), dysfunctional or fundamentally disturbed women (*28 Days, Murder by Numbers*), women who are not really women (*Miss Congeniality*), or unpersons (*The Net*). As the same film will show her as an expert nurse, cop, lawyer, or computer analyst or simply as someone who is very good at thinking on her feet, like Annie in *Speed* (1994), these clear signals of her incompetence at life stand in direct contrast to her impressively skilled professional persona. The Sandra Bullock character is outstanding at what she does; what remains questionable is who she is. In many of her films, part of her or all of her has gone missing and has to be retrieved. Her violently divergent relationship with the world sometimes manifests itself in the image of pursuit: either she is running after (a criminal and, as the audience is well aware, a piece of herself) or running away (from utter annihilation).

Speed. Directed by Jan de Bont. Twentieth Century Fox. Release Date in the United States: June 10, 1994. Total U.S. Gross: $121,248,145

Speed, the film that made Sandra Bullock a star, does not focus on her as the main character and for that reason is not one of the films in which she regains that missing piece at the end. But Annie in *Speed* already shows the same competence and determination that in other films enable the Sandra Bullock character either to complete her identity or to prevent it from being erased.[1] *Speed* is a breathless thriller in which FBI agents Jack Traven (Keanu Reeves) and Harry Temple (Jeff Daniels) try to catch a bomber, disgruntled retiree Howard Payne (Dennis Hopper).[2] The film consists of three hostage stories in which Payne consecutively holds captive an elevator full of people, a bus full of people, and finally Annie (Sandra Bullock), who has emerged, in the bus episode, as the secret heroine of the film. In the end, she replaces Jack's old partner Harry, who has been killed by one of Payne's bombs. As the film progresses, Payne's opponents become fewer but mightier: in the elevator episode, he is thwarted by Jack and Harry, who are supported by an entire FBI SWAT team. In the bus episode, his opposition is down to Jack and Annie, with the FBI and police reduced to the role of helpless observers. And in the final episode on the train, it is Jack alone who busts him, an unavoidable solution given the relationship between Jack and Payne.

On the surface, *Speed* is not a film that deals with female identity. On the contrary, the film abounds in clearly male-defined sexual imagery, from phallic symbols (the elevator shaft, the bus, and finally the subway train), male orgasms (exploding bombs), male homoeroticism (the relationship between Jack and Payne and also, to some extent, between Jack and Harry), and male impotence (Payne's premature explosion of the first bomb is compared with a premature ejaculation). All of the dialogue between the men employs sexual imagery: Payne threatens to drop his stick but later turns out, as Jack puts it, to have shot only blanks. After the first explosion Harry asks Jack the stereotypical postcoital question, "Was it good for you?" and speculates that Payne had to let the bomb go early because he could not hold his wad long enough. In contrast to Jack's decidedly oversexed character, the man with balls (his recurring exclamation under stress is "Fuck me!"), Payne, the film's terrorist, is frequently characterized as castrated, not least because of his missing thumb—the limb that is supposed to make us human. The castration metaphor reaches its climax in the fight scene on the subway in which Jack decapitates Payne. From beginning to end, the two male couples, Jack and Payne and Jack and Harry, are matched in a pissing contest that expresses itself in aggressive and highly sexualized language.

Jack's character, compared with the two older men he is played off against, is that of the youthfully exuberant, oversexed, and adventurous daredevil who jumps down, runs ahead, or rappels down as Harry is still weighing his options. Both Harry and Payne, his main mentor and his main opponent, misinterpret Jack's spontaneity as thoughtlessness, even stupidity (Harry: "You've got to start thinking!"; Payne: "Do not attempt to grow a brain!"). But the film shows Jack from the outset as a man who can think on his feet as well as run with them: his plan to attach the elevator to a cable saves the first batch of hostages, and his idea to create a fake film for the bus's onboard camera, which is being monitored by Payne, saves the second. The older men, Harry and Payne, become Jack's opposing forces, the men who hold him down, Harry with his hopelessness, depression, and lack of initiative, and Payne with his constant sadistic taunts. It is this strangely homoerotic symbiosis first with Harry and later with Payne from which Jack must be liberated to live as what he is: a man with "big, round, hairy cojones," a man who is quick-witted and quick-footed, someone whose defining characteristic is *speed*. And it is these unproductive homoerotic relationships from which Annie rescues Jack.

From the outset, Annie is portrayed as someone who can keep up with Jack. We meet her at full run, yelling for the bus to stop, and we find out later that she is only on the bus because she has lost her license for speeding. Once on the bus, she quickly establishes herself as a woman who refuses to back down: she stands up to Jack when he comes on board and informs the passengers that there is a bomb on the bus.[3] When the bus driver is shot, she takes the wheel and spends a large portion of the rest of the film in the driver's seat, literally and figuratively. Annie's driving skills may have gotten her on the wrong side of the law, but in this situation, even her most girlish squeals of panic cannot fool the audience about the fact that she is saving the day.[4] She handles the obstacle course composed of sharp curves, busy traffic, and huge gaps in bridges with spirit and verve, calms down her passengers, and strategizes with Jack. She releases anxiety in healthy bursts of squeals and curses, but she always regains her calm, no matter how hair-raising the situation, quickly enough to keep the bus above 50 mph, the speed that is needed to prevent the bomb from exploding. Pleasing expressions of femininity such as her slight hysterics, her fear when she thinks she has run over a baby carriage, and her grief and guilt when one passenger is killed make her competence and courage acceptable to the viewer. She is always sensitive but never panics. When the other passengers turn against each other, she provides a stabilizing influence together with Jack, thus establishing herself as his ideal partner. As soon as Jack leaves the bus temporarily, she immediately becomes the boss on board, the person who is responsible for keeping the passengers not only alive with her driving skills but also in good morale. Annie is last to leave the bus, with Jack, after all the other passengers have been rescued. Most important, she saves Jack from giving up and resigning them all to their fates after Harry's death. She keeps Jack from sinking into the same hopelessness that killed Harry and gives him the courage that ultimately saves all of their lives. (Jack's final rescue of her in the subway episode can be seen as him returning her favor.)

Jack's transition from two male partners to one female partner is expressed in a not-so-subtle change in the sexual imagery. Not that Annie's involvement would result in a more feminine vision of sex: sex continues to be symbolized through bombs and phallic symbols. But what reemerges here is a topic alluded to earlier in the recurring castration metaphors, namely, the difference between productive and unproductive sex. To the bomber Payne, the bomb is its own point; its entire purpose, its becoming, is in the explosion. A bomb that does not explode, he tells Jack, is nothing. There is nothing productive about this: Payne is indeed shooting blanks. The bomb symbolizes the bomber who is also unproductive because he is utterly self-centered: "This is about *me*," he screams, "It's about *my* money, it's about money due *me*," and later: "I wish I had some loftier purpose, but I'm afraid it really is just the money." Thus the central question of the film is: How can we have the explosion without becoming Payne? How does one make the explosion productive?

This is beautifully symbolized in the implied sex scenes between Jack and Annie. They shoot out of the bus on a little metal board like a child from the womb, as the bus races into an airplane parked on the runway and the bomb goes off, giving us the biggest and undoubtedly most satisfying explosion of the film. Immediately after this dramatic rescue, Jack and Annie discuss the question whether they will make it as a couple, because relationships begun under extreme circumstances never last; later, Annie comes up with the answer to the dilemma: "We'll have to base it on sex, then." Sex between Annie and Jack is never unproductive: in the final scene, the subway train shoots through the billboard like a penis through a hymen, delivering the couple once again. Annie and Jack end up tightly embracing and kissing in the rubble, with an appreciative audience looking on delightedly, pointing fingers, laughing, and applauding. It may seem somewhat of a minor miracle that the sight of a kissing couple should be so much more interesting than the sight of all that havoc, but such is the message of the film: all that energy (explosions, sex, any kind of speed) has to lead somewhere, it has to end in something productive rather than destructive. Even more than the endlessly overdetermined difference between good and evil, between Jack Traven and Howard Payne, the difference is that between the all-male and the male–female couple, between unproductive homoerotic and productive heterosexual love. It is this aspect of the film, its blatant heterosexism, that assures the viewer that Jack and Annie are safe even if they base their relationship on nothing but sex. Once they have stopped running, jumping, driving, bursting through, boarding, rappelling, or speeding somewhere, once they finally hold still, they will still be the only viable alternative to Jack's earlier unproductive relationships with castrated and impotent men.

The Net. Directed by Irwin Winkler. Columbia Pictures. Release Date in the United States: July 28, 1995. Total U.S. Gross: $50,621,733

If Annie's purpose in *Speed* is to complete Jack, Angie in *The Net* can manage fine without a man, indeed without all human company. Angela Bennett (Sandra Bullock), professional debugger of programs, loner, and computer genius extraordinaire, is sent a computer disc by a coworker who, ominously, crashes in a plane on his way to her to discuss the program. On vacation in Mexico, she meets handsome Jack Devlin (Jeremy Northam). Their budding romance comes to a premature end when it turns out that he was hired to retrieve the diskette and kill Angie. She spends the remainder of the film running from him and trying to regain her identity, which has meanwhile been erased and replaced with a fake persona, that of prostitute and drug addict Ruth Marx. But her determination, her expertise with computers, and her survival skills prevail; she succeeds in killing Jack, uncovers a conspiracy to infiltrate government computers through a gatekeeper program, saves the world, and wins her life back. The end of the film shows her away from her computer, peacefully planting flowers with her mentally demented mother.

Even if Angie was not told constantly, by her customers and her coworkers, that she is the best there is at her job, the audience would be able to surmise this from the unbelievable speed with which she types and clicks her way through complicated algorithms. Clearly, her life is computers. But her impressive performance at the terminal has a flip side, as well: she is clad in an L. L. Beanish man's shirt and sweatpants and turns down a date only to order pizza for herself. As if that were not enough, scenes in which she opens the door to the FedEx man and in which she and her next-door neighbor all but ignore each other define her as someone who has virtually no contact with the outside world. We find out later that she has a therapist, Alan Champion (Dennis Miller), with whom she has slept to combat her increasing loneliness. Her innermost feelings are voiced in chat rooms where she describes her ideal man to people she knows only by their log-in names; even her attempts to make her home comfortable, a cozy fire burning in a fireplace on a computer screen, are technological imitations of the real thing. Her single human contact off-line, other than the misguided sexual fling with her shrink, is with her mother (Diane Baker), who suffers from Alzheimer's disease and no longer recognizes her only daughter.

Both her mother's dementia and the modern disconnectedness from her next-door neighbor already hint at what Angie will experience in the technological

She who fights and runs away lives to fight another day. Sandra Bullock in The Net *(1995).* COLUMBIA/THE KOBAL COLLECTION.

realm: that a life, an identity, can be completely erased, even replaced with one that did not exist before. Angie's lack of human contact in the real world is not only lamentable but dangerous. Her existence as a loner, the absence of friends or family who could recognize her and vouch for her, allows Jack to erase her identity in the world of computers. Angie, who used to be in control of technology, has to stand up not only to Jack Devlin but to technology itself, the computer programs that now define who and what we are. But even in a situation in which her identity has ceased to exist to the outside world, Angie holds on to it, and this ultimately enables her to turn the situation around. Unlike Kafka's Josef K., she never harbors any real doubts about her own identity. Aside from one brief glimmer of self-doubt ("It's like I'm not even me anymore," she confesses to Alan), she never allows the external definition of herself to gain precedence over her own inner conviction of who she is. When the computer at the hotel informs her that she has checked out, when the government computer renames her Ruth Marx, and when the hospital computer kills Alan by misdiagnosing him as a diabetic, Angie consistently pits her memory against the computer's version. This is presented as a remarkable achievement, for in every other contest between human knowledge, human judgment, or human testimony and computer records the computer ends up winning. To everyone else in the film, the computer's version represents the undisputable truth; nobody ever considers the possibility that computer records could be doctored, manipulated, or simply erroneous.

Angie is a survival artist who puts her instincts as well as her intellect to good use.[5] We get a taste of this when she finds Jack's gun and removes the bullets even before she has any real reason to mistrust him. She escapes, gets off the yacht, and crashes the boat into Jack, thus proving that she is quite willing to hurt him to save herself. This motif recurs several times: in a later scene she takes the steering wheel from a fake cop who was sent by Jack and crashes his car into Jack's. The turning point in the movie occurs when Angie stops running and turns her defense tactics into a counterattack. She infiltrates her own place of work, finds the impostor who has assumed her identity (Wendy Gazelle), and uses her computer to copy the parasite program that she then sends to the FBI. The solution to Angie's problems run on a parallel track, one in the virtual, one in the real world: Angie tricks Jack into deleting the program that stole her identity and turned her into Ruth Marx, a scene that affords Angie (and us) the tremendous satisfaction of watching the fake Ruth Marx ID dissolve on the screen. Shortly thereafter, Jack himself mistakes the real Ruth Marx, his coconspirator, for Angela and shoots her IRL (In Real Life).

The Net asks some harrowing questions about human identity: How do we know who we are? And how do we make other people believe our version of who we are? IRL identities, the ones that rely not on the computer's say-so but on our own judgment and memory, seem just as dubious as those established by the computer. In "real" life, Angie's mother has no memory or recognition of her daughter. Our own erroneous assumption that Jack will become Angie's lover disintegrates early in the film. The film visualizes our disorientation by quickly intercutting disjointed fragments of his face as he sarcastically quotes her chat room dreams of the perfect lover back at her. We are bombarded with jarring shots of his hate-filled eyes, his twisted mouth, never his entire face. The implication is clear: he is a part, not a whole human, and he is not who we thought he was. If real-life identities are just as fragile as computer-generated ones, the question becomes who defines who we are: the outside world or us, through our own sense of self.

To women, this question holds a different meaning and urgency than it does for men. More often than not, women's identities are other-defined rather than self-determined: everyone tells women who they are. The film turns this insight into one of its major plot devices. Jack spends most of his time trying to define Angie; even her friend Alan projects his own wishes, for example, his preference for Chinese food, onto her. A female audience is likely to derive great satisfaction from watching the fake Ruth Marx being deleted, because we are all too aware that this persona was forced on our heroine. Interestingly, accepting the fake identity leads not to greater societal approval but into even greater danger: Angela Bennett, in signing her passport as Ruth Marx in order to be allowed back into the United States, becomes a fugitive from the law and plays right into her pursuer's hands. One might even wonder whether Angie ends up single because the two men in her life also present a danger to her sense of self. Can Angie only survive once both eligible men, dashingly handsome but murderous Jack and pedestrian but sweetly supportive Alan, are out of the picture? Both Alan, whose saving grace is his support of Angie although he does not believe her story, and Jack, who desires her almost as much as he wants to kill her, are brutally removed from the film. Jack's death guarantees Angie's survival, and to a lesser degree, so does Alan's, as the film insinuates that Angie's relationship with Alan failed because he never saw the "real her." This resolution is far more radical than claiming that a woman is complete without a man: The more you are yourself, the film seems to suggest, the less you can be with somebody else. In the struggle between the individual and the world that so many Sandra Bullock films describe, *The Net* comes down wholly on the side of the individual, showing her own sense of self as valid even when the entire world disagrees. This new female self-confidence requires a sacrifice from us, as well. The film withholds what every audience craves: the final close-up of the kiss in front of a glorious sunset or a romantic fire in the fireplace, in "real" life.

Miss Congeniality. Directed by Donald Petrie. Warner Bros. Release Date in the United States: December 22, 2000. Total U.S. Gross: $106,887,607

Miss Congeniality addresses the question of female identity explicitly. The film is a mixture between cop thriller and romantic comedy; its two goals seem to be, at least initially, to catch the bad guy and turn the good girl into a real woman. FBI agent Gracie Hart (Sandra Bullock) is a supercompetent cop with ample brain and ample brawn who is nonetheless dissed by her coworkers. The reasons for this contempt are twofold. On the one hand, Gracie is "just a woman" and lets herself be treated like one. She is sent out for coffee and donuts, passed over for promotions, and confined to boring paperwork while her male colleagues devote themselves to the exciting work of chasing the bad guys. On the other hand, she is never perceived as a "real woman" because she is ugly and disheveled, dresses badly, and behaves like a klutz, constantly running into doors and falling over her feet. She snorts through her nose when she laughs, has a "bad hair decade," and wolfs down pizza, messy dinners smothered in tomato sauce, and ice cream by the pint: she is Dirty Harriett, by far the least appetizing female on the force. Gracie is presented as a woman because she is a victim of sexual discrimination; simultaneously, she is presented as no "real" woman because she is not the object of male desire: when she asks her colleague Eric Matthews (Benjamin Bratt) whether she is disrespected because she is a woman, he disingenuously informs her that "nobody thinks of you that way." Small wonder that nobody considers Gracie when the FBI needs an undercover female agent to catch a beauty pageant killer. Gracie only ends up with the assignment because the only other female field agent under thirty-five is currently pregnant. She undergoes beauty boot camp at the hands of pageant makeover artiste Victor Melling (Michael Caine); wins second place at the pageant in her disguise as Miss New Jersey; catches the killer, who turns out to be the sexist son (Steve Monroe) of the pageant organizer herself, Kathy Morningside (Candice Bergen); and learns in the process that not all beautiful women are airheads. At the end, Gracie embarks on a cautious romance with her brother cop Eric Matthews.

Although it alludes to both, the film is neither a Dirty Harry cop flick with a female hero nor an ugly-duckling-transformed-into-a-swan fairy tale. In its very first scene, we are shown a side of Gracie that her colleagues do not recognize: that of a passionate defender of justice. In a playground scene, seven-year-old Gracie knocks out a boy for bullying another little boy but gets no gratitude from the boy she has rescued: he yells at her because now everyone thinks he needs a girl to protect him, and in response, she knocks him out, as well. This brief scene foreshadows Gracie's entire character and situation as an adult. Barely in kindergarten, she already protects and serves, takes no crap from anyone, fights gender stereotypes, and expertly knocks the boys out, sidestepping and kickboxing: this is no scene with little children writhing on the ground; Gracie clearly has the upper hand as a fighter. But her response to the little boy's rejection shows us another side of her as well: she has not yet found a way to resolve conflict other than knocking everybody out. As an adult, she blows off steam by boxing with the punching bag or taking her male colleagues to the mat.

The next scene shows us grown-up Gracie in pigtails on an undercover assignment, still cute, childlike, wearing the same glasses as she did at age seven, and still protecting the world from male bullies. She handles her assignment with astonishing competence; excepting her smarts (she speaks perfect Russian), she is a female copy of Dirty Harry. Just like Dirty Harry, she seizes her chance to take the bad guys out, disobeys a direct order, and takes the lead. In her case, however, another cop is wounded in the shoot-out, and although the operation is a success, she is made to assume the blame for that. In some ways, then, she faces the same dilemma as Dirty Harry, because like him, she constantly battles the boss behind the desk who does not know what it is like "out there." But Gracie gets shot down not only as a cop but also as a woman when Matthews tells her it was the wrong choice "and by the way, you look like hell." This, of course, is stuff that Dirty Harry never has to listen to. Clearly, the Dirty Harriett part is not an exact parallel: Gracie, in her endless and seemingly fruitless fight against sexism on the job, is up against the good guys as well as the bad guys.

Unsurprisingly, Eric Matthews gets rewarded for the success of the Russian hostage operation, whereas Gracie is grounded for it. He ends up as lead detective on the case she wants to work: the Citizen case, which involves a bomber threatening to blow up the Miss United States pageant. Gracie is not only bighearted enough to congratulate him but also savvy enough to steer the operation in the right direction. She is the most competent cop on the force but also, problematically, willing to do the work without receiving credit for it. Although she should be in charge of the investigation, she works quietly behind the scenes and leaves all the glory to the men. Gracie's problematic status as a (non)woman is worked through when she is pushed into the limelight as undercover Miss New Jersey. Gracie initially refuses the assignment because of her aversion to beauty pageants in general, which, according to her, pander to "some misogynistic Neanderthal mentality." She has no desire to parade around in a swimsuit like some airhead bimbo named Gracie Lou Freebush, the name, of course, implying rather crudely that beauty pageant contestants are no better than prostitutes. But as the assignment is forced on her, we understand that part of the motivation is to complete Gracie. Having already established her as an unquestionably competent police officer, we now want to see if she can be transformed into a woman.

Thus begins Operation Thong: Gracie, who does not own a hairbrush, a dress, or lipstick, is sent to a Frankenstein-like beauty factory where she undergoes the tortures of hair removal, waxing, face masks, manicure, and pedicure. She emerges from the factory looking gorgeous (tempting the viewer, of course, to think the torment has been worth it) but thankfully sounding exactly the same and still falling over her feet. Consequently, beauty consultant Victor Melling must embark on the gargantuan task to get Gracie to eat with her mouth closed, say "yes" instead of "yeah," and glide instead of stomping. But lest the audience is tempted to rejoice that Gracie is finally being "fixed," the film issues a warning that Gracie's newfound femininity is not only out of character but also dangerous: obediently gliding across the street, she is almost run over by a taxi.

As one of forty-nine contestants for the Miss United States title, "Gracie Lou Freebush" has to confront her own stereotypes about these "airhead bimbos." Initially, nothing disproves Gracie's prejudices. The "hoochie mamas," as the cops call them, are all presented as cloyingly sweet, silly, and exclusively concerned with keeping their good looks. They live on diet foods, openly discuss their ways of keeping their figures (including bulimia), sing the Miss United States song on command, and shrink in horror when Gracie shows up with pizza, beer, and chocolate. Their "talents" consist of singing, dancing, and twirling batons, and the "cause" they all support is the least controversial, most generic cause on the globe, "world peace." Later, however, we learn that these airhead bimbos are endowed with academic achievements and social concerns. One of them turns out to be a major in nuclear physics with a minor in "elementary particles," another is a theater major working with underprivileged children, and a third works in a homeless shelter: these women all have their brains and their causes. One of the top ten finalists actually turns out to be a militant lesbian who declares her love for her darling Karen from the stage. As Gracie discovers all this, she bonds with the contestants. In her case, this means corrupting their focus on body image by taking them out for pizza, boosting their self-confidence, and instructing them in self-defense. In one of the most subversive scenes of the film, Gracie offers a self-defense class to the women in the audience as her pageant "talent": one of the rare scenes on film in which a woman mistreats a man in public and is applauded for it. As Gracie expertly beats up her colleague Matthews on stage and teaches the audience to S-I-N-G (to hit "a man's four most sensitive areas: solar plexus, instep, nose, groin"), we cannot help but see this as a payback for every slight she has endured on the job because she is a woman.

In the end, Gracie declares that her participation in the pageant was "one of the most rewarding and liberating experiences of my life," and the beauty contestants present Gracie with the "Miss Congeniality" award for being the coolest and nicest girl at the pageant. As the airheads are recognized as intelligent human beings, they in turn show their understanding that there are qualities beyond external beauty worthy of awards. Gracie, in becoming more beautiful, has become more like them; they, in valuing her character rather than her beauty, have become more like her. The rift between bimbos and feminists has finally been healed. Or has it? Clearly, this is what the film purports to do: her fellow contestants treasure the same qualities for which Gracie's cop colleagues put her down. But in the end, the film does not do enough to establish the beauty contestants as anything but airhead bimbos. We get to see them having fun once, eating pizza and sloshing down beer, but we never see a scene in which they have a serious conversation about what they really want (other than world peace). The pseudoemphasis on their unique individuality is destroyed when they all march out onto stage, dressed up as the Statue of Liberty and looking absolutely identical, to the tune of "You're One in a Million." If liberty is individuality, the right to self-determine, these women are anything but free. The Miss United States crown, the ultimate in societal approval for a woman, is designed to single out one of these women from the crowd. But to get that approval, all women are well advised to practice absolute conformity: Gracie's "cause" (harsher punishment for parole violators) is greeted with shocked silence, whereas the other forty-nine all get thunderous applause for the world peace line, precisely because the audience has heard that one before and expects nothing else.

Miss Congeniality shows not what women are like but how they are *seen*. We spend much of the film watching men watch women at the pageant, through the cops' surveillance cameras, or at the Dress-Up-Sally-Website, always accompanied by a running commentary from the men that runs the gamut from leers to insults. This is already established during the Russian hostage situation at the outset of the film, in which a waitress gets in front of a surveillance camera and is called "the broad with two asses" by the man at the other end of the camera. Gracie's story teaches us that women are constantly monitored and ridiculed if they ever let on that they have a brain or any individuality. Thus *Miss Congeniality* could be seen as a film about smart and savvy women who delete every shred of their individuality because they know they will not be accepted with it. Being female, in the world of *Miss Congeniality*, is seen as a losing proposition because anything perceived as "feminine" is viewed as opposed to intellect or individuality and anything perceived as "unfeminine" (Gracie speaking with her mouth full and snorting when she laughs) is perceived as socially ill-fitting. In this world, there is no way that Gracie, or any woman, can gain any respect. The only way out of this dilemma is realizing that the problem lies merely in how women are viewed—hence Gracie's eye-opener with regard to the bimbos (a move that the audience cannot entirely replicate), hence the contestants' new acceptance of feminist Gracie, hence even Agent Matthews's transformation at the end: if he can learn to see Gracie as a competent and lovable character, so can other men.

As the movie emphasizes seeing with new eyes over actual change, Gracie, who has been transformed from ugly duckling to swan, does not have to remain one. It is enough that she has learned to respect the swans. The final scene, in which she negotiates her romance with Matthews, has her snorting through her nose once again. Having realized that she is safer stomping than gliding, she goes back to stomping at the end. Even if her hair looks a whole lot better at the finish than it did in the beginning, we understand that the swan has metamorphosed back into the ugly duckling she used to be. And finally, even Matthews compliments her on her good police work. When they kiss, in a public place surrounded by people who ignore them, we realize that much has changed: Matthews becomes aware of her breasts, seeing her as a woman for the first time. But the rest of the world does *not* see them. For once, Gracie is not under acute observation; for once, the lovers do not have their choice confirmed by an applauding round of bystanders. Societal approval, the final message seems to be, is beside the point.

For women, *Miss Congeniality* presents a strange mixture of liberating and constricting images. On the one hand, it shows us that the image of femininity can be manipulated; on the other hand, it leaves us with the somewhat disheartening message that if a woman wants to be taken seriously on the job *and* noticed as a woman, she would have to be at least a Miss America contestant—a waitress with two asses would stand no chance to be recognized as a competent human being with breasts. *Miss Congeniality* assigns men their share of the blame for the oppression of women: the many locker-room scenes around cameras where women are paraded for the men's crotch-grabbing amusement and disparaging commentary leave us little doubt about that. But the villain of the film, the Citizen, turns out to be sexist pig Frank, who is characterized as completely under his mother's thumb. This transfers the blame from men to mother and implies that if women are hated, they must have done something to deserve it: behind every woman hater, there is a woman. Gracie is accepted at the end although she goes back to overeating, snorting, stomping, and falling over her feet, but could we do the same and expect the same latitude? The compromised female type that Sandra Bullock so often plays—Gracie's clumsiness, unsightliness, and professional competence make her the twin sister of Lucy in *Two Weeks Notice*—is vindicated once again. But we are left wondering whether this privilege would be extended to the rest of us, who have never been Miss America contestants.

Murder by Numbers. Directed by Barbet Schroeder. Warner Bros. Release Date in the United States: April 19, 2002. Total U.S. Gross: $31,874,869

In *Murder by Numbers*, Sandra Bullock plays homicide cop Cassie Mayweather, who investigates the murder of a schoolgirl. Cassie is a hypercompetent policewoman but nonetheless so unpopular on the force that everyone refuses to be her partner.[6] Cassie, in return, makes relentless and occasionally vicious fun of her brother cops. It turns out that she has slept with virtually all of her partners but coldly rebuffs any attempts at intimacy beyond that of sex. When she gets involved, initially in the same fashion, with her new partner, Sam Kennedy (Ben Chaplin), we find out that Cassie has some biographical baggage. Stabbed savagely and left for dead by her husband Carl Hudson, Cassie survived, changed her name (from Jessica), and repressed any memory of her past. Cassie's trauma as a victim of sexual assault and nearly of murder, which resurfaces during the investigation of the schoolgirl's murder, is responsible for her two major flaws: her pathological behavior toward men and her obsessive attitude on the job.[7] Although Cassie's police work is universally recognized as "brilliant," even among colleagues who hate her personally, she is repeatedly criticized for her tenacity. But it is precisely this inability to give up that helps her solve a case that everyone else has long since resigned to the "unsolved" pile. Her colleagues also attack Cassie's tendency to identify with the female victim rather than the male perpetrator of the crime. Cassie treats the victim as a person rather than a case. This is unanimously interpreted as a sign of Cassie's emotional overinvolvement because a good investigator is supposed to be able to "think like the perp." But the film does its share to destroy these cop myths: although Cassie's romantic relationships are indeed shown to be problematic, even pathological, her police work leaves nothing to be desired. In the end, Cassie single-handedly solves the murder case and also finds the strength to face her own past. In the final scene, she returns to her identity as Jessica and serves as a hostile witness at Carl Hudson's parole hearing.

Cop Cassie is a serious version of droll Cop Gracie in *Miss Congeniality*. Both are portrayed as professionally competent but personally damaged, and even some minor facets that define the character in *Murder by Numbers* are taken straight from *Miss Congeniality*. Whereas Gracie was reduced to the gopher who gets coffee for the entire force in *Miss Congeniality*, a huge box of donuts serves as "a very important crime scene tool" in *Murder by Numbers*. In order to keep her colleagues from messing up her crime scene, Cassie distracts them with donuts. This scene reveals that Cassie does not work with the force but, rather, without or even against them and sets her off against her donut-munching colleagues. Cassie is not only highly competent and committed; she is the only one who really wants this crime solved.

The question of identity also resurfaces in this film. Whereas Cassie sheds an identity that she can no longer live with—that of murder victim Jessica—the two perpetrators of the film, schoolboys Richard (Ryan Gosling) and Justin (Michael Pitt), have to merge identities to be able to commit their crime.[8] Richard and Justin see murder as an expression of the philosophical freedom to commit evil. Both Justin's intellect and Richard's ruthlessness are needed to get away with murder. The film visualizes their symbiosis through the digital superimposition of their faces. The identity merger between Justin and Richard functions as a mirror image of Cassie's rejection of her former identity as Jessica: in both cases, the new identity interacts with the outside world in disastrously aggressive ways.

Unlike the boys, however, Cassie has turned some of her aggression to good use, namely, the pursuit of murderers. But on a personal level, her aggression against men leads to some appalling scenes. After her first time having sex with Sam, she literally kicks him out of bed. The next day at work she does not even register him as a human being, but she attempts to seduce him again, at the earliest opportunity, in the crudest way imaginable. She thwarts his attempts at real intimacy through merciless ridicule ("You want a ring?" she taunts him) or by making him aware that she is merely playing the part: "I really respect you as a person," she assures him with a straight face and then bursts into giggles. Sam, aghast, breaks off the encounter, and she goes right back to watching *Matlock* on TV. Throughout the film, Cassie is portrayed as completely unwilling, or unable, to have a personal conversation with anyone. Indeed, her running dialogue with TV detective Matlock, whom she reminds that he will be hard-pressed to solve his case because he has neither fingerprints nor powder burns, seems more authentic and meaningful than many of her conversations with actual people.

Part of Cassie's problem, as diagnosed by the film, is her decided masculinity, and in this as well, she is an amplified version of *Miss Congeniality*'s Gracie. Cassie's nicknames in the force are "Scorpion" and "Hyena" because female hyenas have a mock penis; the standing joke among her male colleagues is that Cassie pisses standing up. If Gracie's colleagues could not perceive her as a woman, Cassie's brother cops do them one better and define her as a man. In her interaction with Sam, she consistently assumes the male role. The bait-and-switch tactics, the sex bare of any intimacy, the coarseness, the brutality with which she rejects Sam, and the ridicule she heaps on him are all things we have seen before at the movies: this is the way mean guys routinely treat women. However, if the audience is to accept such behavior from a woman, her motivation has to be overdetermined: a male character who was left by his wife would be traumatized sufficiently to excuse similar abuse of other women. In Cassie's case, extreme violence and a near-death experience are barely enough. Her disturbing scenes with Sam are highly instructive because they show a woman sexually and emotionally mistreating a man, instead of what we are used to seeing, the opposite.

Gender reversal for instructional purposes is not limited to Cassie's character. Both Sam and Justin are portrayed as highly feminized: Sam is a supportive but also submissive partner, who follows in Cassie's footsteps and carries her coffee on the job while submitting to her sexual and emotional abuse in private life. Justin is described as a longhaired weakling who is intimidated into action by Richard and throws up on the crime scene because he cannot stomach the physical brutality of murder. He plays woman to Richard's man in the sense that Richard desires his exclusive attention and affection and flies into a jealous rage as soon as Justin betrays him by beginning an affair with his classmate and one-time sexual partner Lisa. When Justin attempts to leave Richard, Richard responds in precisely the same way in which Carl Hudson responded to Jessica's attempt to leave him, by trying to murder the "woman" who is about to walk out the door. Clearly, the dysfunctional relationship between Cassie and Sam is far from unusual: all sexual and emotional interactions in the film are portrayed as severely disturbed. The ones in which a gender reversal takes place—between feminized Justin and masculine Richard, between masculine Cassie and feminized Sam—are characterized by emotional manipulation of the worst sort. If no gender reversal takes place and men remain "real men" like Richard and Carl Hudson, then abuse culminates in murder. He-men in the film are defined by their brutality toward women: Cassie identifies Richard instantly as the schoolgirl's killer because she recognizes his mode of interaction with women, based on her knowledge of Carl. The final scene, in which Richard tries to murder Cassie, is overlaid with Carl's voice threatening to kill Jessica.

Watching all this abuse makes us wonder whether it is possible to have a relationship with anyone that is characterized by trust rather than mistreatment. The test case is the relationship between Cassie and Sam, who try to move on to something else after their disastrous sexual affair. When Cassie tells Sam the story of Jessica Hudson, she uses the third person—"this girl I knew in high school"—which demonstrates the degree of her detachment from Jessica. Jessica had to die so that Cassie could get on with her life. Cassie refuses to return to being Jessica and therefore cannot go to Carl Hudson's parole hearing. Of course Sam, and the audience, easily discern what Cassie's problem is: she cannot escape Carl because he has become every man, every perp, every case in her life. The Cassie identity is unreal because it is a mere reversal: in shedding Jessica, Cassie metamorphoses from hunted to hunter, from monogamous to promiscuous, from housewife to professional, from a woman in a nice house to someone who lives on a boat and is thus, at least potentially, always on the go. Nor is Cassie complete: she has lost her past and thus condemned herself to an existence where there is always something missing. Even her name has its first part missing—*Cassie* is an anagram of *Jessica* minus the first letter.

In the end, Cassie solves her case by showing the same disregard for her boss that is also a trademark of Gracie in *Miss Congeniality*. In the best Dirty Harry tradition, both Gracie and Cassie continue to work, without any authorization or support, on closed cases. Just like most male cops of the genre, Cassie finally confronts the perps alone. She catches both of her perps in character-appropriate ways, by killing Richard physically and by outsmarting Justin intellectually. When the reinforcements finally arrive, Cassie no longer needs their help. It would appear that Cassie's rejection of all contact or communication is a personal, but not a professional, problem. Because the other cops consistently obstruct and belittle Cassie's good work, we feel that she was right to go it alone.

But then, we knew all along that Cassie was capable of solving her case and catching her perps. What is really at stake is whether Cassie can make herself whole again, whether she can find the missing piece that completes her as a person. As Justin pleads with her to give him a second chance, her answer is addressed more to herself than to him: "There are no second chances. You get one life—and whatever you do with it, whatever is done to you, you gotta face that. You can't pretend it didn't happen." The next scene shows her at the parole hearing, answering to Jessica Hudson: she, too, has stopped pretending that it did not happen to her.

Cassie's ability to save herself makes her a true Sandra Bullock heroine. Very often, self-preservation is all the Sandra Bullock character gets. When the danger to her life is greatest, such as in *28 Days*, *The Net*, or *Murder by Numbers*, we do not see her paired off in the end. In other words, these films give us what she needs but not what we want for her. Perhaps this is the main reason for the varying success of the Sandra Bullock character: all the films that offer a romantic ending (*Two Weeks Notice*, *Speed*, *While You Were Sleeping*, *Miss Congeniality*) were unequivocal box office hits, grossing between $81 and $121 million in the United States alone. But the films in which she "merely" saves herself, displaying admirable spirit, determination, and competence in the process, were unmitigated flops. *The Net* was a moderate failure at the box office with $50 million gross and was slammed unmercifully by movie critics across the country. *Murder by Numbers* and *28 Days*, in which the danger to her character is shown to be the most extreme, grossed in the $30 million range. Neither so much as recouped production costs ($50 million for *Murder by Numbers*, $43 million for *28 Days*). Sandra Bullock's career, as measured by box office success, is a great deal more spotty than that of Julia Roberts. In some Sandra Bullock movies, it seems that for once, Hollywood is showing us something we are not quite ready to see. It may be some time yet before we, the audience, perceive the spectacle of a woman saving herself—not the world, not some man, just herself—as worthy of our attention.

NOTES

1. Anthony Lane calls Bullock a "Julia Roberts with guts" (*Nobody's Perfect: Writings from the* New Yorker [New York: Alfred A. Knopf, 2002], 67).

2. Richard Dyer characterizes *Speed* "the movie as rollercoaster: all action and next to no plot" (*Only Entertainment* [New York: Routledge, 2002], 65).

3. Yvonne Tasker argues that "Annie—as victim/bargaining chip/feisty heroine (dubbed 'Wildcat') and tomboyish cheerleader—is symptomatic, an indicative composite of agency and passivity" (*Working Girls: Gender and Sexuality in Popular Cinema* [London: Routledge, 1998], 67). She also notes: "Ultimately Annie shifts from the driving seat to heroine awaiting rescue" (*Working Girls*, 78). However, although Tasker draws attention to the imperfect nature of the heroine, she also believes that in *Speed* "both central characters are composites of agency and passivity, active and reactive in turns" (*Working Girls*, 78).

4. Although *Speed's* gender politics are intriguing, its depiction of race is problematic. Dyer points out that the movie celebrates straight white men. It is left to "Keanu and his white helper to save the busload of mainly non-white passengers" (Dyer, *Only Entertainment*, 66). On the other hand, they are being *saved*. In *Speed*, it is things, not non-white characters, that are expendable.

5. The fact that the film focuses on the victim Angie, not on the perpetrators, fits in with a general trend in crime thrillers of the 1990s. See Ron Wilson, "The Left-Handed Form of Human Endeavor: Crime Films during the 1990s," in *Film Genre 2000: New Critical Essays*, ed. Wheeler Winston Dixon (Albany: State University of New York Press, 2000), 145.

6. This isolation marks her as a masculine hero. In her analysis of action movies, Yvonne Tasker points out that "the hero of the action narrative is often cast as a figure

who lacks a place within the community for which he fights" (*Spectacular Bodies: Gender, Genre and the Action Cinema* [London: Routledge, 1993], 77).

7. Tasker's analysis shows that this is a stock feature of crime movies with female investigators: "The criminal investigations which structure the narratives of *Impulse, Blue Steel* and *Bodily Harm* all involve an exploration of the sexuality of the female investigators alongside, and complexly intertwined with, the central case itself" (*Working Girls*, 93).

8. Both perpetrators grew up under extremely privileged circumstances. *Murder by Numbers* thus provides a variation on the theme of "corruption in high places," popular in crime films of the 1990s (Wilson, "The Left-Handed Form of Human Endeavor," 156).

☆ **3** ☆

Sleeping with the Enemy
Meg Ryan

"Don't you think that daisies are the friendliest flowers?"

—*You've Got Mail* (1998)

Although Meg Ryan has appeared in a variety of roles, ranging from prostitutes to drug addicts, she is most identified with the genre of romantic
comedy. The typical Meg Ryan heroine is cute and fresh as a daisy and has a
touch of Doris Day about her. She is a working girl who teaches history, writes
articles for a local paper, or is even the owner of a little store. Although she
knows how to make a living and may even occupy a position that requires great
competence, such as a surgeon in *City of Angels* (1998), she is usually not very
ambitious or obsessed with her career.[1] Her focus is on romance and family,
and she often appears old-fashioned. It is no coincidence that several Meg
Ryan films are remakes of or allude to movies from the 1930s and 1950s (*The
Shop around the Corner* [1940], *An Affair to Remember* [1957]). In *You've Got
Mail* (1998), Kathleen Kelly belongs to a bygone era in which people shopped
in corner stores and owned handkerchiefs made of actual fabric. In *Sleepless in
Seattle* (1993), Annie not only tries on her grandmother's wedding gown, but
she also wears flowery flannel nightshirts that might well stem from the same
source. In *Kate and Leopold* (2001), she achieves a happy ending when she
leaves modern-day New York and time travels straight back to the nineteenth
century. Clearly, the Meg Ryan heroine belongs to an era that knew nothing of
today's gender trouble. Because she is not really of our time, our feminist
struggles cannot touch her. She does not avoid them; rather, they are simply
not her problem.

Never a tomboy, the Meg Ryan character is a master of female values and virtues. The realm of emotions and interpersonal relations is her true area of expertise. She is loyal and strictly a one-man kind of a gal, although it may take some time until she identifies the right candidate. More interested in love than sex, she knows how to connect, to share, to communicate, and to take care of others.[2] Even as a soldier in *Courage under Fire* (1996), she is most lauded for her ability to protect her crew and for her motherly dedication to her daughter. Usually, all her hopes and wishes are directed toward the right combination of home, house, and family. Because of this desire to grow roots, her movies often exhibit a strong sense of location—or at least purport to do so. She falls in love with "Sleepless in Seattle," walks the streets of New York in *You've Got Mail*, and communes with angels in Los Angeles. Even when she agrees to spend the rest of her life on a French vineyard, there is something very American and apple pie about her. She is frank, honest, and willing to engage. She expresses her feelings openly and always says what is on her mind. Her optimism is relentless, and so is her capacity for denial. We cannot help but admire her desperate courage when she refuses to accept that she has been abandoned by her beloved fiancé, when she claims that her tiny little bookstore and the Fox Books megastore will complement each other most wonderfully, or when she insists that she is in love with her fiancé Walter long after we have realized that the two of them will never make it. In the usual Meg Ryan fare, the heroine will be mistreated, but she will never give up, and her stamina will be rewarded in the end.

Unlike Julia Roberts or Sandra Bullock characters, Meg Ryan heroines do not usually set out to find their true identity. The Meg Ryan heroine is also not on a quest to liberate or emancipate herself. Rather, she already embodies a promise of wholeness and integrity. What few problems she has relate to her lack of self-esteem. She may not realize that she is fine the way she is. She tends to be far too nice and accommodating and hence is easily victimized by others. In many of her movies, the Meg Ryan character is the object of abuse and betrayal. Other characters walk all over her: in *French Kiss* (1995) and *Addicted to Love* (1997), she is cheated on and abandoned for another woman; in *You've Got Mail*, her competitor drives her out of business; in *City of Angels*, she is run over by a truck; and in *Courage under Fire*, she is shot at by her own subordinates. Consequently, personal growth for the Meg Ryan heroine is often defined as a process of learning to stand up for herself. But no matter how hard she tries to fight back, her acts of self-assertion always remain harmless and cute. Even when she points a long, sharp knife at her arrogant and insulting competitor Joe Fox in *You've Got Mail* or when she shouts in frustration that all men are bastards in

French Kiss, we are more inclined to feel protective toward her than threatened by her. Frequently, schoolgirl outfits of plaid skirts and white blouses emphasize her childlike innocence. She possesses a "Jeffersonian purity" (*You've Got Mail*) that keeps her from harm.

If she has any kind of power at all, it is usually the power to save others. The Meg Ryan persona can be counted on to rescue her man. She will come to his aid in every possible way: financially and sexually (*French Kiss*), emotionally (*You've Got Mail*), when he is lonely (*Sleepless in Seattle*), and when his life is threatened (*Courage under Fire*). More often than not, she trades protection for redemption.[3] But no matter whether she rescues her man or her man protects her, the Meg Ryan heroine always embodies the promise of reconciliation with patriarchal structures.[4] Her sunny demeanor helps to gloss over sadism and abuse of the worst kind. When the Meg Ryan heroine sleeps with the enemy, we cease to perceive mistreatment and injustice. Watching Meg Ryan allows us to partake of her wholeness and integrity and to let go of the gender wars that define our own time—at least for a while.[5]

Sleepless in Seattle. Directed by Nora Ephron. Sony Pictures. Release Date in the United States: June 25, 1993. Total U.S. Gross: $126,680,884

Sleepless in Seattle comforts us with the promise that our lives are part of a larger destiny. In Nora Ephron's romantic comedy, the magic of true love is not the sole precinct of movie characters but, in fact, is available to everyone.

Sam Baldwin (Tom Hanks), an architect and the father of the eight-year-old Jonah (Ross Malinger), has moved to Seattle because he felt that a change in location would help him cope with the death of his beloved wife Maggie. At the other end of the country, Annie Reed (Meg Ryan), a reporter for the *Baltimore Sun*, announces her engagement to her colleague Walter (Bill Pullman) at a family Christmas party. But much as Annie tries to convince herself that she wants to marry Walter, she keeps wondering about the possibility of a different kind of love. When she accidentally listens to Jonah talk about his father on a radio show, followed by a surprised and hesitant Sam sharing memories of his dead wife on the air, her dreams crystallize in the longing for Sam. She writes a letter to "Sleepless in Seattle" in which, inspired by the movie *An Affair to Remember*, she proposes that she and Sam meet on Valentine's Day on top of the Empire State Building. Sam has no intention of responding to the letter of a woman who might be "a crazy lunatic," but Jonah is enchanted with Annie and determined to meet her in New York. Jonah's resourceful friend Jessica, the daughter of two travel agents, books the boy on a flight to New York, and Sam has to follow to retrieve his son. Against all odds, Sam and Annie finally meet and immediately know that they are right for each other.

It is likely that the box office success of *Sleepless in Seattle* is directly connected to its preoccupation with signs, fate, destiny, and reincarnation.[6] Early on in the movie, when Annie tries on her grandmother's wedding gown and causes a big tear in the fabric, we begin to wonder with Annie whether such occurrences are merely accidental or whether we are indeed privy to a sign. But believing in signs and fate is no license for inactivity on our part. *Sleepless in Seattle* does not advocate the kind of belief in destiny whose appeal lies in its promise to absolve us of responsibility for our lives. In fact, Annie has to mobilize all her resources and energies in her pursuit of Sam, from online databases to detective agencies. She even flies all the way across the country to meet the man of her dreams. In order to catch up with her fate, Annie has to be on her toes. One might even claim that Annie's pursuit of Sam to the point of stalking him makes her the man in this relationship. Clearly, it is not the prospect of quiet resignation that attracts us to Nora Ephron's version of fate. Rather, *Sleepless in Seattle* responds to our desire to feel embedded in a meaningful universe in which everything happens for a reason. The ultimate source of suffering is the belief that there is no rhyme or reason to our lives. "If we start asking why, we go crazy," says Sam's voice-over during the funeral scene at the beginning of the movie. Nonetheless, by the end of the movie, we have come to believe that even the tiniest little detail, for example, when Jonah forgets his backpack on top of the Empire State Building, fulfills its purpose in a grand cosmic scheme.

As a whole, *Sleepless in Seattle* insists on personal responsibility. But there are also moments when this sense of embeddedness in a grander cosmic scheme, visualized by the concluding representation of the United States as a map dotted with stars, absolves Annie from responsibility. Most important, it frees Annie from the responsibility of breaking up with her fiancé Walter. Of course, we, the audience, know from the start that Walter and Annie are not meant for each other—just as we know that Sam and Annie are right for each other when we see how Annie peels an apple in one long curvy strip, a highly desirable skill that Sam's dead wife also possessed. As to Walter, even if we had been willing to grant for a second that somebody with the name of Walter might make a suitable partner, the latter's consuming allergies and tepid jokes are clear signals that he is not the man of anybody's dreams. If Annie were to marry him, she would not only be obliged to explain nonexistent punch lines to an uncomprehending audience for the rest of her life; she would also be saddled with a man who needs a mini pharmacy by his bedside, drowns in Kleenex, and snores like a lumberjack. Still, Walter is a nice guy, and when Annie wonders whether it is fair to expect more than that, many in the audience will identify with her conundrum. Unsurprisingly, the desire to live the dream and not settle for a man like Walter is identified with the wish to live the life of movie characters. "You don't want to be in love; you want to be in love in a movie," says Annie's girlfriend Becky (Rosie O'Donnell). All throughout *Sleepless in Seattle*, the characters admonish each other and themselves to grow up, get real, and overcome their desire for the kind of happiness that exists only in the movies.[7] In the end, of course, Annie is rewarded with "movie happiness," and movies and their promises are reaffirmed as an unfailing source of wisdom and guidance amid the challenges of real life. Ironically, in this focus on movies as the best guide to life, *Sleepless in Seattle* deviates radically from its much-quoted source of inspiration, *An Affair to Remember*. To the characters of *Sleepless in Seattle*, the 1957 Cary Grant–Deborah Kerr vehicle is the I Ching that holds all the answers to life's fundamental questions. All Annie has to do to achieve happiness is allow herself to believe in the kind of love that is depicted in *An Affair to Remember*. To the characters of *An Affair to Remember*, happiness does not come quite as cheap. Both Nickie (Cary Grant) and Terry (Deborah Kerr) are used to a life of luxury paid for by their respective lovers. When they admit to their feelings for each other, they realize that, if they want to be together, they will have to give up their previous lifestyle and find gainful employment. Clearly, in 1957 movies strove to depict "real life," whereas in 1993 even movies strive to imitate movies. Of course, as survivors of the postmodern 1990s, we are as inclined to feel bamboozled by the movies as tempted to concede that movies are indeed more real than "real" life.

Even for those of us who are not devotees of movie magic and cosmic destiny, *Sleepless in Seattle* has some pleasures in store. Although the movie presents the usual cast of ridiculous female caricatures—ranging from Sam's would-be girlfriend, who laughs like a hyena, to his neurotic client who is kept awake by the thought that her dinner plates will not fit in the refrigerator of her new house—there is also an appealing undercurrent of female bonding. First and foremost, Annie is supported by her good-humored friend Becky, who nurses Annie's fantasies for romance and facilitates the pursuit of Sam by mailing Annie's letter to "Sleepless in Seattle." In addition to the stock character of the female best friend/ally, *Sleepless in Seattle* shows women from all walks of life and all parts of the country united in a common cause. Independent from each other and in different contexts, both Suzy (Rita Wilson), Sam's married friend, and Annie refute the chauvinist statement that it is easier for a woman to be killed by a terrorist than it is to get married over the age of forty. *Sleepless in Seattle* also takes time to debunk sexist clichés and poke fun at some of the most grossly misogynistic cultural products of the 1980s, such as *Fatal Attraction*. Instead of *Fatal Attraction*, every female in *Sleepless in Seattle*, including Suzy, Jonah's friend Jessica, and the wife of the guard at the Empire State Building, has seen *An Affair to Remember* and is inspired by it. Although this common fascination with a movie is wholly noncommittal and serves as yet another example of the obsessive self-referentiality typical of *Sleepless in Seattle*, it still creates a sense of a female community united by shared hopes and wishes.

Tellingly, one of the desires that the women of this fictional world share is that for a man like Sam, as evidenced by the thousands of letters Sam receives after his radio interview. Sam's most attractive quality consists in his love for and dedication to his deceased wife and his son Jonah. Sam's character shows the film's preference for emotionally expressive, urbane, charming men with a sense of humor over adventurous macho he-man types with a touch of brutality. In other words, it celebrates Cary Grant at the expense of Clark Gable. Although this shift from Gable to Grant is in line with the movie's preferencing of romance over sexuality, Ephron is not completely inattentive to female sexual desire. Sexuality is clearly not the focus of her movie, but there are some hints that it is an issue—from passing references to women's interest in the shape of male butts to remarks by Annie's mother, whose definition of magic is pretty much equivalent with "being good in the sack."

All in all, *Sleepless in Seattle* has a lot to offer. We get female bonding; a romance with a compassionate, emotionally competent man; and a universe filled with meaning and purpose. So why is it that in spite of all this we still do not feel satisfied in the end? Maybe Annie's sadness about her average life, her less-than-enchanting fiancé, and a job that does not seem to fulfill her is a little too convincing to be easily forgotten when Mr. Right finally makes an appearance. And maybe Annie's admonishments that great love and happiness exist only in the movies are a little too real for comfort.

French Kiss. Directed by Lawrence Kasdan. Twentieth Century Fox. Release Date in the United States: May 5, 1995. Total U.S. Gross: $38,863,798

French Kiss takes place in a mythical France where the crooks are princes in disguise, the policemen are fairy godmothers, and true love is just one vineyard away. Kate (Meg Ryan), the American heroine of this European adventure, is engaged to the Canadian doctor Charlie (Timothy Hutton), who is about to embark for Paris. Kate, terrified of flying and of life in general, prefers to stay home and wait for his daily phone calls while she cleans the keyboard of her computer with Q-tips. Soon Charlie's calls grow more infrequent, until he finally informs Kate that he has met his destiny: a French goddess (Susan Anbeh) whom he loves with a passion he has never felt before. Finally propelled into action, Kate boards the next plane to Paris determined to win Charlie back. Aboard, she meets the Frenchman Luc (Kevin Kline), who instructs a reluctant Kate in the French art of *savoir vivre*. In the end, Kate rejects Charlie for a life with Luc on a French vineyard.

When we first meet Kate, she is in a state of transition. Soon-to-be ex-American and soon-to-be ex-single, she is in the process of receiving Canadian citizenship and of entering the state of marriage. The fact that she chooses Canada, a country often reputed to be the most pedestrian and homely of all industrialized nations, already indicates what the movie defines as Kate's biggest challenge. Kate's longing for a life in the world of Mounties and maple leaves is but one aspect of her overarching desire to shut herself off from life's excitements. Kate is not just afraid of flying, she is afraid of new experiences and, ultimately, of life itself. Her character is designed to mirror women's worries about the stability of their home and marriage. But as viewers identify with Kate's plight, they also share in Kate's learning experience. *French Kiss* teaches its heroine that such permanence is not only undesirable but also impossible. Kate's soon-to-be ex-sister-in-law (Renée Humphrey) explicates this lesson just a few minutes into the movie: "You think you own something when really it ends up owning you, and one day it all burns to the ground." In Kate's case, disaster strikes when she loses her fiancé through no fault of her own. Consequently, women viewers who identify with this sympathetic heroine are vicariously absolved of any feelings of guilt for their failed relationships. If it happens to her, then no wonder it happens to us! But *French Kiss* offers more than absolution. It reassures us that although bad things may happen to good people, at least they did not deserve them and did not bring them about. It also promises that such bad spells are but fleeting moments on the way to greater rewards.

The locale chosen for Kate's self-discovery is France or, rather, some Hollywood version of France: a fictitious land filled with suspicious dairy products and dangerous sexual knowledge where thieves and police officers live in blissful harmony. Thus, *French Kiss* creates a humorous contrast between Kate, who does everything by the book and fills out a customs declaration form for chewing gum, and the French, who, at least according to this movie, continually steal everything they can lay their hands on: bags, passports, money, Kate's fiancé, a diamond necklace, cars, motorbikes, credit cards, and the birthright of their own brothers. In France, crime appears to be a popular pastime that does not really hurt anybody and in which the police themselves participate with a wink and a smile.

One wonders, of course, why France, a country filled with "nicotine-saturated and hygiene-deficient" small-time crooks and pouting sex goddesses, is chosen as the proper environment for the completion of Kate's education. Does Kate's destination symbolize the dire need to liberate a sexually repressed individual? After all, France is the land of erotic sophistication, as opposed to Kate's homeland, the empire of puritanical hypocrites, as the hotel manager informs us. But France is also the land of sexual deviancy, where strangers volunteer to arrange for a threesome including urination for sexual pleasure and, more important, where even the most desirable man turns out to be impotent. Although Kate's fear of flying is explicitly interpreted as fear of sex, the movie does not focus on inhibited sexuality.[8] Rather, Kate's challenge to open herself to new experiences is translated as the task of adapting to another culture.

Initially, Kate's desire to shut herself off from life finds expression in her xenophobic prejudices. When we first meet her, she hates France and the French, who smoke and engage in unspeakable culinary crimes, ranging from hiding horsemeat under delicious-looking sauces to the production and consumption of suspicious cheeses. One might thus expect that Kate's gradual acculturation would be symbolized by her changing eating habits. However, aside from first devouring and then vomiting huge quantities of *fromage*, Kate is not shown eating. Rather, her changing attitude is visualized through her literal inability to see the Eiffel Tower. Upon her arrival, Kate passes the Eiffel Tower several times but consistently has her back turned. Gradually, she begins to sense its presence, but by the time she turns around, the tower, brightly lit just moments before, is enveloped by darkness. Finally, she glimpses its reflection in a shop window and, ultimately, perceives the monument itself in its full splendor. Clearly, though the movie purports to portray openness to new experiences and other cultures, it also feels compelled to reassure its audience that the challenge involved is infinitesimally small. What started out as an encounter with a foreign culture is soon reduced to daring to catch a glimpse of one of the most widely publicized tourist attractions in the world. And lest we be too scared of the perils of intercultural intercourse, *French Kiss* makes sure that the Frenchman with whom Kate falls in love is portrayed by an American actor.

To Kate, acculturation comes at no cost at all. Although the movie presents her as currently without country, she remains as American as apple pie. *French Kiss* both ironizes and admires the relentless optimism that marks Kate as typically American. Devastated by the news of Charlie's engagement with the sex goddess, Kate still manages to hold up a vaguely triumphant fist in delusional anticipation of a future reconciliation with Charlie. In addition to this positive attitude, Kate also exhibits the straightforward honesty that is often associated with her nation of origin. Repeatedly, the movie emphasizes the French fondness for pretense. French women say yes when they mean no and no when they mean yes. When Kate interacts with the hotel manager, she marvels that "the words come out, but the meaning is completely different." Kate, on the other hand, always expresses what she feels inside, and the movie champions her way of being as the right one.[9] However much *French Kiss* purports to celebrate openness to other cultures, its basic structure and choices validate the American way of life. But if the movie's portrayal of cultural encounters is phony, should we not conclude that Kate's personal growth is equally spurious?

In the beginning, Kate is both infantilized and victimized. Her skirts, woolen jackets, and white blouses make her look like a little schoolgirl. Everybody in her life, from the hotel manager to her own fiancé, walks all over her. Clearly, Kate needs to learn to stand up for herself, and there are some hints that she does. In her second confrontation with the insouciant hotel manager, Kate emerges victorious. The final encounter with the French goddess who stole her man also proves more satisfactory than the two previous ones, in which Kate first fainted and got her bag stolen and then fell over a cart with desserts and had to crawl away covered in *mousse au chocolat*.[10] There is no denying that Kate does make progress, but there is also no denying that all of her attempts to fight for herself are completely innocuous and purely defensive. When Kate mutters that "all men are bastards," she gets away with it precisely because we know that she does not really mean it. Kate does not really change, and she does not really learn to assert herself. In the end, she is still "the old me" who happily gives herself and all her money to her man. Only this time she chooses the right guy.

The relationship between Luc and Kate is presented as a chain of mutually beneficial learning experiences. Kate not only teaches Luc commitment and some (very moderate) degree of honesty, she also empowers him sexually. When Kate tells Luc that he cannot stick it out, she has identified the cause of his sexual malfunction in his inability to commit, and the movie confirms her analysis. But Luc finally realizes that there is one man meant for one woman and that the woman for him is Kate. This turns him into the ideal man for Kate and into an ideal panacea for the female viewers' worries about the stability of home and marriage addressed in the beginning. Whereas Kate teaches Luc to choose only one partner, Luc teaches Kate to choose the right partner. Luc's gift to Kate, and the movie's gift to us, is that there is nothing wrong with women like Kate. They just haven't found the right guy yet, but they will! We could dismiss this message as yet another empty promise of the Hollywood dream machine, but we could also value it for what it is worth: namely, for telling women, the gender that is more easily inclined to take the blame and to engage in prolonged acts of self-accusatory soul-searching, that men like Charlie are hopeless cases, that they themselves are fine, and that the right guy will come along eventually. And if he doesn't? Well, there are always woman's best friends, the movies.

You've Got Mail. Directed by Nora Ephron. Warner Bros. Release Date in the United States: December 18, 1998. Total U.S. Gross: $115,821,495

You've Got Mail, a remake of Ernst Lubitsch's delightful *The Shop around the Corner,* tells the story of real-life enemies who, unbeknownst to themselves, are engaged in an online romance. Kathleen Kelly (Meg Ryan), cyberpseudonym "Shopgirl," meets Joe Fox (Tom Hanks), alias "NY152," in a chat room for over-thirties. Although they harmonize perfectly in virtual reality, in real life Kathleen—whose children's bookstore, The Shop Around the Corner, is threatened by the newly constructed Fox Books Superstore—despises everything Joe and his "mega moccacino discount land" stand for.[11] Coached by an expert in cutthroat business strategies, namely NY152 himself, Kathleen decides to "go to the mattresses" and fight for the survival of her store. In the end, she loses her shop but falls in love with Joe, and the two of them live happily ever after.[12]

There are few movies that thematize capitalism as explicitly and directly as *You've Got Mail.* Aside from the James Bond franchise, there are also few movies

Sweet and innocuous, Meg Ryan characters frequently hold out the possibility of reconciliation and harmony. Meg Ryan and Tom Hanks in You've Got Mail (1998). WARNER BROS./ THE KOBAL COLLECTION/BRIAN HAMILL.

that could top the number of product placements displayed in Nora Ephron's box office success. From Starbucks to AOL, Apple, Microsoft, and Baby Gap, everything in this movie spells consumption. Moreover, the plot itself is taken from the ur-narrative of capitalist economics: the destruction of small independent players by oversized corporate monopolies. This theme is introduced toward the very beginning of *You've Got Mail* when Joe Fox's gleeful report that another independent bookstore is going under is greeted with much merriment in the Fox family circle. Consequently, ruining The Shop Around the Corner is not an unintended by-product of the Fox family strategy but, rather, its distinct goal. "Crush it," shouts Joe's grandfather enthusiastically when Joe reminds him of the existence of a children's bookstore in the vicinity of their new Fox outlet.

The movie's stance toward this steamroller approach to business is somewhat ambiguous. *You've Got Mail* does take some time to depict the losses that the triumph of the Fox superstore carries in its wake. Kathleen's store is staffed with employees who know a good deal about the products they sell. They provide excellent service, know their customers by name, and create a warm and friendly atmosphere. Like her mother before her, Kathleen sells more than just books. She helps people develop their identities. Fox Books, on the other hand, offers nothing of the sort. It gains its competitive edge through cappuccinos and discounts. The Statue of Liberty that lies flat on the ground next to the Fox construction site appears to be a not-so-subtle hint at the way in which the elimination of choice imperils the concept of freedom. Later, when the statue is reerected as store decor, she no longer holds a tablet commemorating the birth of freedom but has become a dedicated reader of Fox books. However, aside from such discreet criticism, *You've Got Mail* might more justly be said to enact a jubilant celebration of the endless possibilities of consumer capitalism. When Kathleen loses her store, she starts writing children's books. In the rose-colored world of *You've Got Mail*, losing one's livelihood and heritage releases creativity and stimulates personal growth. The Fox Books Superstore is not the end of civilization as we know it but simply the beginning of something new—a newness, moreover, that is associated with the rejuvenating power of spring. The movie's emphasis on the change of seasons aligns economic callousness with the inevitability of the natural life cycle and thus obscures the human agency at the helm of the Fox empire. Moreover, the focus on the impact of the big bad chain store on the good little bookstore also deflects attention away from far more nefarious problems tied to the megastore phenomenon, such as the devastating impact of book monopolies on the publishing world—to name but one.

Like most relationships in romantic comedies, the one between Joe and Kathleen unfolds as a mutual learning process. Joe teaches Kathleen how to be brave and fight for what she wants, whereas Kathleen teaches Joe empathy and love. Interestingly, although Joe is as rich and successful as is humanly possible, he is in some ways much more in need of being rescued than Kathleen. Kathleen's life is "small but valuable." Her shop is more than a workplace. It is the home of a little urban family of employees and associates who offer each other comfort and help. The all-male Fox family, on the other hand, is about as messed up as it gets. Joe has an eight-year-old aunt, the daughter of his grandfather, and a four-year-old brother, the product of one of his father's many affairs with Joe's former nannies. The current partner of Joe's father "studied decorating at Caesar's Palace," takes every opportunity to make sexual advances to Joe, and finally runs off with the nanny. Joe is continuing the Fox tradition of catastrophic choices of partners in life by initially joining his fate to that of Patricia, a supremely neurotic publishing executive, so hectic that she "makes coffee nervous." Clearly, female viewers are meant to derive satisfaction from the implication that Joe would be a lot worse off than Kathleen if the two of them had never met.

One of the aspects of the Joe–Kathleen relationship that most likely speaks to a contemporary audience is its preoccupation with the fragmentation of modern identities. Joe's mantra-like comment that "it's business, it's not personal," initially his only response to putting Kathleen out of business, epitomizes what is at stake here. At the bottom of all the complications that defer the happy ending is the question whether we are what we do. Do our jobs define us? Can Joe Fox be both a ruthless businessman and a lovable person? Or, as in the case of Birdie (Jean Stapleton), Kathleen's septuagenarian employee who once had a crush on General Franco, can a decent person fall in love with a fascist dictator? Unsurprisingly, *You've Got Mail* answers that yes, most certainly, a decent person can. Although Joe's personal growth is manifested by the fact that he finally asks for Kathleen's forgiveness "for this tiny little thing of putting you out of business," this forgiveness is granted without a demand for restitution and hence at no cost at all. Consequently, the price to be paid is that of narrative integrity. As Joe and Kathleen become friends, Joe's professional activities vanish from sight. Neither the corporate office nor his megabookstore, Joe's natural habitat during the first part of the movie, makes another appearance. In *You've Got Mail*, life is full of compromises, and it appears to be our job as audience to ignore them. This would be a tough job indeed if it were not assuaged by the promise of wholeness and integrity embodied by Meg Ryan's character. In Ephron's movie, the happy union of the couple, of the daisy and her enemy, disguises—or in movie speak, "heals"—both Joe's "phallic sadism" and the brutal effects of big business.[13] There are plenty of lies, tricks, and bankruptcies, but all we are meant to see is love and daisies.

Courage under Fire. Directed by Edward Zwick. Twentieth Century Fox. Release Date in the United States: July 12, 1996. Total U.S. Gross: $59,003,384

At first glance, *Courage under Fire* appears to be very different from the standard Meg Ryan fare. Upon closer inspection, however, and although it purports to sketch a picture of female heroism, *Courage under Fire* ends up confirming the stereotype of woman as victim.

The story of the Gulf War medevac pilot Karen Emma Walden (Meg Ryan) is embedded in the story of Nat Serling (Denzel Washington), a tank commander who, in the heat of battle, mistakes one of his own tanks for an enemy vehicle and gives the order to shoot his own men. The investigation into this incident of "friendly fire" ongoing, Serling is assigned to write a report on the validity of Karen Walden's posthumous nomination for the Congressional Medal of Honor. As he conducts interviews with her crew, numerous discrepancies arise. By uncovering the truth about Walden, Serling finds a way to deal with his own pangs of conscience and is finally able to rejoin both the army and his own family.

Karen Walden, the object of Serling's investigation, is an extraordinary soldier in every respect. Although we are first presented with contradictory accounts of her skills and character, the movie establishes in the end that Walden was indeed an officer of exceptional moral courage. Her own men confirm that she never displayed any doubt or fear and got calmer when pressure increased. *Courage under Fire* presents a picture of female heroism, but this picture is tarnished with so many grains of salt that it is difficult to enjoy it. Karen Walden may emerge as the only true and untainted hero in this movie, but she is also the only one who is never in control of her own story: she is dead before the movie even begins. In the official version of her story, Walden's claim to the Medal of Honor is founded on the courageous acts that led to the rescue of a Black Hawk crew downed by Iraqi fire. In truth, however, it is Walden's unswerving commitment to the military maxim to "defend with all your heart the lives of the men and women under your command" that makes her more deserving of the Medal of Honor than most eye-catching acts of bravery ever could. Interestingly, the representation of a female hero is combined with the redefinition of military heroism as female, that is, as taking care of others. Because the best officer is the one who never leaves a man behind, women, who for centuries have been culturally identified with the task of caring for others, are ideally suited to fill this role. The stereotypically female predisposition to self-sacrifice is put in a new context when the gravely injured Walden insists that all attempts to rescue her be postponed until her subordinate Rady, who was shot in the lung, is transported to safety. Moreover, Walden's physical toughness is itself associated with distinctly feminine skills and qualities. When she is shot in the stomach, Walden brushes aside her crew's concerns with the comment: "I gave birth to a 9-pound baby. . . . I can handle this." It is also significant that Monfriez (Lou Diamond Phillips), the morally dubious soldier, who refuses to acknowledge Walden's authority and is responsible for Walden's wound, is also least committed to the moral imperative of "leave no man behind." The good guys in this movie know about the moral and physical strength of women and about the validity of "female" values.

There is a lot to be said for the way in which *Courage under Fire* represents female valor and accomplishments. If in the end its portrayal of gender remains less than satisfying, this is largely because of the movie's narrative structure. The decision to focus on Karen Walden to the total exclusion of all other female soldiers or medics turns her into the quintessential token woman and deprives the character of all forms of female support and companionship. But Walden's status as an exception to her gender is less problematic than the fact that she has no agency and voice in her own story. Walden may be in command in the story within the story, but she is long dead when the plot of *Courage under Fire* starts. If this had been the story of a male chopper pilot, portrayed by Dennis Hopper or Robert De Niro, we can rest assured that said pilot, though presumed dead, would have returned from the dead and become the agent of his own revenge and vindication. But not only is Karen Walden truly dead, her story is also not really her own story but, rather, serves a greater purpose in Nathaniel Serling's quest for redemption. *Courage under Fire* draws attention to the ways in which Walden's candidacy for the Medal of Honor is employed for political purposes: "The first woman in history to be nominated for a Medal of Honor, it's gold," rejoices the White House representative. But the film is oblivious of its own complicity in this process. Nat, forced by military authorities to hide the truth about the friendly fire incident that caused the death of his friend Boylar, finds redemption in his dedication to unveiling the truth about Karen Walden. Walden, as it turns out, also died in a "friendly fire" incident. Trapped in a pocket of enemy territory, Sergeant Monfriez urges Captain Walden to leave the wounded Rady behind and make an escape during the night. When Walden refuses, the situation escalates. As she points her gun at Monfriez, demanding his weapon, an Iraqi soldier appears behind Monfriez. Walden shoots the Iraqi, and Monfriez, thinking that she is shooting at him, shoots her in the stomach. When the rescue team arrives, Monfriez claims that Walden is already dead in order to avoid being court-martialed for mutiny. By showing us that Karen Walden was killed so that she would not be able to tell her version of the story, *Courage under Fire* establishes just how important it is to be the author of one's own story. Moreover, Walden's inability to speak for herself finds its mirror image in the official military policy that keeps Nat from telling the truth about Boylar's death. But unlike Karen Walden, Nat is finally given an opportunity to present his account of the events when the tape of all conversations aboard his tank resurfaces. Karen Walden, on the other hand, never gets to set the record straight. All she is granted is a voice-over of a letter to her parents, reiterating her dedication to her men. The last scene, which shows Walden as the pilot who was present at the scene of Boylar's death, exemplifies one last time Walden's subordinate part in Serling's story.

In the end, we are left with a hybrid: the female hero as victim.[14] Karen Walden's moral courage proves superior to that of every other officer, and she truly deserves the Medal of Honor. But she is also the only soldier who never gets to tell her own story. We can read this as an accurate representation of the plight of a woman in a man's profession. But we can also read it as yet another example of a cultural product that is guilty of reinscribing the structural problems that it pretends to unveil.

It is no wonder that daisies are Kathleen Kelly's favorite flowers. In all four movies, the Meg Ryan character combines the harmless innocence and inconspicuous gentleness that characterize this most unpretentious of flowers. Like daisies, Meg Ryan characters, who are "small but valuable," are easily ignored, passed over, and victimized. In spite of their initial vulnerability, however, they generally triumph in the end. To women viewers, this holds out the promise that one day they too will be noticed and appreciated for what they are. But Meg Ryan characters also embody a promise of wholeness and integrity that seems wholly foreign to our modern times. In watching Ryan characters, we partake of an old-fashioned sense of feminine virtues and values that seems more rightly to belong to the era of our grandmothers than to our own. Meg Ryan heroines reconcile us with abuse and take us on a vacation from modernity. When the Meg Ryan heroine gets in bed with the enemy, hostility and injustice fall by the wayside. If she wasn't occasionally shot in the stomach or run over by a truck, we might forget that there was any kind of problem at all.

NOTES

1. See Peter William Evans, "Meg Ryan, Megastar," in *Terms of Endearment: Hollywood Romantic Comedy of the 1980s and 1990s*, ed. Peter William Evans and Celestino Deleyto (Edinburgh: Edinburgh University Press, 1998), 193.

2. This conforms to a general trend in romantic comedies of the 1990s: "Romantic comedies of the 1970s and early 1980s often ended with the characters getting married but they usually had sex along the way. This is not the case with romantic comedies of the 1990s" (Catherine L. Preston, "Hanging on a Star: The Resurrection of the Romance Film in the 1990s," in *Film Genre 2000: New Critical Essays*, ed. Wheeler Winston Dixon [Albany: State University of New York Press, 2000], 233).

3. It is of interest to note that the Meg Ryan heroine never enjoys the protection or companionship of a mother. This makes her all the more susceptible to male influence because "mythically, the absence of the mother continues the idea that the creation of the woman is the business of men" (Stanley Cavell, *Pursuits of Happiness: The Hollywood Comedy of Remarriage* [Cambridge: Harvard University Press, 1981], 57).

4. Meg Ryan and Tom Hanks exhibit many of the features of what Martha P. Nochimson calls the "Iconic Couple": a couple that energizes "a formulaic script and makes submission to cultural stereotypes seem like a party" (*Screen Couple Chemistry: The Power of 2* [Austin: University of Texas Press, 2002], 11).

5. Evans makes a similar claim: "To look at Meg Ryan is to contemplate a world free of demons and terror" ("Meg Ryan, Megastar," 190). See also Evans, "Meg Ryan, Megastar," 200.

6. According to Anthony Lane, "*Sleepless in Seattle* is a gentle meditation on fate, on what must come to pass, but there's no hint of a genial God pulling strings from on high; it's up to the characters to plot their own course toward a triumphant union" (*Nobody's Perfect: Writings from the* New Yorker [New York: Alfred A. Knopf, 2002], 12.

7. Lane makes a similar point when he asks, "What does it say about a movie that its funniest and most delicious moment comes from the fond remembrance of cinema?" (*Nobody's Perfect*, 13).

8. In her readings of screwball comedies, Kay Young maintains that "conversations work as performances of vibrant, uncontrolled, interactive, sublimated sexuality" (*Ordinary Pleasures: Couples, Conversations, and Comedy* [Columbus: Ohio State University Press, 2001], 165). One might claim that this also holds true in *French Kiss*, that is, that the verbal sparring of Kate and Luc is a signifier of future sexual fulfillment.

9. See Evans, who speaks of the film's "wariness of the exotic and the pursuit of sincerity and tenderness" ("Meg Ryan, Megastar," 202).

10. Kate's embarrassment echoes that of the heroines of screwball comedy. For example, Susan (Katharine Hepburn) in *Bringing Up Baby* (1938) finds herself in public with her bottom bared because the backside of her dress is torn. As Cavell points out, it is "a virtue of our heroes to be willing to suffer a certain indignity, as if what stands in the way of change, psychologically speaking, is a false dignity" (*Pursuits of Happiness*, 8).

11. Interestingly, in *You've Got Mail*, the Internet functions as a form of what Frye, with respect to Shakespearean comedy, calls "the green world," "a place in which perspective and renewal are to be achieved" (Cavell, *Pursuits of Happiness*, 49). Joe and Kathleen's online romance allows for the kind of doubling or splitting of identities that is a stock feature of many screwball comedies, for example, *The Lady Eve*.

12. *You've Got Mail* is reminiscent of a fairy tale. The story of Joe and Kathleen conforms to what Young has called the "Cinderella plot of narrative where poor girl not only deserves wealthy man but effects his spiritual transformation" (*Ordinary Pleasures*, 48).

13. Nochimson makes a similar claim about Clark Gable, whose undeniable appeal served to disguise an "apologist narrative for male violence, insensitivity, and pigheadedness" (*Screen Couple Chemistry*, 25). The Meg Ryan–Tom Hanks relationship in *You've Got Mail* also resembles that of Errol Flynn and Olivia de Havilland in *Captain Blood* (1935) or *The Adventures of Robin Hood* (1938), in that Kathleen too challenges masculine prerogative until Joe "humbles her to his will and simultaneously raises her to the level of his acquired power" (Nochimson, *Screen Couple Chemistry*, 27).

14. Yvonne Tasker makes a similar point. Comparing *Courage under Fire* with "male" action movies, Tasker draws attention to the enormous difference between the male protagonists of the *Terminator* movies and the "suffering, betrayed female hero" of *Courage under Fire* (*Working Girls: Gender and Sexuality in Popular Cinema* [London: Routledge, 1998], 73).

☆ **4** ☆

The Real World
Is Not Enough
Renée Zellweger

"I know there's something special out there for me."

—*Nurse Betty* (2000)

Renée Zellweger's characters are very often women trapped in the ordinary and seeking the extraordinary. Zellweger plays inconsequential accountants (*Jerry Maguire* [1996]), diner waitresses (*Nurse Betty* [2000]), junior editors (*Bridget Jones's Diary* [2001]), or housewives (*Chicago* [2002]) who have not had much of a life so far but who believe, steadfastly and starry-eyed, that there is something else "out there." The Renée Zellweger persona is quite different from other working women in movies. She is the exact opposite of the highly educated, impressively competent, and usually (over-) ambitious professional woman of many Hollywood films—the female lawyers, policewomen, doctors, or academics whose professional aspirations contrast with their personal failings as "women." Renée Zellweger characters tend to be uneducated or undereducated and work in lowly positions, if at all. Their ambitions and dreams are not usually work re-lated. They are not professional go-getters. What they look for is rather vague, no more clearly defined than "something special," something "out there"; it is more a general expression of discontent with the real world than a specific desire. Pro-pelled from the security of their workplaces or homes by crisis, they set out to seek that nameless something with heartwarming naïveté. It is no coincidence that two of these characters are identified, in different ways, as "Dorothy," the timeless heroine of *The Wizard of Oz* (1939), whose travels through fairy and munchkin land conclude with the realization that "there's no place like home." But whereas Dorothy's main opponent in her travels is a wicked witch, the

Dorothies of Renée Zellweger films encounter white (and occasionally black) male anger. In *The Wizard of Oz*, the sober black-and-white reality of Dorothy's Kansas appears drab in comparison with the brilliant colors of Oz. In the end, Oz turns out to be nothing but a dream that leaves real life reaffirmed but also unaffected. In contrast, Renée Zellweger films attack precisely that sovereignty of the real world: reality is a matter of perception and representation—and as such is subjected to virtually limitless manipulation.

Jerry Maguire. Directed by Cameron Crowe. Sony Pictures. Release Date in the United States: December 13, 1996. Total U.S. Gross: $153,952,592

Jerry Maguire is the story of an angst- and anger-ridden sports agent (Tom Cruise) who grows a conscience.[1] In a burst of ethics, Jerry composes a mission statement in which he demands "more personal attention" for the firm's clients and "less money" for their agents. Initially, his courage is hypocritically applauded, but it promptly costs him his job and nearly all of his clients. Jerry leaves the firm to found his own agency, supported and accompanied only by a minor accountant, Dorothy Boyd (Renée Zellweger), and a single remaining client, the washed-up football player Rod Tidwell (Cuba Gooding Jr.). Both Rod, whose most insistent demand of Jerry is to "show me the money," and Dorothy, who has given up a steady income and health insurance for herself and her child, absolutely depend on Jerry's success. Interwoven with the professional are the personal entanglements of the characters: Jerry's failed relationship with his dominatrix fiancée Avery (Kelly Preston), Rod and Marcee's (Regina King) overly effusive conjugal love, Jerry's touching affection for Dorothy's son Ray (Jonathan Lipnicki), and Jerry's somewhat hesitant attraction to Dorothy. When Dorothy and Jerry marry, their bland companionship represents the exact opposite of the fervent romance between Rod and Marcee. Jerry's success on both a professional and personal level is endangered when Rod's fate hinges on a single game and Dorothy, finally questioning Jerry's feelings for her (and perhaps also influenced by her sister's divorced women's group), decides to separate from Jerry. But all's well that ends well: Rod scores the touchdown and a major contract, and Jerry, realizing belatedly that he loves Dorothy, takes possession of his wife and rescues her from the clutches of feminism. Fame, fortune, and public acknowledgment follow as a matter of course.[2]

Sweet and supportive Dorothy Boyd, accountant, twenty-six-year-old widow, and single mom of a precocious six year old, is the only person trusting and naive enough to believe in Jerry's idealistic vision born out of his own exploitative business practices. His previous brutal treatment of his athletes, who were forced to play even when severely hurt, has turned Jerry into an angry white male plagued by angst and bad conscience. "I hate myself," he confesses at the outset of the film, "no—I hate my place in the world." Jerry the oppressor is thus smoothly transformed into Jerry the victim, who would readily choose ethics over exploitation if given half a chance. The problem is not really his character but the fact that nobody appreciates his sensitive inner child: "I had so much to say and no one to listen." Enter Dorothy, a character whose only function consists in listening to Jerry and enabling him to turn his newly developed ethical business ideas into practicable, and profitable, reality. She supports Jerry's seemingly hopeless business venture, and later falls in love with him, because of his newly found moral stance. Unfulfilled in her dead-end job, she is now part of something meaningful, something she believes in, for the first time in her life. Naive and idealistic, Dorothy builds her hopes not on the way things are but on the way things ought to be: she is inspired by Jerry's ethical behavior and loves Jerry not for who he is but "for the man he wants to be—I love him for the man he almost is." Prepared to leave the man she loves, she decides to move because Jerry cannot afford her services; faced with the prospect of losing her, Jerry marries her out of loyalty. When Jerry learns to be successful in a cynical world full of tough competitors without sacrificing his ethics, he realizes that he owes his reformation to Dorothy's unwavering confidence in him. The final scene shows him triumphant, untroubled by angst or anger, gleefully announcing to the world: "I love my wife! I love my life!"

Beyond Dorothy's refreshing championship of the moral high ground, her role is limited to the traditional "Stand by Your Man." In *Jerry Maguire*, men, such as Jerry and his mercenary and exploitative colleague Bob Sugar (Jay Mohr), must confront the problems of the modern work world; they are in danger of being destroyed ethically and emotionally by the cynicism and competitiveness of the capitalist workplace. Women, on the other hand—Dorothy, her divorced sister Laurel (Bonnie Hunt), and the pathetic jilted women in the women's group—are still caught in a nineteenth-century predicament: being without a man. The women's group in *Jerry Maguire* represents one of the most mean-spirited portrayals of feminism in recent decades. With the help of frumpy clothes and unappealing makeup, a shaky handheld camera, and swift cuts between speakers, the women are made to appear as quacking geese. They spout feminist clichés of mutual support but do not actually listen to each other; they bitch about men but would date any man confused enough to ask them. If fierce competition and unethical business practices are shown to be the downfall of men, then feminism is presented as the pitfall for women and a danger to children. Dorothy keeps her son away from the group, as if he were in danger of contamination. We are told in no uncertain terms that Dorothy is different from these women: rather pointedly, she is widowed (whereas we must assume that all the other women were abandoned by their men). Refuting the tenets of the women's group, Dorothy becomes the mouthpiece of the patriarchal credo: "You all think that men are the enemy, but I still love the enemy." Naturally, when the "enemy" shows up in the form of Jerry, who declares his love for Dorothy in moving words, even the feminists' eyes tear up; one of them mutters, sniffling, that "this is the best talking group I've ever been in." *Jerry Maguire* essentially rehashes an idea about women's role that goes all the way back to the beginning of the industrial era. The message to women is clear: forget all that feminist nonsense about the battle of the sexes and stand by your man so that he can survive the ravages of the modern workplace unharmed.

The only redeeming feature of this rather nauseating portrayal of men and women, the home and the workplace, is that the "real world" is consistently played off against the imaginary world created by the media. It is the media world that furnishes the basis for Jerry's and Rod's success in the "real" world. Rod's career depends not so much on his talent as a player as on the way the media represents his performance and character; at stake is not his ability but his image. Consequently, his final triumph manifests itself as media coverage: thousands watch breathlessly as he lies injured on the football field, having risked life and limb for a particularly perilous play. When he regains consciousness, he is no longer a halfhearted performer but everyone's hero. After the game, he is surrounded by television cameras and mobbed by the same reporters who used to ignore him. Both his ultimate triumph, the longed-for $11 million contract, and his acknowledgment of Jerry also take place in a media setting, on a talk show featuring him as special guest. Male success, facilitated by the loving support of women like Marcee and Dorothy, is only "real" when it is also a show. Unlike women, who find their purpose in life in the privacy of their homes (after all, there's no place like it), men seek fulfillment, victory, and completion in the most public arena imaginable. Men's transformation *will* be televised. Unlike other Renée Zellweger films, *Jerry Maguire* does not launch an all-out attack on "reality," but it does show that the "something else" that can make real life "special," that is, financially profitable *and* morally tolerable, is made possible by image management and successful manipulation of the media.

Nurse Betty. Directed by Neil LaBute. Gramercy Pictures. Release Date in the United States: September 8, 2000. Total U.S. Gross: $25,167,270

At the beginning of the film, Betty's (Renée Zellweger) life is in urgent need of repair: she is a diner waitress in Nowhere, Kansas, married to an abusive used car salesman (Aaron Eckhart) who cheats his customers, cheats on her, runs drug scams on the side, and forbids Betty to realize her dream of becoming a nurse. Betty is afflicted with nonexistent self-esteem, which manifests itself in sweet supportiveness toward every man in town and bashful obedience toward her husband, and her only release from her miserable existence is a doctor show on TV, *A Reason to Love*. As if her innocent demeanor were not enough, she appears in a child's dress with puffy sleeves, complete with a basket, bow tie, and apron, as the spitting image of little Dorothy in *The Wizard of Oz*. On her way to California, Betty is dubbed "Dorothy" by a waitress in a bar who shares with Betty her fond memories of a long-ago trip to Europe and is amazed to hear that Betty has never been out of Kansas. Betty is so engrossed in her TV show, in which her hero, the show's heart surgeon (Greg Kinnear), has to battle sexual allegations, that she completely misses the fact that, in the next room, her husband is rather noisily tortured and murdered by a father-and-son team of hit men (Morgan Freeman, Chris Rock). When she finally opens her door to the carnage, she is unable to face this gruesome reality and does what she always does: she retreats into the world of her show. This time, however, she loses all memory of her actual life and firmly institutes the world of the show in its place. Her fugue state launches her quest for "something special," and "Dorothy" leaves Kansas in search of the TV doctor, whom she now believes to be her fiancé. Pursued by the contract killers and the police, she ends up in Los Angeles and finds a job as a nurse in a hospital and a friend and roommate in Rosa (Tia Texada), who promises to help her locate her fiancé. When Betty first meets George McCord, the actor who plays her TV hero, he offers her a part on the show, charmed by the incredible "realism" of what he believes to be improvisational acting. Her first day on the set destroys her illusion; Betty regains her ability to distinguish between fiction and reality and thus becomes able to put up a real act in the show. With the money she makes as a TV nurse, she manages to carve out a new life for herself: she fulfils two of her dreams, traveling to Europe and training as a nurse in real life.

Like *Jerry Maguire*'s Dorothy, this "Dorothy," too, encounters male anger in various forms. Her skill at coping with male anger grows progressively and marks the development of a healthy self-assertion that ultimately enables her to survive in the real world. Initially, she is utterly defenseless when faced with male aggression, responding to her husband's abuse in a submissive and appeasing manner. By the end of the film, she assuages the anger of Charlie (Morgan Freeman), the older hit man, to such an extent that he sacrifices himself rather than killing her. Her ultimate act of self-assertion occurs when she responds to George's anger about what he takes to be her refusal to act. In addition to being able to distinguish between fiction and reality, she is also able to see—and confront him with—the difference between the kind and sensitive man he plays on TV and his less-than-perfect real-life persona.

But media-created illusion and reality are not nearly as dissimilar as they appear. Betty is not the only person in the film who is unable to see life for what it is. The ability and willingness to fall for an illusion, even privilege it over reality, characterize virtually every figure of the film. When Betty declares her love for George's soap opera character, Doctor David Ravell, his fellow actors mistake her heartfelt confession, which to her is the absolute truth, for accomplished acting. On the other hand, when Betty mentions details from her real life, for example, her marriage to a used car salesman, the actors mistake them for the plot of a soap opera. In *Nurse Betty*, even those few who do not mistake illusion for reality privilege glossy fantasy over the drab routine of their everyday existence.[3] The movie opens and concludes with a scene in which a waiter, Betty in Kansas and the *cameriere* in the bistro in Rome, are so engrossed in the *Reason to Love* reruns on the restaurant TV that they barely pay attention to their customers. The showdown between the cops and contract killers in Rosa and Betty's apartment is briefly interrupted by breaking news on their favorite TV series. Spellbound by the shocking fact that Nurse Chloe on *A Reason to Love* is a lesbian, all present—the hit man Wesley (Chris Rock), his potential victims, and the policemen in his pursuit—peacefully watch the show together. The soap opera achieves something that real life cannot, namely, a temporary truce among the killer, his victim, and his pursuer: the lamb lying down with the lion *and* the watchdog. The illusion is so pervasive that it briefly succeeds in creating a Paradise on earth. Once the show ends, reality reasserts itself, and murder and mayhem return.

The fusion of illusion and reality within Betty's character complicates the viewer's perception of what is real and what is not. "You're so real," says George to Betty, the person in the film who most consistently lives an illusion, and he is right. Because she utterly believes in her illusion, Betty plays her role and then *becomes* the person she has played. The job offer from an L.A. hospital, which she receives without degree, credentials, or experience, is the result of an illusion—but one that turns into truth: she saves a man's life in an ambulance and emerges covered with his blood but smilingly conscious of a job well done. There is no question in the viewer's mind that Betty, in "real life," has a calling as a nurse, and thus the distinction between life and fiction loses its validity.

Our belief that childlike, naive, and vulnerable Betty is likely to fall for every form of make-believe that comes her way represents the last hope for a clearly recognizable and privileged reality. But this, too, is rebuffed by yet another twist in the plot. Hired killer Charlie, presumably the most hardheaded, cool cus-

Betty, mesmerized by her favorite soap, still never spills a drop. Renée Zellweger in Nurse Betty *(2000). ABSTRAKT/GRAMERCY/IMF/ THE KOBAL COLLECTION/BRUCE BIRMELIN.*

tomer of the film, is trapped in an illusion about Betty that is no more rational than Betty's fantasies about Dr. David Ravell. An educated lover of books, art, and music, Charlie defends his ideal, based on Betty's diary, against his son Wesley's down-to-earth assessment of Betty as a crazy housewife who is in love with a soap opera character. Charlie's Betty, born of the written word, is respectable, beautiful, and innocent. In Charlie's imagination, Betty is "no showgirl" but, rather, a decent and cultured person who would find falling in love with a soap opera star, or even watching a soap, entirely beneath her. Wesley's more realistic view of Betty acknowledges the pervasiveness of the media illusion (after all, Wesley, too, is a fan of the show) and does justice to Betty's real life: "The bitch ain't nothing but a fuckin' housewife," he informs his father, "ain't nothin' beneath her." In the end, both die of their respective illusions: Wesley because he takes time out from his job to watch the show, Charlie because he is unable to see the real Betty behind the ideal he has created.

Unlike in many Hollywood movies, where "there's no place like home," in *Nurse Betty* it is illusion that carries the day. Even the lowbrow fictions of a soap opera are capable of propelling our heroine from an unbearable reality to self-actualization, self-assertion, and a happier life. They lead to the demise of the bad guys and offer us a brief glimpse of Peace on Earth. Real happiness is a consequence of believing in the illusion. The soap opera, or—for the educated elite—the literary imagination, turns average people into ideals of perfection. It is significant that Betty awakes from her fond dreams of a kind and loving Dr. Ravell when the man who portrays that character, George McCord, begins to scream at her on the set. He calls her a crazy person and tells her to get a fucking life—in short: he treats her the way her husband used to. In this scene, Betty is disabused of not one illusion but two: the illusion that her favorite show is "real" and the illusion that the love of her life is a man who will treat her kindly. To Betty, being abused by a man is an unmistakable sign of real life. Thus *Nurse Betty*, in its disturbing commentary on what constitutes women's reality and in its cheerful championing of mostly benevolent illusions, reminds us of something that the facile conclusion of *Jerry Maguire* glosses over. Once we entertain the thought that monotony, violence, abuse, and a lack of prospects make up the reality of many women, we might also consider that women, who constitute the overwhelming majority of America's soap opera viewers, may have a *reason* to prefer TV to reality, perhaps even a reason to want reality changed.

Bridget Jones's Diary. Directed by Sharon Maguire. Miramax. Release Date in the United States: April 13, 2001. Total U.S. Gross: $71,500,556

Bridget Jones (Renée Zellweger) is a junior editor with a massive self-esteem problem who spends much of her diary-writing time obsessing about losing weight and getting a guy. Her family considers her, at age thirty-two, a ticking biological clock and tries to set her up with Mark Darcy (Colin Firth), a wealthy, good-looking, and high-powered human rights lawyer. But Bridget is busy exchanging tips on career, love, and sex with her friends Shazzer (Sally Phillips), Tom (James Callis), and Jude (Shirley Henderson), when she is not otherwise occupied with her doomed office romance with suave boss Daniel Cleaver (Hugh Grant). When she catches Daniel with another woman, she quits her job. Embarking on a new career as a TV reporter, she has her big break when Mark grants her an exclusive interview in a sensational court case. After Bridget rejects her "user" boyfriend Daniel and Mark drops his competent but coldly scheming lawyer girlfriend Natasha (Embeth Davidtz), the path is clear for romance between Mark and Bridget.

Bridget Jones, whose last name indicates that she is a sort of Everywoman, is insecure enough to make even the most self-doubting women viewers feel like paragons of self-assertion. Bridget also has a great talent for making a colossal fool of herself. She shows off her insecurity by babbling inanities, sings karaoke out of tune in a bar, and appears at a garden party dressed as a playboy bunny because she thought it was a "tarts and vicars" costume party. At a book-launching reception, she reveals herself to be the worst public speaker in the history of oratory. She spends an entire evening carefully rehearsing appropriate questions for famous authors but cannot think of anything to ask Salman Rushdie other than directions to the bathroom. Bridget is well aware of her social incompetence, but her response to it alternates among sinking into depression, getting drunk and eating junk food in front of the telly, and devouring books on self-help, weight loss, and increased self-confidence. This endless back-and-forth hints at another problem commonly perceived as "typically" female: the yo-yo effect of mood swings, dieting, and bingeing. But Bridget's problem is not only one of self-confidence; there are real deficiencies in her character that may form the basis for her negative self-image. For someone employed in a literary agency and a TV network, she is astonishingly badly read and uneducated in the most basic terms. She has never heard of El Niño or of a famous human rights case that has occupied the British press for five years, and she has only the vaguest idea of contemporary political events or geography. Nor is she a potential housewife: cooking at her birthday party reveals her to be a disaster in the kitchen. Bridget's portrayal as more deficient and more insecure than most women is meant, paradoxically, to empower women. If Bridget, with her middling figure, her professional incompetence, her self-assurance issues, and her bad cooking, can land a rich and handsome man like Mark Darcy, then surely there must be hope for the rest of us. Bridget's incompetence and her talent for embarrassing herself are intended as an exaggerated expression of the character's humanity (compare Bridget with ice-cold but obviously intelligent and professionally accomplished lawyer Natasha), but her humanity comes with a gender label. Neither Daniel Cleaver nor Mark Darcy has to be dumbed down to appear human.

Bridget's amiable humanity plays a familiar part, namely, that of assuaging male anger. Daniel Cleaver turns out to be promiscuous yet possessive, sleeping with other women but reluctant to let Bridget go. The enmity between him and Mark dates back to Daniel's seduction of Mark's former wife, an affair that led to Mark's divorce and forms the basis for his role as the film's angry white male. Mark's aggression and rudeness toward Bridget are motivated by his feelings for her and by his anger over having to watch Daniel, yet again, walk off with a woman he desires for himself. The only way Bridget can assuage this anger is, of course, by rejecting Daniel for Mark. All ends happily when Bridget sees behind Mark's angry facade and recognizes him for the kind and gentle man he really is.

Perhaps we can understand why a good-looking, wealthy, accomplished, and intelligent man like Mark Darcy falls in love with a dimwit like Bridget, why he loves her "just as you are," as he confesses. For aside from her many deficiencies, Bridget is also portrayed as warm, honest, and funny—and these are qualities that, unaccompanied by good looks and impressive smarts, are not often celebrated. What we might find a little more difficult to swallow is how Bridget, with her deficits of knowledge and intellect, can hold down a job first as an editor and later as a reporter. In a film that rather directly offers its heroine as a figure of identification for women viewers—we all want to be loved "just as we are"— every female character's job is strangely void of content. Bridget's friend Jude has a high-powered job herself but is never shown in a professional capacity. Instead, she spends most of her time bonding with her girlfriends (ostentatiously gay Tom fits right in with the girls) or crying in the company toilet over her "fuckwit" boyfriend, Vile Richard. Work life, like private life, is made up of sexual encounters. For Bridget, sexual harassment, both on the job and at family parties, is a recurring experience throughout the film.

For all we know, Bridget the junior editor has never read a book; Bridget the TV reporter is ignorant of world events or nationally important court cases. She gets her big break, an interview with the main protagonist of a prominent human rights case, not through any achievement of her own but through Mark's intervention. During the interview, she proves herself ignorant of the political context and asks mushy "human interest" questions that are completely irrelevant to the case. The second pinnacle of her career as a TV reporter occurs when she slides down a fireman's pole in a miniskirt, with her butt landing on the camera. To the viewer, Bridget as a professional appears ludicrous; in the film, however, she is celebrated as "the new face of British TV reporting." There is no resolution for this discrepancy and no convincing explanation for it. We are left with the distinct impression that what matters in Bridget's professional life is not substance but surface; "reality" pales beside its representation, its manipulation first in print and then on TV. Books are not there to be read, as is apparent at the booklaunching reception, but to be packaged, endowed with an image, and sold. In Bridget's TV career, makeup, and length of skirt are of greater consequence than her job performance. Bridget's career also demonstrates the media hierarchy, for progressing from print media to TV is presented as a move up, not to mention a move away from her unhappy love affair with Daniel. Tellingly, her mother, who is also unhappy in her marriage, falls for a man who offers her a chance to appear on TV. The more devoid of content a medium is, the higher its societal prestige and the higher its ability to offer a dreamworld to those like Bridget, or her mother, who are unhappy with their real lives.

Curiously, the film *Bridget Jones's Diary* is itself the product of media manipulation. It is an adaptation of Helen Fielding's *Bridget Jones's Diary* (1996), which is itself a comic modernization of Jane Austen's *Pride and Prejudice* (1813). With respect to Austen's novel, the film is highly self-referential: Colin

Firth, who plays Mark Darcy, also portrayed Fitzwilliam Darcy, the model for Mark Darcy, in the BBC adaptation of *Pride and Prejudice* (1995); in Fielding's book, Bridget is a big fan of Colin Firth, the actor. As an adaptation of Fielding's novel, the film tries to be literal but fails because Bridget's story does not lend itself to transfer from one medium to another. Fielding's book is told from Bridget Jones's perspective, and we remain aware, throughout the book, that Bridget may not be the best judge of her own character or abilities. In the film, the camera acts as a narrator and turns Bridget's self-flagellation into objective reality. In Fielding's book, she thinks of herself as stupid, and we doubt her; in the film, she appears stupid, and we believe it. The transfer of Bridget's diary reality onto film effectively cancels what the film tries to achieve. Bridget is set up as a model of identification for every self-doubting woman, in short, all of us. But with whom do we identify if we are even moderately intelligent, knowledgeable, or competent at our jobs? Is being an accomplished and smart woman, like the film's manipulative ice queen Natasha, still portrayed as a defect? Is *Bridget Jones's Diary* a film about a wonderful woman, who does not need to be anything other than a nice person to find happiness, or just about a dumb blond? Identifying with Bridget is an ambiguous experience: we appreciate her warmth and her sweetness, but even if we are not high-powered career women à la Natasha, most of us are likely to know what El Niño is and to put our noses into a book or a newspaper from time to time. The film intends to show us imperfect humans as lovable: Bridget, with her talent for self-embarrassment and her insecurities; Mark, with his repressed feelings and occasional bursts of anger and violence; Shazzer, with her dirty mouth; Tom, with his vanity; Jude, with her hysterics and her dependence on Vile Richard. What is perhaps unusual about *Bridget Jones's Diary* is that it does not counter our dissatisfaction with our real lives by presenting us with a media-created fiction about beautiful people, perfect love affairs, and glamorous lives. Rather, it shows us an exaggeration of our own problems and shortcomings. Our professional predicaments, from lack of advancement to sexual harassment, our personal troubles, from cheating boyfriends to general feelings of inadequacy, pale beside Bridget's. In answer to life's rather large problems, *Bridget Jones's Diary* offers us identification with someone smaller than life.

Chicago. Directed by Rob Marshall. Miramax. Release Date in the United States: December 27, 2002. Total U.S. Gross: $170,684,505

Chicago, a musical set in the prohibition era, is perhaps the most barefaced indictment of what reality is worth when it is not touched up by a good media makeover. The film's heroines, Roxie (Renée Zellweger) and Velma (Catherine Zeta-Jones) are murderesses who would do absolutely anything for a spot in the limelight. Roxie, a housewife with dreams of a career on stage, is incapable of perceiving people or events around her as anything other than vaudeville performances. The film adopts her perspective and duplicates her inability to perceive offstage life as "real" by accompanying every major twist of the plot with song and dance intervals. Roxie murders her lover Fred (Dominic West) because he promises her a career on the stage in order to get her to go to bed with him. In jail, she meets her idol Velma and the corrupt warden Mama Morton (Queen Latifah), who, if generously bribed, provides her jailbirds with goods and services, ranging from everyday comforts to media attention and legal representation. She puts Roxie in contact with Billy Flynn (Richard Gere), who easily obtains Roxie's release by manipulating her image and her story in the newspapers. In the end, Roxie and Velma, who has also beaten the rap with Billy's help, start a successful vaudeville act entitled "The Killer Dillers."

Chicago is one of the rare Zellweger films in which her role is not limited to assuaging male anger. Indeed, the film deals more with female than male anger. Velma, for example, kills her husband and her sister when she finds them in bed together. Like Roxie, she is absolutely remorseless and exclusively concerned with her release and media image. This lack of penitence also characterizes the other female killers imprisoned in Roxie's jail. In "Cell Block Tango," they justify their various murders of men with the hook line "He had it coming." The reasons why "he had it coming" range from the understandable (such as bigamy) to the ridiculous (such as popping his bubble gum). Female anger toward men is not always motivated by men's mistreatment of women. Roxie, for example, murders her lover not because he betrays her love but because he cannot jump-start her stage career. The only truly "nice" man in the film, Roxie's husband Amos (John C. Reilly), hardly fares any better than the other male victims: Roxie first cheats on him, then uses him to obtain her release, and finally abandons him. Amos exhibits no signs of the ruthlessness that defines every other character in the film; whereas everybody else struggles for a spot in the limelight, he is content with his unglamorous offstage existence. Paradoxically, the fact that Amos refuses to participate in the media circus and lives fully in the real world makes his character strangely unreal. In fact, to others, Amos hardly exists at all: nobody notices his presence, and the lawyer Billy keeps forgetting his name. Amos's song, "Mister Cellophane" ("You can look right through me and never know I'm there"), establishes invisibility, lack of reality, as his primary characteristic.

If the portrayal of Amos, the only character without a media image, is any indication, the film endorses Roxie and Velma's conviction that you are only visible when onstage or in the newspaper. Existence is being seen by others; life in the "real" world, outside of media-generated images, is beside the point. Lack of media attention or projecting the wrong image can be deadly, as evidenced by Katalin Helinszki's "disappearing act," a musical trapeze number juxtaposed with a real-life hanging. The fact that media matter and real life is irrelevant also accounts for the film's disturbing moral emptiness: the harmless and loyal husband Amos is neither rewarded nor endorsed; nor are the ruthless killers Roxie and Velma, the corrupt Mama, and the manipulative shyster Billy Flynn condemned. Thus the film practices what it preaches; it not only privileges illusion over reality but also distances itself from the moral concerns of the "real world."

In the film's juxtaposition of the real world, characterized by the absence of music, with media-created fiction, expressed through musical interludes, there can be no question which part counts. It is the media world that shows the "true" story and has the power to effect change. Roxie's song about her husband ("He follows me around like a droopy-eyed pup") tells us more about her relationship with Amos than the nonmusical scenes in which she pretends to be his loving wife. Mama Morton, who in her speech to her charges hints at her greed and corruptness rather indirectly, lays it all out in her song: "If you're good to Mama, Mama's good to you." If we were taken in by the showy press conference Billy puts on with Roxie, the accompanying rag, in which Billy acts as ventriloquist and Roxie acts as his dummy, soon disabuses us of any illusions we might have had. Billy understands that "the world is show business." All that needs to be done to obtain Roxie's release, although she is clearly guilty, is to "razzle dazzle" the jury, to whom he refers as "the audience." And razzle dazzle them he does: he turns the facts of the case on their head with an unmatched skill that is visualized—how else—in a tap dance. What may be veiled or confusing in the real world becomes crassly obvious in the "show." When unable to interpret reality, we turn to the media; we grant them the power not only to translate but also to *shape* events. Because the media produces representations of the real world, and because the media can be manipulated, the real world becomes inconsequential: in the end, any version of events might be "true." Thus Roxie's verdict appears in the papers before the jury has made up its mind. On the morning of the verdict, two editions of the same paper, with the headlines reading alternately "Guilty" or "Innocent," lie ready to be sold. Fortunately for Roxie, "Innocent" gets the sale. Roxie exchanges the "real world" for a glitzy existence on the vaudeville stage, from which she and co-star Velma inform their adoring audience—quite correctly—that they could not have done it without them.

Renée Zellweger films show us little women discontent with their lives in the real world. Relying on the help of the media, these hapless drifters attempt to give reality a face-lift. Once Dorothy has left Kansas, she is headed for the modern incarnation of Oz: the stage or TV. In *Nurse Betty* and *Chicago*, the heroine leaves real life behind altogether. The recurring evocation of *Oz*'s Dorothy shows in no uncertain terms how much the real world has changed. In 1939, there was no place like home; in the early 2000s, "home," the point of departure of our modern Dorothy, is a dead end, a place of intense suffering or boredom. None of our heroines returns home; most of them, having escaped it, never look back. The fact that "home" is the point of departure but no longer the goal shows us that the real world, which in Oz still wins out over the colorful illusion, is no longer enough. But media-created illusions can be just as dangerous because they are subject to interpretation, adaptation, and manipulation. Thus Renée Zellweger films leave us emotionally homeless: they mirror, on the one hand, our own discontent with the real world, but they also comment on our apparently limitless naïveté, our never-ending willingness to be manipulated.

NOTES

1. *Jerry Maguire* is but one of a flood of recent movies that depict the crisis of concepts of masculinity (see Elisabeth Krimmer, "Nobody Wants to Be a Man Anymore? Cross-Dressing in American Movies of the 90s," in *Subverting Masculinity: Hegemony and Alternative Versions of Masculinity in Contemporary Culture*, ed. Russell West and Frank Lay [Amsterdam: Rodopi, 2001], 30–37).

2. *Jerry Maguire* offers a variant of the comedy of remarriage because "the drive of its plot is not to get the central pair together, but to get them back together, together again" (Stanley Cavell, *Pursuits of Happiness: The Hollywood Comedy of Remarriage* [Cambridge: Harvard University Press, 1981], 2). Cavell points out that in "questioning the legitimacy of marriage, the question of the legitimacy of society is simultaneously raised, even allegorized" (*Pursuits of Happiness*, 53). It is of interest to note that *Jerry Maguire* carries traits of the genres of both comedy and drama. It would appear that, in the 1990s, examining the validity of the institution of marriage was too grave a matter to lend itself to the levity of the genre of screwball comedy.

3. The world of *Nurse Betty* bears all the essential traits of what Susan Faludi calls a display culture, a culture that is "constructed around celebrity and image, glamour and entertainment, marketing and consumerism" (*Stiffed: The Betrayal of the American Man* [New York: Perennial, 2000], 35).

☆ 5 ☆

Highlights and Low Points
Affairs of State and Kung Fu Bunnies

Unlike all previous chapters, which focus on the work of individual actresses, the analyses below are guided by a thematic approach. In the following, we want to take a close look at two female screen personae that recur in movies of the 1990s, the kick-ass Bruce Willis–style superwoman and the politically and socially aware thinker. Because women are not usually perceived as either, one might be seduced into thinking that, through these types, Hollywood finally presents truly progressive heroines, who serve as ideal role models for ambitious and independent women. It will be part of the purpose of this chapter to investigate if these heroines are indeed harbingers of a bright new future for women in movies or if—despite the prominence of these new types—nothing much has changed at all.

Part of our interest in these two types of heroines stems from the conviction that both make explicit what is merely implied in romantic comedies. Generally, "women's films" are considered unpolitical.[1] But clearly, film romances *imply* a form of politics. One need only call to mind the corporate image defining the heroine of *My Best Friend's Wedding* (1997), or the strange discrepancy between Kathleen Kelly's modest job as a bookstore owner and her luxurious New York City apartment in *You've Got Mail* (1998), or the simple fact that most romantic comedies have as their heroes and heroines, without exactly advertising the fact, the well-to-do, if not the immensely rich. If not, the purpose of the film is often not only to get the happy couple together but also to make the fairy tale complete by endowing bride and groom with immense riches or at least substantial material comforts; this is implied in the endings of *Pretty Woman* (1990) and *Jerry Maguire* (1996), for example. Other films state that money isn't everything, that, in fact, money can't buy you love (*Notting Hill* [1999]), but they do so from a perspective of considerable wealth, which remains part of the happy couple's endowment package at the end of the film and thus loses none of its attraction for the viewer. One could read the two "political" films we discuss below as a more direct discussion of these genre conventions. By the same token, one could read the action heroines we analyze as exaggerations of other instances of female competence in romantic comedies—the sassy, no-nonsense, professionally competent, and slightly defensive heroines of *The Net* (1995) or *Runaway Bride* (1999), for example.

It seems appropriate that in our analysis of "political films," we should make our own politics explicit. Our discussion of political and action films will make no pretenses at "bipartisanship," as our title already indicates. We think of some of these films as "highlights" and others as "low points," both in terms of the portrayal of contemporary politics and in terms of how women's roles are used to arrive at this interpretation. Thus we admit openly that our reading of action heroines and women in political films is influenced by comparisons with films of other genres, the incorporation of feminist sociological works, and—yes—our own political convictions.

AFFAIRS OF STATE: *TWO WEEKS NOTICE* AND *MAID IN MANHATTAN*

The twentieth century ended with an electoral debacle: the December 2000 selection of George W. Bush as U.S. president despite a clear minority in the popular vote and a questionable outcome in the electoral vote. Exactly two years later, in December 2002, Bush's politics made it into romantic comedies. *Two Weeks Notice* and *Maid in Manhattan* appeared a week apart in December 2002 and were seen by a comparable number of people (the films grossed within half a million dollars of each other). Both portray the love story between an ultrarich and clearly Republican politician/entrepreneur and a woman who serves as his humanizing influence. But both films offer a radically different picture of Republican politics in the new millennium and its influence on American society.

Highlight: *Two Weeks Notice*. Directed by Marc Lawrence. Warner Bros. Release Date in the United States: December 20, 2002. Total U.S. Gross: $93,354,918

Even as youngsters, the future lovers Lucy Kelson (Sandra Bullock) and George Wade (Hugh Grant) are presented as political opposites. Old photographs show

Lucy waving signs reading "Peace" and "Impeach Nixon," whereas George is portrayed in uniform, seated next to Nixon. She grows up to be a tree-hugging, granola-crunching rabid feminist environmentalist, a stereotypical protester complete with rucksack and Birkenstock sandals. When we meet the adult Lucy, she straddles a wrecking ball to prevent it from tearing down a historic landmark. Lucy's protests are heartfelt but inefficient. At her self-organized protest of the wrecking site, only two other people show up, and they are more concerned with getting into each other's pants than with saving the building. Lucy is dragged off the building site and put in jail, where her supportive left-wing parents bail her out, and the building is torn down. George's career, on the other hand, seems wildly successful at first glance: the first shot of George as an adult shows him as "Man of the Year" on the cover of *Forbes Magazine*. But appearances deceive. Crazy Lucy turns out to be a competent lawyer with a degree from Harvard who cares more about doing good than making money. Hotshot George is revealed to be nothing but the pawn of his ultrarich, ultraconservative family, who uses his charming playboy image as a front but reserves the right to make all decisions, including the decision to cut George out of his lavish lifestyle.

When George's brother Howard (David Haig) sternly admonishes him to hire a competent lawyer, rather than the beautiful dumb blonds he usually hires for their looks, George offers the job to Lucy. Lucy accepts not because of the quarter-million-dollar salary and sumptuous benefits but because he guarantees to save the Community Center in her neighborhood, slotted to be torn down to make way for a much more profitable commercial building. The way in which George negotiates the deal shows him to be shrewder than his playboy image suggests. He lures Lucy in with a chance to do good, the promise of millions of dollars to her favorite charities, and, perhaps most important for an unsuccessful activist, the chance to "win occasionally." Already at this early stage, the capitalist/conservative agenda appears all-powerful. Protest or opposition is shown to be ineffectual to the point of ludicrousness; it can only prevail if sanctioned by the conservative power itself, which might let you "win occasionally" the way indulgent parents let their children win at board games.

Lucy's job description in George's firm expresses this power differential clearly. She serves George's firm as a lawyer and George himself as his personal assistant, selecting everything from his ties and office stationery to his mattress. George's demands and dependence on her become so overbearing that she determines to quit, only to find him unwilling to let her go. She persuades him to accept her two weeks' notice and is promptly charged to hire her own replacement. The candidate favored by George turns out to be the exact opposite of

Lucy: blond and beautiful but incompetent June (Alicia Witt), clearly determined to sleep her way to the top, represents the possibility that George might return to his old dissolute lifestyle. Indeed, George soon caves in to his family's demands to have the Community Center knocked down. The happy ending thus hinges not only on George's realization that he is dependent on Lucy but also on his willingness to give up immeasurable riches to become an ethical person.

Repeated allusions define George as a Republican: his appearance on the cover of *Forbes* as "another George," his stunning wealth—he owns the hotel in which he lives—and his pursuit of profit, regardless of human consequences. On the other hand, he is presented as much more sympathetic than the snobs who make up the moneyed elite of the film. Whereas George's brother Howard, for example, never even notices the hired help, George flirts charmingly with middle-aged housekeeper Rosario. One of the most important aspects of George's character is his indiscriminate generosity. He offers his ex-wife an opulent settlement, pays his employees extremely well, and flings money at the poor and lower service employees by the fistful, ranging from an expensive party for the concierge to a $100 tip for a hot dog man. This defines George as unthinking rather than uncaring, as indiscriminate rather than rapacious: he is the greedy capitalist's boyish alter ego. The audience accepts him unproblematically because his indifference to causes is funny rather than harmful. His relentless pursuit of profit and his devil-may-care attitude never hurt anyone. The movie treats his behavior rather nonchalantly. Asked how he sleeps at night, he answers: "Well, I have a machine that simulates the sound of the ocean." When Lucy accuses him of being the most selfish person on the planet, he protests innocently that she can hardly claim this because she does not know everybody else. George comes across as good-natured, boyishly handsome, and charmingly harmless, and we are never quite sure whether he has ever thought about the consequences of his actions. But to Lucy, who wants him to use his wealth for a purpose, his playful indifference presents a problem. "All you have to do is use your power for good rather than evil," she tells him, indicating to him, and us, that random generosity is not good enough.

For a substantial part of the film, rabid feminist/activist Lucy is the only person who objects to George's indifference. Whereas it is not obvious what might be wrong with George, there is clearly lots wrong with Lucy. She eats enough for ten—whenever she orders Chinese, she has to confirm that yes, these eight dishes are for just one person—and bosses George around as if she were his superior, not vice versa. She dresses badly, snores like a log cutter, runs into plants, and spills drinks down her front. She overeats to the point of illness and finds herself stuck in traffic badly needing to defecate. George organizes a potty break in an RV two car lengths ahead, but she does not quite make it and finishes the scene with stains all over her tennis dress. Her sometimes klutzy, often embarrassing behavior counteracts her obvious competence as a lawyer and makes her image as a professional female more palatable to the audience. Still, Lucy is the moral authority of the film, even though many viewers might consider her commitment to the environment and women's rights as exaggeratedly PC and clichéd. She emerges as the hero of the film, without any detraction from her views. In the end, George wins her by being true to his word and saving her Community Center, even though his family disinherits him for it. No such fundamental change is required of Lucy: although the film presents her as a cliché at the outset, the audience is ultimately forced to adopt her perspective.

Lucy is unabashedly anti-Republican throughout the film. When she is in tears over George's treachery, a concerned friend comments, "I've known you since Brownies, I've never seen you cry. Except when Bush won." Her parents, admonishing Lucy to keep up the fight, remind her that she has past achievements to live up to: after all, she was on the White House's enemies list at age five. Such open anti-Republicanism, even anti-Bushism, comes as a surprise in an America with a Republican president and a Republican majority in House, Senate, and Supreme Court. But *Two Weeks Notice* goes a step further: it defines anti-Bushism not as political correctness but as ethical behavior. Lucy's deliberate commitment to the people offers direction and purpose for George's lavish but indiscriminate generosity toward people. The difference between Lucy and George is simple: George views the people he helps as individuals, whereas Lucy sees them as part of a community. Ultimately, it is the community, not just the Community Center, that is at the heart of Lucy's concern: understanding people as a group who can only thrive if they work together.

Perhaps for this reason, *Two Weeks Notice* is one of the rare films that can do without an applauding community in the final love scene. In other movies—from *Speed* to *Notting Hill*—there is a somewhat artificial and dilettantish attempt to fold the lovers into the community: the public kiss or declaration is routinely greeted by the applause of bystanders. Lucy and George, on the other hand, are by themselves in the final scene. Because commitment to the community brought them together in the first place, there is no need to create an artificial connection between the lovers and their community. Thus *Two Weeks Notice* challenges us to practice that ability on which all political activism depends: the willingness to do without community approval. And what could make more sense in a film that openly advocates minority rather than majority views and champions the ethical over the popular?

Low Point: *Maid in Manhattan*. Directed by Wayne Wang. Sony Pictures. Release Date in the United States: December 13, 2002. Total U.S. Gross: 93,932,896

Maid in Manhattan is a modern Cinderella story depicting the romance between Latina hotel maid and single mother Marisa Ventura (Jennifer Lopez) and high-society playboy and Republican politician Chris Marshall (Ralph Fiennes). When Chris first meets Marisa, he mistakes her for someone of his own class because Marisa, in a moment of weakness, has tried on a wealthy hotel guest's clothes. But as the film relentlessly repeats, anything is possible: the ultra-rich Republican stays in love with Cinderella once she is revealed to be nothing but the chambermaid, untroubled by this revelation. Nor is Chris's political career hurt by his liaison with the maid: at the end of the film, he has been elected senator, and he and Marisa live happily (and wealthily) ever after.

As a document of early-twenty-first-century Republicanism, *Maid in Manhattan* does its best to idealize Bush's America and to distract attention away from the actual content of Republican politics. The extensive opening shots of the Statue of Liberty to the strains of Paul Simon's hit "Me and Julio Down by the Schoolyard"—"I'm on my way—I don't know where I'm going, I'm on my way"—evoke an America to which immigrants are lured by the promise of a better life. It is the land of unlimited opportunity for everyone, where, no matter how dismal the log cabin of your humble beginnings, hard work will take you to the White House without fail. Marisa Ventura belongs to several disadvantaged groups simultaneously: her Latina origins define her as an immigrant and as nonwhite, she works in a subordinate and badly paid service job, and—to top it all off—she is a single mother. But lest we fall into the trap of underestimating her, her last name, *Ventura*, already indicates that Marisa is different from the stereotypical mass of lazy, drug-addicted, alcoholic, ever-breeding, and never-working dark-skinned immigrants of American popular imagination. She ventures out to win a better life for herself and her child.

In many ways, Marisa already lives better than workers in her income group can generally afford to: whereas most of America's working poor live in weekly rentals, shelters, cheap hotel rooms, or even cars, Marisa actually has an apartment, and the movie does not bother to explain how Marisa obtained the several thousands of dollars she would have needed for a security deposit as well as first and last month's rent on minimum wage.[2] Marisa is a good mother who reads about education, enrolls her son in the gifted students program of his school, checks his homework, and supports his academic endeavors. She also instills the correct right-wing values in her child, for at age ten, Ty (Tyler Garcia Posey) has read a Kissinger biography, and his number one hero is—who else—Richard Nixon. In addition to being a good mother, Marisa is conscientious and efficient on the job, hardworking, energetic, unassuming, modest, and lightheartedly witty on the subject of her own poverty: she is portrayed as an upbeat kind of gal, just the kind who deserves to make it to the top. She works her ten-hour shifts smilingly, interrupted only by cordial banter with her coworkers (and occasional bursts into song and dance evocative of Coca-Cola commercials), and spends the remainder of her time with her son, as a good mother should. Until Chris comes along, we do not ever see her having a love life, a social life, drinking, eating (although she is seen feeding her son), or relaxing.

Though her image as an acceptable lower-class nonwhite person depends on her representation as a hard worker, her image as the ideal woman is defined, somewhat paradoxically, by her "refreshing" lack of self-confidence. In the extremely modest fashion in which this is possible for a maid, Marisa dreams of moving up. But when a job opens up in management, she does not dare apply for it although she is well qualified. The film does not link Marisa's fearfulness to the "invisibility" she is trained to perform as part of her job, for that would imply a social aspect of her victimization.[3] The problem, rather, is her mother, who holds her down and destroys her self-esteem whenever possible. Apparently, this is a regularly occurring dilemma among hotel maids, who repeatedly discuss the possibility of "getting out of uniform"—that is, moving up into the managerial ranks of the hotel hierarchy—as a way of "proving our mothers wrong." We witness this firsthand when Marisa' s own mother denies her every right to professional ambitions and personal dreams. Thus the film transfers blame for the plight of the working poor: in today's Republican America, anything is possible. If you haven't made it to the top, you're not working hard enough. If you work hard enough and you still haven't made it to the top, don't blame Republican politics, cuts in health care, or the elimination of social programs. Blame your mother.

As a modern Cinderella story, the film advocates sympathy for a certain segment of the poor population, that hardworking, uncomplaining, and easily governable segment that Marisa represents. Curiously, its open promotion of Republicanism combined with contempt for the rich is not represented as a contradiction. This corresponds exactly to real-life politics: although the ranks of the rich are largely Republican, Republicans like to represent themselves as solidly middle class. In the film, the ultrarich are seen through the eyes of those who serve them and who know their every dirty secret: the married men with girlfriends, the thieves and con men, and the exhibitionists living in the hotel's most expensive suites are hardly likely to inspire the respect and admiration of the staff. Clearly, the rich are not superior. As Marisa's friend, the hotel manager, puts it: "They're only people with money." The maids, too, repeatedly state that there is no difference between them and the goddess in the Park Suite.

Although *Maid in Manhattan* incessantly denies the existence of any real difference between rich and poor, it shows that difference in exaggerated, even clichéd, ways. The rich not only harbor embarrassing secrets, they are also the only truly prejudiced people in the film. They harass maids sexually in the crudest terms imaginable, require extravagant services, inconsiderately ask them to work extra hours, or discuss intimate details in front of them as if they were not even in the room. The poor, on the other hand, are portrayed as an idealized community dedicated to serving the rich and helping each other. Marisa's coworkers, for example, take care of her son Ty without complaint while she works her ten-hour shifts; there is no backbiting or nasty gossip among the maids or other hotel staff; the racial slurs that are common among the rich in the film are entirely absent here. And of course, in the lower-class service community every race is painstakingly represented, from the stereotypically overweight and buxom black maid—a descendant of the "mammy" in Civil War films—to the slender Asian woman in the tailoring department. To upbeat tunes whose message is all too obvious, from "I'm Coming Out" to "(If Only You Believed in) Miracles," the maids kick up their heels, dance happily around their carts while cleaning, and assert their lower-class self-confidence. Just as the entire hotel service community works together to take care of Ty, they all help to dress up Marisa for her date with Chris in a borrowed dress that none of them could ever afford. "For one night, you're living it for all of us," one of them tells Marisa as she drives off in a limousine to play guest at a party where she would normally be serving the drinks. If the moneyed elite in the film is defined by prejudice, intolerance, rudeness, arrogance, and sexual transgression, the poor offer a pleasing spectacle of solidarity, friendship, and mutual support. In spite of this, the film holds fast to its philosophy that there is no essential difference between the haves and have-nots. Aside from their bank accounts, they are equal in every respect.

The film does not invite us to identify with the haves; in fact, the contrary is true. In this film, Republicans run on a platform of support for the poor. Unlike the Republicans of our world, *Maid in Manhattan* Republicans do not cut social programs and destroy the welfare system, the school system, and social security to increase military funding. Rather, they support inner-city literacy campaigns, show their benevolent faces in the slums and ghettos, and support the socially weak in every way they can. Chris Marshall, the central Republican in the film, is also rescued from the negative image Americans generally have of

Maid in Manhattan *(2002) makes low-wage jobs look like one big party: fun, fun, fun.* COLUMBIA/THE KOBAL COLLECTION/K.C. BAILEY.

politicians by being "refreshingly" indifferent to politics. While his staff desperately tries to get his attention and approval for the next visit in the housing projects, he plays frisbee; he skips out on a sumptuous League of Women Voters lunch to walk the dog. His image on the covers of political magazines is that of a rich scandal-besieged playboy, but the audience knows better: he is just a regular guy with money. Again, the love story between Maid Marisa and Mighty Marshall is possible because there is no "class" difference here; the difference is just money. This, of course, is the reason why it is possible for anyone to make it in equal-opportunity America. The final scenes show Marisa in a managerial position, dispensing autographs and press interviews full of good advice "to other maids looking to trade up." Chris is elected into the U.S. Senate despite the fact that he has "friends in low places." And as though this were not enough, the movie repeats its gratifying portrayal of American egalitarianism in the story of Marisa's friends, who all metamorphose from maid to manager within a year. Hard work and talking back to your mother make up the recipe for success: in Bush's new America, anything is possible.

It comes as no surprise that *Maid in Manhattan* requires no change or development of any kind of the Republican figurehead to make the love story work. Right from the start, Chris embodies the "correct" distance to the political machinery, mirroring the American voter's skepticism toward "big government." And it is even less surprising that the film drags the love story of Chris and Marisa even further into the public arena than is customary in romantic comedies. Normally, an approving and applauding audience in the film suffices to signal to the audience viewing the film that it, too, should bless this union. *Maid in Manhattan* makes doubly sure that we get it: Chris's pursuit of Marisa takes place in a crowd composed of bystanders and reporters; their love is consummated in every newspaper and tabloid in the country. A year later, headlines document their thriving as a couple, validating the Republican credo of "we're all just the same."

What *Maid in Manhattan* offers the viewer is a new version of the old American dream: in order to deserve society's support, you must be hard working; but if you are hard working, you will not need it. The working poor in the film toil happily and are unresentful of the rich who treat them well, good-naturedly humorous toward the rich who treat them badly, and quite able to pull themselves up by their own bootstraps. Among Marisa's coworkers, the success rate of maids trying to make it into managerial positions is 100 percent within one year. Minor setbacks are merely seen as a test of character that should not diminish one's resolve: although Marisa is fired from her job for stealing, she does not end up on welfare. Rather, she performs the somewhat unlikely feat of getting another job and moves up to boot. Serious problems are always personal, never social: Mother is the great imposing presence holding the maids down, and the Republicans, who govern this exceedingly fair society, do everything in their power to support the poor. In addition, the stereotypical and distasteful characterization of the rich in the film creates a distance between them and the "average" millionaire, supporting the Republican credo of the wealthy as middle class. Thus *Two Weeks Notice* and *Maid in Manhattan*, viewed as Hollywood's commentary on Bush's politics, leave us with contradictory messages. One suggests that a fair society can only be achieved through opposition against or at least radical modification of the Republican stance. The other assures us that the world is fine as it is and that a bit of ineffectual ranting against the ultrarich should purge us of our remaining doubts or rebellious inclinations.

KUNG FU BUNNIES: HOLLYWOOD ACTION HEROINES

Recently, feminist cultural critics Susan Faludi and Susan Bordo have pointed to a widespread trend to ornamentalize and sexualize the male body.[4] Movies, television, and commercials now depict male bodies in poses that were previously reserved for women. From the Coke ad that has female office employees gaze at the naked upper body of a construction worker to *Buffy the Vampire Slayer*, in which Buffy's male love interests frequently display their naked torsos (and more) whereas the heroine herself is always properly attired, the male pinup has become a staple of today's mass media. Conversely, women have conquered the realm of action and thriller, previously the sole domain of men. From *Charlie's Angels* (2000) to *Lara Croft: Tomb Raider* (2001), the 1990s and 2000s in particular have seen a surprisingly large number of action heroines. Women heroes now ride motorbikes and fly helicopters; they are equipped with fancy combat technology and trained in Asian martial arts. They can beat their opponents to a pulp or outrace them in cars.

And yet it is at times difficult to rejoice wholeheartedly when Lara Croft triumphs over another conspiracy of devious men. Many of these action chick flicks drown their woman power message in a sea of sexist stereotypes. Even Tarantino's Beatrix Kiddo in *Kill Bill* conforms to the stereotype of the mother who fights claw and teeth because her baby girl has been hurt. In short, the bigger the budget backing a particular action venture, the greater the likelihood that the heroine will perform her extraordinary feats in a rigidly patriarchal setting. More often than not, she not only abets this system but even fights to uphold it. In *Lara Croft: Tomb Raider*, for example, the heroine is doing it all for Daddy. In *Charlie's Angels*, the original task to free a kidnapped millionaire inadvertently turns into the mission to save the Angels' employer and benefactor Charlie. Even Trinity, the spirited heroine of *The Matrix*, devotes all her energies to finding and protecting the male hero Neo, who, in turn, is in charge of saving humankind. If, on the whole, Trinity is still a much stronger female role model, it is because her body is not subject to the same relentless commodification and sexualization that characterize both *Lara Croft* and *Charlie's Angels*. There is a good deal of fighting in both of these movies, but there is a good deal more screen time devoted to breasts, hips, and buttocks in various states of undress. The result is an uneven blend of a Hong Kong action movie with a Victoria's Secret commercial. Beatrix Kiddo, on the other hand, is not sexualized but, rather, walks the tightrope between the female archetypes of Black Mamba and Sweet Mommy, poisonous snake and aspiring homemaker.

It is not surprising that, in order to find a convincing and strong female action hero, we have to turn to a movie that was not part of the summer blockbuster circus. One of the most impressive action heroines of recent years, Mace (Angela Bassett) in *Strange Days* (1995), plays a supporting role in a thriller focused on a male protagonist. Mace is not nearly as omnipotent as Lara Croft or Charlie's Angels, but she is certainly far more real than the four of them together. Comparing Mace with Lara and the Angels clearly brings to the fore the final frontier of the female action movie: to create a physically and emotionally strong character who is neither a shamelessly sexualized bimbo nor so completely removed from the realm of the everyday that identification becomes nearly impossible. Once such a character can draw a crowd, we will indeed kick butt.

Low Point: *Lara Croft: Tomb Raider.* Directed by Simon West. Paramount Pictures. Release Date in the United States: June 15, 2001. Total U.S. Gross: $131,144,183

One might be tempted to mistake Lara Croft (Angelina Jolie) for the ultimate female omnipotence fantasy. She is beautiful, sexy, rich, intelligent, educated, and a superior fighter. A James Bond–Batman hybrid, Lara Croft combines cultural refinement and supreme riches with physical superiority and the finest of combat technology. She owns a stunning castle with eighty-three rooms and an equally oversized fleet of cars and motorcycles. She speaks every language known to man, is an authority on archaeology and mythology, knows how to decipher the most obscure ancient inscriptions, listens to Bach in her spare time, and identifies a Blake quotation at first glance. Clothed in silk pajamas and relying on nothing but her wits, a pneumatic gun as weapon, and screwdrivers as bullets, she prevails against a small army of special combat forces who have come to raid her home. Shouldn't women viewers be excited about this paragon of female competence?

Unfortunately, the answer is no. Far from a female role model, Lara Croft is the ultimate male fantasy. There are several reasons why it is nearly impossible for female viewers to identify with this Über-woman. First of all, Lara is clearly one of the guys. She has a male butler, a male computer wizard, and male enemies. When she needs to get to Cambodia in record time, she calls on her male military network for help. Lara is not only an exceptional woman; aside from the ghostly apparition of a little girl, she is the only woman in this movie. Second, Lara is still a cartoon character. She has no inner life, no emotions except the ones for her father, no relationships, and no friends. Lara's splendid isolation proves that the movie takes the omnipotence fantasy too far. Lara is too rich and too competent. There is nothing human about her, and nobody is her equal. In the beginning, she does not even have proper enemies but, indeed, has to fight a machine to get some exercise. Furthermore, unlike her male counterpart James Bond, Lara does not have affairs. Hints at a previous relationship with fellow tomb raider Alex (Daniel Craig) are sparse and remain utterly unconvincing. Third, Lara's exaggerated competence reduces the risk involved in her fights. Practically invulnerable, Lara is never in danger of being hurt. Even the tiny little scratch on her upper arm sustained during one of her adventures is magically healed by a potion administered by a mysterious monk. There is no effort, no struggle, and no fear. Because there is never anything at stake, all her fights ultimately leave us cold.

The relentless sexualization of her body also makes it difficult for a female audience to identify with this heroine.[5] The camera simply cannot get enough of her breasts, thighs, crotch, and ass. There is hardly a shot that does not zoom in on her bosom or take its departure from between her legs. Lara Croft's fights are heavily eroticized. Her weapons are strapped to her naked thighs. When she reloads her guns, she presses them against her buttocks. The first fight scene with the robot is presented as a sexual encounter in which Lara moves from the missionary position to that of woman on top, all the while gasping as though she were having an orgasm. Lara is the ultimate male fantasy, and the $131 million U.S. gross testifies to her enormous appeal.

Lara Croft does not represent a fantasy of female empowerment but, rather, one of patriarchal containment of female power. She is not only a projection of erotic desire, she is also a quintessential daddy's girl. *Lara Croft: Tomb Raider* overemphasizes its heroine's relationship with her father. Lara may be fighting a secret society of devious, dangerous men, but she is certainly doing it for daddy. Her mother, on the other hand, is reduced to a pale, silent image. We can rest assured that, given the power of God, the ability to control time and the world, Lara would not use it for her own aggrandizement but only to be reunited with her deceased father. Consequently, the penultimate scene of the movie shows Lara's visit to her father's mausoleum. Lara's body may be the object of every

Although marketed as a woman warrior, Lara Croft is presented as the ultimate sex kitten. Angelina Jolie in Tomb Raider: The Cradle of Life *(2003). PARAMOUNT/ THE KOBAL COLLECTION.*

man's fantasies, but her heart belongs to daddy. She is beautiful, sexy, rich, intelligent, educated, and a superior fighter—and we couldn't care less.

Low Point: *Charlie's Angels*. Directed by Joseph McGinty Nichol. Columbia Pictures. Release Date in the United States: November 3, 2000. Total U.S. Gross: $125,305,545

Charlie's Angels and Lara Croft have much in common. Although they do not inhabit the same highbrow British world, Charlie's Angels, like Lara Croft, are meant to be both sexy and competent. Between the three of them, Dylan (Drew Barrymore), Alex (Lucy Liu), and Natalie (Cameron Diaz) speak numerous languages fluently, excel at car racing and parachuting, win on *Jeopardy*, go to outer space, and know how to handle every piece of sophisticated technological equipment they can get their hands on. They can beat up a crowd of men while tied to a chair, make their way into the mainframe of a computer company safer than Fort Knox, or fix the intercom at a McDonald's drive-through. Throughout all their ordeals, they manage to look stunning in their numerous fashionable outfits. Again, Hollywood purports to give us the ultimate dream: not one but three women who are strong and desirable—a great idea, only it is not so. Unlike, for example, *Legally Blonde* (2001), *Charlie's Angels* is not a movie about the stereotypical blond ditz who turns out to be intelligent and competent at heart. Rather, it is the story of three competent women who, so the movie assures us, have remained dumb ditzes after all. In order to achieve this effect and yet retain its superficial shine of woman power, *Charlie's Angels* engages in a good deal of double speak.[6] Repeatedly, the characters in the movie ponder the threat posed by strong women. Alex, for example, pretends to be a bikini waxer because she is worried that her boyfriend will leave her if he finds out that she is one-third of an elite crime-fighting team: "They are all lovey-dovey until they find out I can shatter a cinderblock with my forehead." In response to this, Dylan formulates the pseudomessage of the movie: "You don't want to be with a man who is intimated by a strong woman anyway." However, even as it discusses harmful gender stereotypes, the movie itself turns its elite crime fighters into bikini waxer equivalents. Alex, who can hack into the most challenging computer but is unable to produce edible muffins, inspires one of the running jokes of the movie. Natalie, who speaks Japanese fluently, is trained in Asian martial arts, and possesses vast ornithological knowledge, exhibits a verbal and physical clumsiness that borders on idiocy. Even Dylan is caught hopping about naked in somebody's backyard, barely covering herself with an inflatable swim ring while imploring two teenaged boys for help. Clearly, these inadequacies counterbalance the Angels' potentially intimidating skills. Don't be scared, the movie tells its audience, they are just as silly as the next girl. Moreover, although the Angels are experienced fighters and tricksters, they still rely on their sex appeal to get what they want. In order to distract their male opponents, they bare their breasts, shake their hair, belly dance, and perform a yodeling routine in butt-baring dirndl outfits. Of course, the way in which this is presented is highly ironic and self-conscious. They do not just shake their hair, they shake it over and over again. When Dylan bares her breasts to seduce her opponent's chauffeur while Alex breaks into the car's trunk, she does not just unzip her blouse to the navel, she lusciously licks his steering wheel to boot. Similarly, the Angels do not just fulfill one male fantasy, they embody them all.[7] They are belly dancers in a seedy bar and geishas at Madame Chong's House of Blossoms. They wear the sexy evening gown of the society lady, the black leather outfit of the dominatrix, and the dirndl of the blond ingenue. We can choose to read such excess as deconstructive parody or be put off by the fact that *Charlie's Angels* capitalizes on what it pretends to critique. Like so many other Hollywood movies, *Charlie's Angels* wants to have it both ways. As the camera savors the Angels' breasts and buttocks, the audience listens to woman power rhetoric. The movie glorifies female bonding among the Angels, but the few other female characters are either villainized—Vivian Wood (Kelly Lynch), the evil partner of the criminal mastermind—or ridiculed, like the fat secretary at Red Star Systems. If these

The antics of the three Angels are supposed to highlight their fun-loving nature. Often, however, the three simply look stupid. Drew Barrymore, Cameron Diaz, and Lucy Liu in Charlie's Angels *(2000).* COLUMBIA/THE KOBAL COLLECTION/DARREN MICHAELS.

compensatory devices do not quell lingering doubts, an audience that might "be intimidated by strong women" is reassured that the Angels are doing it all for Charlie. Whereas Lara Croft remains in the patriarchal fold because she is a daddy's girl, the Angels are unthreatening because they are Charlie's girls. *Charlie's Angels* may want to be an action flick, but it has the rhythm and harmlessness of a fashion show. Its heroines do not represent the new woman of the twenty-first century; rather, they are relics of the 1970s from whence they derive and where they truly belong.

Highlight: *Strange Days.* Directed by Kathryn Bigelow. Twentieth Century Fox. Release Date in the United States: October 6, 1995. Total U.S. Gross: $7,918,562

The powerhouse production team associated with *Strange Days*—a big-budget movie, produced and cowritten by James Cameron and directed by Kathryn Bigelow—should have guaranteed box office success.[8] Instead *Strange Days* tanked at the box office and did not even recoup the initial investment ($35 million versus $8 million at the box office). Although it later acquired a dedicated cult following, it was never graced with mainstream success.

Strange Days was variously marketed as "action thriller," "murder mystery," "erotic thriller," and "science fiction." Set in the not-so-distant future of 1999, that is, only four years after the movie's release date, the film's urban dystopia clearly wants to be perceived as uncomfortably real and close. Bigelow depicts Los Angeles as a war zone wrought with interracial tension. The brutal execution of the rap star Jericho One that sets the plot in motion is reminiscent of the Rodney King beating. Scenes with rioters, heavily armed policemen, and soldiers echo the L.A. riots of the early 1990s. Throughout the film, we see guns, barricades, and streets on fire. In Bigelow's bleak vision of the future, fifth grade kids shoot each other at recess, and even Santa Claus is the victim of a mugging.

As living in the real world has become too dangerous, virtual reality functions as a welcome substitute. Many people prefer watching clips to real experience. They get wired using SQUID, a "superconducting quantum interference device" that records "a piece of somebody's life, straight from the cerebral cortex" and allows playback later. Lenny Nero, the male protagonist played by Ralph Fiennes, peddles software for this device. Whenever he gets into trouble, Lenny calls his friend Mace (Angela Bassett), a professional chauffeur and security specialist trained in defensive combat.[9] Mace is an impressive fighter. During the course of the movie, she triumphs over the vicious bodyguards of a music tycoon and beats two murderous policemen into submission. When her car is set on fire, she drives it into the ocean, shoots the trunk open, and swims to safety. As an action heroine, Mace is as good as they come. But it is her strength of character more than her superior combat skills that compels our admiration and respect.

Whereas Lara Croft is life in a clip, *Strange Days* thematizes what it would be like to live in a clip. Because of this self-conscious quality, the movie's heroine Mace possesses a realness that makes her much more appealing than her video game sister Lara. Mace is the only person in this world who refuses to be wired and insists on living in the real world. Because of this, the Afro-American Mace has been read as yet another instance of the "problematic tradition in film and literature of locating authenticity with women of color."[10] But one might also claim that Mace disapproves of SQUID because she is the only person in the film who knows of the difficulty of truly understanding the experience of an "Other."

Mace is a hero, not because she is authentic or because she can beat people up but because she takes care of her child, pays the rent, and simply manages to hang on. We are told repeatedly that her combat skills are of a defensive nature. In a chaotic and violent world, Mace stands out because she is mature and responsible. She possesses dignity, self-respect, and ethics. Although she is in love with Lenny, she is willing to lose him when he offers to pawn the precious clip that documents the racist murder of rapper and political activist Jericho One committed by the Los Angeles Police Department. Amid violence and corruption, Mace upholds ethical standards, but she is no Uncle Tom. Although the movie burdens its preeminent black character with the role of racial conscience, it does not relegate her to that of martyr for the cause. In the end, Mace triumphs twice: when she defends herself successfully against the two homicidal cops of the movie who killed Jericho One and when the white deputy director, whose appearance saves the day, stands by Mace and has the maniac cops arrested. Although this scene with its timely "intervention of the white patriarchal figure" has been criticized as a cop-out, the deus ex machina qualities of his descent in a helicopter might also be read as an ironic quote of conventions that have long lost their validity.[11]

In Bigelow's movie, the power of the cinematic gaze is shattered.[12] A black heroine saves the day, whereas her white male companion is a masochistic spectator who has no power over what he sees. And yet the disturbing violence that is often cited as one possible reason for the film's lack of popularity is invariably perpetrated by white men and directed against women and black men.[13] Mace's strength and ethics stand in stark contrast to the deficiencies of the male protagonists, who are either cruel, insane, or both. Even Lenny, though charming and a good soul, is ethically problematic. Although he refuses to deal in blackjack clips, that is, clips that end with the death of the person recording the tape, Lenny's ethics do not transcend the realm of the personal. His acts of kindness tend to be limited to caring for the well-being of his former lover Faith (Juliette Lewis). Mace, in contrast, has a vision of a better world, and she does everything in her power to realize it. She can be tough and bossy, but she is also vulnerable, soft, and caring. She may be prone to outbursts of anger, but she is a loyal and reliable friend and a wonderful mother. She pampers and massages Lenny when he is hurt and protects him when the bodyguards of his ex-girlfriend's new lover try to beat him up. Mace represents an omnipotence fantasy, but she is also a model of strength in the real world. She is impressive not because she is super-human but because she is more human than all other characters in *Strange Days*. Neither female replica of the traditional muscleman à la Schwarzenegger and Stallone nor action heroine *qua* sex kitten à la Lara Croft and the Angels, Mace truly is a new kind of action heroine.

Highlight: *The Matrix*. Directed by Andy Wachowski and Larry Wachowski. Warner Bros. Release Date in the United States: March 31, 1999. Total U.S. Gross: $171,479,930

Like Mace, Trinity (Carrie-Anne Moss) compels our admiration. But unlike Mace, Trinity comes with a downside. She is both a fascinating image of female strength and an elaborate male fantasy.

From the beginning, Trinity is portrayed as an extraordinarily skilled computer hacker and superb fighter. She can float through the air, kickbox her opponents unconscious, jump across rooftops, throw knives, ride motorbikes, and fly helicopters. In the opening scene, she single-handedly beats up an entire contingent of policemen. Trinity's superpowers are the effect of the Matrix, in which the success of a fighter is not dependent on one's real-world muscle strength and body mass. The Matrix is a Cartesian world in which mind triumphs over matter, but it is a Cartesian world without gender hierarchies. Women are not identified with the bodily realm and excel in the same kind of digital calisthenics that their male counterparts exhibit.

Like Mace, Trinity also possesses dignity and authority. She is second in command on her spaceship and knows how to pull rank when the situation calls for it. Although a classical messenger figure, she is more than an empty go-between. In her relationship with Neo (Keanu Reeves), the unequal distribution of knowledge weighs heavily in her favor. Neo truly is a neophyte, whereas Trinity is familiar with the rules and dangers of the Matrix. She is in a position to answer all of Neo's questions because she has always already been where he is going and done what he is about to do. When they first meet, Trinity knows Neo, but he does not know her identity. Neo looks up to her and entrusts himself to her guidance, and she does his confidence justice.

In addition to being competent and strong, Trinity is also portrayed as sexy. Although her sex appeal is of the dominatrix variety, she never uses it as a means to control or manipulate others. Rather, Trinity is a princess in a dominatrix outfit, whose kiss awakens the hero to his full capacities. Her personality encompasses toughness and softness, commanding presence and timid shyness. Trinity possesses many desirable traits, but she combines impressive strength with utter submissiveness, and one wonders whether this is the reason for her enormous popularity. Trinity is both an innovative model of female strength and a traditional male fantasy. She is in command, but she is second in command and completely accepts her rank in the hierarchy. Actually, as her name indicates, she is not number two but, in fact, number three. She lives to execute the orders of Commander Morpheus (Laurence Fishburne) and to support the supreme talents of the One. Trinity is the ideal servant of the alpha man. Once she has found her man, she is completely devoted to him. She brings him dinner, believes in him implicitly, and stands by him no matter what. She may at times disobey him—but only in order to protect him and serve him better. It is her love that makes him strong. Neo's mission is to save humankind; Trinity's mission is to save him. The fact that Trinity's extraordinary displays of strength throughout the entire movie make us forget the ancillary status of her character is one of the most accomplished stunts of *The Matrix*.

Highlights: *Kill Bill: Vol. 1.* Directed by Quentin Tarantino. Miramax. Release Date in the United States: October 10, 2003. Total U.S. Gross: $69,909,813

Kill Bill: Vol. 2. Directed by Quentin Tarantino. Miramax. Release Date in the United States: April 16, 2004. Total U.S. Gross: $65,535,505

Tarantino's postmodern revenge epic features Uma Thurman as the Bride Beatrix Kiddo, a highly trained and unusually effective assassin. When Kiddo, formerly a member of the Deadly Viper Assassination Squad headed by Bill (David Carradine), learns that she is pregnant, she wants to start all over, lead a normal life, and get married. Unsurprisingly, her efforts are foiled by her former boss Bill and his henchwomen, who massacre the entire wedding party and leave the Bride for dead. When Beatrix awakens from a four-year coma, she embarks on a gruelingly violent vengeance spree that terminates in the killing of Bill.

It is difficult to tell whether Beatrix Kiddo, aka the Black Mamba, represents a new ilk of female action heroine or whether she is a martial arts–*cum*–spaghetti western replay of the maternal avenger à la Sally Field's Karen in *Eye for an Eye* (1996) or Betty in *Not without My Daughter* (1991). But one thing she is not, namely, Bill's Angel. Although Beatrix occasionally sports the fashionable yellow leather outfits that are the clothing *de choix* of Charlie's Angels, she, unlike her lightweight sisters, feels every blow and visibly bears the aftereffects of violence. When Beatrix Kiddo fights, she fights for real. Martial arts scenes of balletic grace are juxtaposed with hard-core slamming that leave the heroine black and blue, drenched in sweat, and besmeared with her own and her opponents' blood. In one memorable scene, Beatrix literally claws her way out of her own grave and, still limping and dripping with dirt, resumes her mission of vengeance.

Unlike Lara Croft and the Angels, Beatrix does not fight for a better world; nor is she motivated by tender love for a father who died too soon.[14] But in eliding one set of stereotypes, the movie conjures up another. Beatrix's orgy of vengeance originates in her devotion to the most sacred of womanly quests, motherhood, and her wrath is fueled by the most heinous crime, the killing of her baby girl in utero, or so she believes until the end of the movie when she finds out that her daughter has survived after all. Beatrix transgresses against every commonly accepted notion of femininity, but she does so because her attempt to sacrifice everything for the best of her daughter and lead a traditionally female life has been thwarted. Conversely, the movie alludes to Beatrix's former career as a cold-blooded contract killer, presumably not stimulated by similarly noble motifs, but we never see her on the job. This renders her previous lifestyle choice rather unreal because, in the movies, only seeing is believing. Indeed, it is hard to tell whether *Kill Bill* constitutes a send-up of the romanticization of motherhood or ardent advocacy of its redeeming value. Is Tarantino poking fun at some of society's most sacred conventions, or is he reproducing mushy clichés for maximum effect? Consider, for example, the following scene from *Kill Bill: Vol. 2*: Beatrix is under attack from a hit woman at the very moment that her pregnancy test comes out positive. Surprisingly, she manages to convince her opponent to back off by making her read the pregnancy strip. On her way out, the Asian femme Nikita, who must have enjoyed some lessons from Miss Manners, peeks through a hole in the door and, still pointing her gun at Beatrix, expresses her heartfelt congratulations. Is this construed to show that our most enduring cultural constructions extend their reach even into the darkest recesses of society? Or does it constitute proof that, even to the most mercenary of villains, motherhood is a cathartic experience? In the Tarantino universe, contract killers have maternal feelings and mothers are assassins in disguise. Thus, the movie leaves us between a rock and a hard place. We are told that motherhood changes everything—"Before that strip turned blue, I was a killer. I killed for you. But when that strip turned blue, I could no longer do any of those things because I was going to be a mother"—and that such a change is not possible because Beatrix is a natural-born killer and she always will be. It would be nice to be done with the idea that motherhood automatically cleanses women of their previous personality and ambitions only to turn them into self-sacrificing lambs. But in *Kill Bill*, the previous self is that of a merciless killer. Given this choice between mommy and Black Mamba, no wonder Beatrix goes ballistic.

The same ambivalence holds true for *Kill Bill*'s representation of male power. Beatrix finishes what Demi Moore's renegade Angel Madison Lee has started. She rebels against Bill, and she wins. *Kill Bill* could be said to retrace the workings of a patriarchy that pits women against each other. Throughout the entire movie, women are the main perpetrators of violence, but their battles are instigated and directed by men: "I could see the faces of the cunts who did this to me and the dicks responsible," Beatrix tells us. Moreover, women are consistently portrayed as superior warriors, and all important duels are fought among women. When Beatrix faces O-Ren Ishii (Lucy Liu), the female boss of the Tokyo underworld, the battle is choreographed according to a strictly delineated hierarchy. Beatrix first defeats O-Ren's army of male underlings, but when the time comes to fight O-Ren's female bodyguard Gogo (Chiaki Kuriyama), the two women go it alone, thus suggesting that one woman warrior equals dozens of men. The sequence concludes with the final showdown, in which Beatrix kills O-Ren herself. One might conclude that women are the only fighters that *Kill Bill* takes seriously. But one might also wonder why the heroine is limited to killing women and hordes of unidentifiable Asian men whereas her only white male opponent gets the better of her by first immobilizing her with shells of rock salt and then burying her in the ground. As Beatrix finishes off Bill by resorting to the legendary five-point palm exploding-heart technique, it would appear that she did not so much kill him as simply break his heart. Tarantino's double movie is not only filled with blood and gore, it is also packed with quotes and pastiche. *Kill Bill* may contain a critique of conventional gender roles, but then again, it is also possible that it says nothing at all. Beatrix is one of the most impressive female warriors ever to grace the silver screen, but she is also a "kiddo" who, like all good women, becomes a bride and then a mommy. Her professional existence, on the other hand, is an aberration that is as poisonous and treacherous to woman's true goals as Beatrix's nom de guerre, Black Mamba, implies.

A survey of recent action heroines is apt to quell any enthusiasm about woman's foray into this previously male-dominated genre. Sadly, the commercial viability of a female action movie is directly dependent on the heroines' availability as sex symbols and on their compatibility with patriarchal settings. Mace, arguably more "real" and impressive than any of the other superfighters discussed here, paled at the box office, whereas kung fu bunnies, action bimbos, and sexualized daddy's girls raked in millions of dollars. Still, it is difficult to interpret the numbers. Does *Lara Croft*'s stunning success of $131 million truly reflect audience preferences, or is it the result of a massive advertising onslaught that has directed all attention toward some very few blockbusters while alternatives remain invisible? In other words, are studios delivering what the audience wants, or are viewers victims of studio manipulation? And who is the audience? Do *Lara Croft* and *Charlie's Angels* draw female crowds, or are they primarily targeted toward men? In any case, if reactionary models of femininity reach their audiences more easily, characters like Trinity and Beatrix might indeed be our best bets. Hopefully, Trinity, who introduces female strength and skill to mainstream audiences, will pave the way for future action heroines whose virtues are no longer adulterated by subservience.

NOTES

1. Political films featuring female heroines were, to some extent, prefigured in some screwball comedies of the 1930s and 1940s, such as *The Farmer's Daughter* (1947).

2. Barbara Ehrenreich took a job as a housemaid in Maine in the late 1990s/early 2000s and documents clearly that low-income earners generally cannot afford apartment living by themselves. While her coworkers at the cleaning service either lived in small apartments that they shared with others, cheap hotels, shelters, or cars, she herself, after a month of working at minimum wage, failed to make enough money to pay next month's rent and had to quit her job (Ehrenreich, *Nickel and Dimed: On (Not) Getting by in America* [New York: Henry Holt and Co., 2001], 51–119).

3. The invisibility of the low-wage worker (Chris first meets Marisa while she is scrubbing his toilet and does not notice her) and the ease with which Marisa impersonates a wealthy woman both have their parallels in social reality. According to Ehrenreich, "The affluent rarely see the poor or, if they do catch sight of them in some public space, rarely know what they're seeing, since—thanks to consignment stores and . . . Wal-Mart—the poor are usually able to disguise themselves as members of the more comfortable classes" (*Nickel and Dimed*, 216).

4. Susan Bordo, *The Male Body: A New Look at Men in Public and in Private* (New York: Farrar Strauss Giroux, 2000); Susan Faludi, *Stiffed: The Betrayal of the American Man* (New York: Perennial, 2000).

5. Thus, Lara too is an embodiment of the "big-breasted sexualized fantasy woman of comic-book tradition" (Yvonne Tasker, *Spectacular Bodies: Gender, Genre and the Action Cinema* [London: Routledge, 1993], 14).

6. Tasker notes a similar problem in her discussion of *Bad Girls* (1994): "*Bad Girls* was marketed as a (sexy) post-feminist Western, employing a language of liberation and independence, of women's rights to control their own bodies in an uneasy combination with cleavage shots and the fetishistic use of whips and weaponry" (*Working Girls: Gender and Sexuality in Popular Cinema* [London: Routledge, 1998], 57).

7. Anthony Lane quips that the Angels "switch wigs, outfits, and, occasionally, languages with such reckless zeal that, were Wim Wenders directing this picture, I would call it a classic study of ontological meltdown and the disintegrating self" (*Nobody's Perfect: Writings from the* New Yorker [New York: Alfred A. Knopf, 2002], 329).

8. *Strange Days* was part of a multimillion-dollar multipicture distribution deal between Lightstorm, Cameron's company, and Twentieth Century Fox. The same deal also included *True Lies* (1994). For a detailed history of the production and distribution of *Strange Days*, see Romi Stepovich, "*Strange Days*: A Case History of Production and Distribution Practices in Hollywood," in *The Cinema of Kathryn Bigelow: Hollywood Transgressor*, ed. Deborah Jermyn and Sean Redmond (London: Wallflower Press, 2003), particularly page 144. Cameron provided a "hybrid between a script and a treatment" (Stepovich, "*Strange Days*," 150). Screenwriter Jay Cock was in charge of producing a complete screenplay (Stepovich, "*Strange Days*," 150).

9. See Steven Shaviro, who points out that Mace's love for Lenny violates the conventional pattern in several respects: "For one thing, she is black and he is white; for another, she is the film's tough guy and action hero" ("Straight from the Cerebral Cortex: Vision and Affect in *Strange Days*," in *The Cinema of Kathryn Bigelow: Hollywood Transgressor*, ed. Deborah Jermyn and Sean Redmond [London: Wallflower Press, 2003], 174).

10. Christina Lane, "The Strange Days of Kathryn Bigelow and James Cameron," in *The Cinema of Kathryn Bigelow: Hollywood Transgressor*, ed. Deborah Jermyn and Sean Redmond (London: Wallflower Press, 2003), 194.

11. Lane, "The Strange Days of Kathryn Bigelow and James Cameron," 196.

12. Shaviro, "Straight from the Cerebral Cortex," 166. See also Laura Mulvey, "Visual Pleasure and Narrative Cinema," in *Film Theory and Criticism: Introductory Readings*, ed. Leo Braudy and Marshall Cohen (Oxford: Oxford University Press, 1999), 833–44.

13. See Lane, "The Strange Days of Kathryn Bigelow and James Cameron," 179.

14. Nor is she sexualized in quite the same way as Lara Croft or the Angels. Tarantino cited his conscious avoidance of this as part of his attempt to create a more progressive female action hero: "I didn't want to sexualize the girls . . . because I wanted them to be empowering women and not eye candy for guys" (quoted in "Here Comes the Bride, Again," *The Washington Post Express*, June 22, 2004, 19).

☆ II ☆

SOME ALTERNATIVES

Traditional Hollywood films frequently portray a lone woman searching—for an identity (Julia Roberts), Mr. Right (Meg Ryan), a way out (Sandra Bullock), an alternate reality (Renée Zellweger), or a way to save the world from certain disaster (Charlie's Angels and Lara Croft). The diva heroine elicits the viewer's identification partly because she is young and unusually attractive and partly by virtue of the fact that she *is* still searching, which means that her life is far from perfect. The viewer accompanies the diva on her quest, and the film ends—usually happily—when her goal is achieved.

So where, one might ask, are the women who do not fit this mold? Where are the older women, the fat women, the failed women, or the ones who have given up the search? Where are the women with whom we can no longer identify? And where, for that matter, are the ones complex enough for us to identify with on a deeper level because we actually see them develop? They do exist—but not as the leading lady in a blockbuster movie. Typically, one encounters these alternatives in one of three venues: in minor roles, at times even cameos, in popular film; as the leading lady in independent film; or on TV. Obviously, not every indie film or TV show makes use of these opportunities, but all three options open up possibilities beyond the traditional Hollywood model. Supporting roles in major movies or major roles in indie films turn the spotlight on women whose age, body, or personality type makes them ineligible to play the young, pretty, and perfectly proportioned blockbuster heroine. TV shows permit the development of a character over time, which in turn allows for many quests, varying goals, shifting perspectives, and complexity of character. Minor roles, minor films, and television allow for more variety in the portrayal of women on the screen, which makes these alternatives to the Hollywood diva well worth a closer look.

☆ 6 ☆

Hidden Alternatives
Judi Dench, Kathy Bates, Parker Posey, Whoopi Goldberg, and Frances McDormand

Our survey in chapters 1 through 5 might well leave us with the impression that the entire landscape of women's Hollywood roles is made up of sexualized superwomen who leave us cold and cute but insecure romantic heroines who warm our hearts while insulting our intelligence. This, however, is not entirely true. There are alternatives to these two types, only they are not in plain sight. Actors like Judi Dench, Kathy Bates, Parker Posey, Whoopi Goldberg, and Frances McDormand appear in many contemporary feature films. But they frequently portray nontraditional body and personality types and have therefore been banished to nonmainstream films or supporting roles.

All actresses discussed in this chapter also offer role models for women, but they are not as obvious as those of the great divas of romantic comedy. Indeed, some of these women embrace roles that most women viewers would never want to play in real life: the hysteric in the throes of murderous insanity (Parker Posey, Kathy Bates), the "failed" mother (Kathy Bates, Frances McDormand), the lonely woman at the top (Judi Dench), or the street-smart woman at the bottom of the social ladder (Whoopi Goldberg).

In spite of the quirkiness of their characters, all these actresses present models with which female viewers are invited to identify. The point of identification, in their cases, lies not in their looks, status, or position but in their unusual character—or in the fact that their stories tell us truths about women's social reality that we are rarely told in real life and almost never at the movies.

THE GRANDE DAME OF CAMEOS: JUDI DENCH

"I know something of a woman in a man's profession. Yes, by God, I do know about that."

—Shakespeare in Love (1998)

Judi Dench is the master of short but memorable scenes and one of the few women who is granted authority in Hollywood movies. She has played the two most influential English queens (Elizabeth I in *Shakespeare in Love* [1998] and Victoria in *Mrs. Brown* [1997]), and she has a recurring gig as Bond's boss M in recent James Bond movies. Particularly in Bond films, which rely largely on close-ups of female body parts and inane sex jokes, M's cool distance and elegant poise counterbalance all the buxom females caving in to the hero's irresistible sex appeal. She is a rock of authority in a sea of writing female bodies. But how much authority can we really allow her to have?

In James Bond films, M's authority is compromised in various ways. M sends her man Bond (Pierce Brosnan) out into the underworld of crime, but she herself remains at headquarters, in the safe, clean haven of technology. Like us, she watches the action as it unfolds on a screen. She is usually in a vulnerable position vis-à-vis her American colleagues, who question her competence and solve international crises with tanks rather than individual derring-do. In this respect, M's cautious rationality is always proven right, and she celebrates her triumph by allowing herself the smallest of smiles. But M, while cool and competent, is not infallible: in *The World Is Not Enough* (1999) and *Die Another Day* (2002), she commits an error in judgment by not recognizing the traitor on her own team. In *Die Another Day*, she is held hostage; in *The World Is Not Enough*, the evil counteragent Elektra (Sophie Marceau) captures and imprisons her. Both times she is rescued by James Bond. Needless to say, the male boss M in earlier James Bond films was never compromised by such lapses in judgment or physical vulnerability. But because this M is a woman, her authority is constantly questioned: she makes mistakes, she is under attack or in captivity, and more than once, she is called on to prove that she has her team under control. She is vindicated in the end, but her victory hinges less on her brain than on James Bond's brawn. Her strategy, it seems, amounts to no more than persuading her own government or the ever-present Americans to hold off nuclear attack so that Bond can do his stuff.

Nonetheless, M offers us something we rarely see on the silver screen. In all Bond films, she makes decisions, gives orders, and is endowed with great charisma, wisdom, and self-control. Whereas all other women are relegated to the worst female stereotypes, she refuses to take on a stereotypical role. Although she is portrayed as someone with a heart, she never lets the safety of her team take precedence over the success of the mission. In *Die Another Day*, she unapologetically abandons Bond to his fate; in *The World Is Not Enough*, she sends Elektra out as bait. She refuses to mother Bond or pity him because he underwent torture (*Die Another Day*), without appearing heartless or unfeminine. M is weak only when she is part of the action and thus in danger of being captured. When she is where she should be, outside of the action, she displays great poise and determination. The real M in Bond films is a modern version of the Greek chorus, an observer and commentator on the action rather than a participant.

Perhaps for that reason, M functions as the mouthpiece whenever Bond films feel the need to critique their own inherent sexism and obsolete Cold War ethics. Self-consciousness of gender or genre conventions does not come easily to Bond films, but very occasionally, these movies purport to question what they portray. In *Tomorrow Never Dies* (1997), M, accused of not having "the balls for this job," answers curtly: "Perhaps, but the advantage is I don't have to think with them all the time." M's cool poise, her quiet authority, is here defined as feminine and superior to the masculine, "ballsy" method of problem solving, from the American nonnegotiation stance to Bond's inflated heroism in the field and his larger-than-life libido. In *GoldenEye* (1995), M dismisses the Cold War ethics of previous incarnations of the Bond genre. When Bond questions her authority, she accuses him of being "a sexist, misogynist dinosaur, a relic of the Cold War." As the film's "chorus," as a noncombatant, she can afford to voice a question that we have been asking ourselves all along: Why, indeed, should we watch Cold War movies in the mid-to-late 1990s or even at the beginning of the next millennium? What is the relevance of these films a decade and a half after the end of the Cold War? M is the only character who could raise this point, briefly, before we are barraged again with huge explosions or huge breasts. No wonder her scenes are so short and so rare.

Judi Dench's queens are equally awe inspiring and equally problematic. As Queen Elizabeth in *Shakespeare in Love*, she takes up all of seven minutes of the 122-minute film, although nobody can deny that she makes those minutes count. Queen Elizabeth is shrewd, wise, and just. She makes it her business to know everything there is to know about her courtiers and her subjects but interferes only when absolutely necessary. She is a competent ruler, but when she is out for a good time, she can be all too human. In her first scene, she coughs and eats throughout a dramatic performance, laughs uproariously at slapstick, and falls asleep to a recitation of Shakespeare's sonnets. She is rouged to the point of vulgarity, reminiscent of a brothel madam rather than a monarch. But when the queen deigns not to be amused, she is direct and upfront with her sub-jects and expects honest answers from them. Her shrewd assessment of her sub-jects makes her appear near-omniscient. She instantly perceives the secret love between Shakespeare (Joseph Fiennes) and Viola (Gwyneth Paltrow). She eas-ily sees through obvious disguises—for example, when she recognizes Shake-speare cross-dressed as a maid at her court—as well as deep secrets, such as the loss of Viola's virginity. She puts overzealous servants in their place and never lowers herself to revealing the secrets she discovers. In the end, she pronounces the verdict on both Shakespeare's love story *Romeo and Juliet* and the love story portrayed in the film, which ends "as stories must when love's denied, with tears and a journey." Her tremendous power, authority, and omniscience would make her godlike were it not for her empathetic humanity. If her humanity was estab-lished in the first scene, in which she is partial to cheap comedy rather than great literature, it is also documented by her kindness. She allows the lovers a final parting scene and prevents the exposure of Viola, who pretends to be Master Kent in order to be admitted to the all-male theater troupe. Most significant, Queen Elizabeth's humanity is indicated by the fact that she has to preserve her power at a cost. Her words to Viola disguised as Master Kent—"I know some-thing of a woman in a man's profession. Yes, by God, I do know about that"— tell us that this queen, apparently so aloof, faces struggles that her subjects will never fully appreciate.

If *Shakespeare in Love*, like the Bond films, shows us a woman of impressive stature for a mere five minutes of the film, *Mrs. Brown* grants its Queen Victoria center stage but divests her of much of her authority. Victoria is not shown as a queen but first as a suffering widow and later as the love interest of her forth-right, plainspoken Scottish groomsman and protector John Brown (Billy Con-nolly). At the outset of the film, Victoria, in deep mourning for her husband, has withdrawn from all government affairs. Her prolonged absence from politics causes her son to hope that she will go into retirement and provokes rebellious thoughts in Parliament about overthrowing the monarchy entirely. Brown be-comes Victoria's personal adviser, assistant, doctor, and chief of staff. He has control over her schedule and can afford to insult the queen's servants, her prime minister, and even her son. Brown is the only one who stands up to her when everyone else curtsys and scrapes; he is the only person who remains straightforward with her when everyone else gossips and schemes behind her back. In his company, she is able to laugh, drink, relax, and recreate, even dance at a ceilidh. When everyone else calls her "Your Majesty," Brown uses the epi-thet that best describes his experience with her, "woman." Victoria is happy in the relationship, but we as viewers realize that it is built on her renunciation of power. She must submit to Brown in everything and follow his every directive. Gossipers at court and in Parliament refer to her as "Mrs. Brown." This nickname implies more than the allegation of an illicit love affair with a social inferior; it amounts to the demotion of the queen to the rank of an anonymous commoner, a Mrs. Smith, or Jones, or Brown. When Mrs. Brown is reinstated into her full powers as Queen of England, she loses her companion, thus suggesting that authority, for women, carries loneliness in its wake.

Judi Dench's queens and spy bosses indicate that portrayals of women in authority are still considered a potential liability at the box office. The most studio bosses dare to sell, it seems, is a five-minute glimpse of a real queen in *Shakespeare in Love* or an equally brief sighting of a competent and charismatic M. If these women are granted too much screen time, either they spend it in jail (like M in *The World Is Not Enough*) or we are watching the drama of a *non*queen: a woman who is not yet a queen or a queen no more. Or is it a coincidence that the only other full-length feature about a queen made during the 1990s, *Elizabeth* (1998), portrays the story of Queen Elizabeth *before* her ascension to the throne? Like "Mrs. Brown," the Elizabeth of this film spends most of her time on screen as a woman in love; like Victoria, Elizabeth can assume power only by relinquishing all claims to a private life. Both *Elizabeth* and *Mrs. Brown* end with the queen's ascension to the throne: her activities as a political figure would presumably not make interesting viewing. The harsh juxtaposition of Elizabeth or Victoria as a queen and as a woman (a friend or a lover) shows that in Hollywood's worldview, femininity and authority are still incompatible. This is the hidden meaning of "a woman in a man's profession": exercising power of any kind *is*, of course, still a man's profession. But even as we are confronted with this most trite of all conclusions, we are cheered by brief glimpses of a rarity: a woman who exercises authority without being presented as power hungry, a woman who exhibits kindness without either mothering or coddling others, a woman who exudes charisma rather than sex appeal, and a woman who relies on wisdom rather than cunning.

MURDEROUS (AND OTHER) MOTHERS: KATHY BATES

> *"Sometimes being a bitch is all a woman has to hold on to."*
>
> —*Dolores Claiborne* (1995)

The role most often identified with Kathy Bates is that of the middle-aged bitch. From *Titanic*'s "unsinkable Molly Brown" to the murderous mothers of

Misery and *Dolores Claiborne*, the Bates character is often uncouth and uneducated, an outcast from her society. But she answers society's contempt of her with astounding reserves of strength and resistance—a resistance that at its most extreme drives her to murder. Intriguingly, the role that provides the background for her unusual strength, resilience, and murderous impulses is the mother, a part undoubtedly considered most proper for someone of her age and body type.

In *Titanic* (1997), Molly Brown is a nouveau-riche widow with a big heart and an even bigger mouth who incurs the contempt of the moneyed elite on the ship. Molly's vulgarity, her coarse directness, and her kindness are unique in someone of her wealth and standing. Whereas the well-heeled passengers on the ship think themselves high above the lower classes, Molly knows that the difference does not amount to much and exhibits both a healthy disdain for the upper class and consistent kindness and respect toward the lower. She plays surrogate mother for Jack (Leonardo DiCaprio), a third-class ticket holder, who is invited to a dinner with the rich as a reward for saving the life of the heiress Rose (Kate Winslet). On this occasion, Molly loans him a tuxedo and instructs him in the basics of table manners and snobbish behavior. Her sarcastic comments are an early indication to the audience of the unhappiness and despair that would await Rose were she to wed her oppressive and arrogant suitor Cal (Billy Zane). In the end, Molly is the only one in her lifeboat who pleads with the others to return for survivors and does not give up until her fellow survivors threaten to throw her overboard.

Molly's role, although only a supporting part, carries great symbolic significance. Most important, she embodies the antithesis of the upper-class snobbishness that leads to the sinking of the *Titanic*. The arrogance that characterizes the behavior of the affluent passengers is the same arrogance that motivated the decision to equip the ship with only half the lifeboats necessary. After all, the lifeboats would have cluttered the deck on which the rich promenade themselves. Ultimately, this selfish conceit condemned thousands of third-class passengers to death because all lifeboats aboard were reserved for the rich. Molly Brown also serves as an example to Rose that is on a par with that set by Rose's lover Jack. Whereas Jack exhorts Rose to live a strong and independent life, to "make it count," Molly provides a living example for how this can be done. Her moniker, the "unsinkable" Molly Brown, is more than merely a pun on the supposedly unsinkable *Titanic*. It is an allusion to her indestructible survival skills, her indomitable determination to be happy in the face of societal contempt—in short, her bitchiness: a trait that Rose will have to develop if she is to achieve happiness.

The psychotic nurse Annie Wilkes in *Misery* (1990) and the title character in *Dolores Claiborne* (1995) are other notable bitches in Kathy Bates's repertoire. These two films, both based on Stephen King novels, can be read as question and answer, call and response. Annie Wilkes and Dolores Claiborne represent two sides of the same coin. Both live as outcasts in a rural society. Both are uneducated, unsophisticated, and dressed in the traditional garb of the 1950s housewife, in shapeless aprons and frumpy cardigans. Both nurse bedridden and incapacitated patients; both exhibit decidedly maternal traits; and both have committed murder. The difference—albeit not the only one—lies in the ultimate verdict: a death sentence for Annie and acquittal for Dolores.

In *Misery*, Annie Wilkes is a psychotic serial killer who rescues romance writer Paul Sheldon (James Caan) from a car wreck. She holds him captive in her house and forces him to write a sequel in her favorite romance series, the *Misery* novels. She is both jailer and mother to Paul. Annie is frighteningly unpredictable: all smiles one moment and murderous rage the next, a combination of masculine power and maternal pampering, of demureness and explosive anger. She is too prim to use real swearwords, instead relying on expressions like "pooh," "oogy," and "cockadoodie," but she is not above controlling her victim through manipulation, blackmail, and brute force. Her artistic sense is hampered by her lack of education: she mispronounces Dom Perignon and has no idea who painted the Sistine Chapel. Accordingly, her aesthetic tastes run to the cheap and the childish; her house overflows with kitsch figurines, and she boasts a complete collection of Paul's third-rate romances. Clearly, Annie Wilkes is the very opposite of a sophisticated reader; she is the naive consumer of the garbage that Paul Sheldon was wont to produce, his "number-one fan."

Annie Wilkes's double role as mother and reader shapes Paul's existence as her dependent and pet writer throughout the film. Her maternal attitude is particularly pronounced in two scenes: when she tenderly shaves him, cooing to him as though he were a small child, and when she breaks his ankles with a mallet. The unparalleled brutality of the latter scene derives precisely from her maternal pity, her "this-hurts-me-more-than-it-hurts-Paulie" attitude.

As a reader, Annie is equally unpredictable. Although she is portrayed as a starry-eyed fan, she is completely unwilling to swallow everything Paul dishes out. On the contrary, she insists on verisimilitude and plausibility. The reason she grants Paul no poetic license whatsoever is simple: Annie reads literally, turning his fiction into her reality. Thus Annie misrepresents her real role when she tells Paul to "think of me as your inspiration." She is also a symbol for the kind of book he is writing. Annie is what is left when you subtract aesthetics, style, and rhetoric from a book: nothing but plot, nothing but text. And finally, she is an externalization of Paul's worst fantasy of his readers: fat, ugly, crazy, stupid, demanding, oppressive, and murderous, she embodies for him the quintessential fan of his romances. Annie represents Paul's inability to accept himself as a writer of trash novels whose only goals are to satisfy his readers and to make money. In his mind, murderous and demanding Annie stands for all those fans who have killed his creativity. Instead of producing great literature, Paul is required to churn out numberless installments in a never-ending sequence of trashy romances. To develop as a writer, he has to kill her. Indeed, killing his number-one fan finally enables him to produce a book that distinguishes itself through its critical rather than commercial success.

In the first scene of *Dolores Claiborne*, we encounter Annie Wilkes again: Dolores towers over the body of a helpless old woman, a rolling pin raised high to deliver the fatal blow. But even before she is accused of a capital crime, Dolores is already a murderous bitch by repute. Kids who pass her on their bikes routinely yell, "Kill anyone else today?" The word *bitch*, scrawled by anonymous hands, defaces the facade of her house. Her arch nemesis, Detective John Mackey (Christopher Plummer), is convinced that Dolores got away with the murder of her husband (David Strathairn) eighteen years ago. Dolores protests her innocence with a lot of lip. Her fierce defiance and bitchiness are the defense mechanisms that help her cope with Mackey's accusations and the hostility of an entire village. Dolores's role as a mother is defined in two ways: she assumes maternal responsibility toward her bedridden employer Vera Donovan (Judy Parfitt), whom she has served for decades and nursed for years; and she tries to reestablish a relationship with her estranged daughter Selena (Jennifer Jason Leigh). Both of Dolores's mothering roles are inextricably tied up with murder: she acts as a mother to the woman she is supposed to have killed, and her daughter hates her because she, too, believes that Dolores is guilty of the murder of her husband.

Dolores Claiborne is a paradox: eternally subservient, she is also consistently insubordinate. When she is arrested on suspicion of murder, she dusts and tidies up the police station and has to be reminded that she is a suspect, not a maid. Scenes from her horrible marriage show that she submitted willingly to her husband's unreasonable demands, his drunkenness, and his verbal abuse. However, he goes too far when he physically abuses her: she threatens to kill him and finally does so when she finds out that he sexually abuses their daughter. Her relationship with Vera is equally contradictory: Dolores accedes meekly to Vera's exacting requirements but also calls her a bitch to her face. Dolores is too uneducated and naive to understand her most basic legal rights and too poor to hire a lawyer, but she nonetheless defends herself most forcefully. She calls

Mackey "Mr. Grand High Pooh-bah of Upper Buttcrack" as she douses him with the contents of Vera's bedpan. In all these instances, Dolores's bitchiness functions as a safety valve that enables her to remain in her subservient role.

The great revelation of the film—that the relationship between Dolores and Vera was defined by love rather than hate—sheds new light on interactions between servant and employer that are easily misinterpreted as scenes of abuse. Instead, they emerge as forms of physical and emotional caregiving, ranging from changing Vera's diapers to engaging Vera in verbal sparring that eases the physical indignities she must endure. "You're poisoning me, aren't you?" asks Vera as Dolores serves her food, every bit the crabby old woman. Instead of feeding into Vera's self-pity, Dolores silences her with a harsh rejoinder: "I'd shove you out of the window, there'd be one less smelly bitch in the world." But when Vera weeps with frustration at her physical weakness, Dolores comforts her with her favorite musical box, a piggy that plays "Happy Days Are Here Again." Like a good mother, she knows what her charge needs.

Dolores Claiborne is a highly unconventional film, in more ways than one. As in *Misery*, the cantankerous bitch assumes center stage. But *Dolores Claiborne* one-ups the earlier film by justifying not only Dolores's bitchiness but also the murder of her husband. Significantly, it is Vera, the second irritable bitch of the film, who inspires Dolores to murder. She convinces Dolores that her original plan, a simple getaway with Selena, would only expose them to her husband's persecution and revenge. In *Dolores Claiborne*, it is open season on abusive husbands. In one of the most memorable scenes of the film, Vera confesses to Dolores that her own husband's death in a car wreck was not entirely coincidental and simultaneously provides Dolores with an MO: "An accident, Dolores, can be an unhappy woman's best friend." The film confronts us with two bitches, one of them already a husband killer, conspiring to murder another. It is difficult to see how any film could justify such crimes and simultaneously portray its criminals as likable characters. Nonetheless, when we get to the final scene, in which Selena splendidly defends her mother, we root for Dolores's freedom and rejoice in Selena's eloquent vindication of her mother.

Vindicating two murderesses is quite a feat in and of itself. But it may be even more courageous to take the potential of female bonding seriously. Unlike more traditional Hollywood films, which portray heterosexual and father–daughter relationships as happy and fulfilling, *Dolores Claiborne* indicts them as miserable and abusive. In *Dolores Claiborne*, only female couples share true intimacy: first Dolores and Vera and later Dolores and Selena, who is, not coincidentally, the only person to see Dolores's association with Vera for the loving relationship it was. If viewers do not perceive this sooner, it is not because the film attempts to mislead: we are free to interpret interaction between Vera and Dolores as infused with either hatred or love. If we cannot perceive the attachment between Dolores and Vera as spirited, supportive, and loving—at least, not until Selena tells us so in the final scene of the film—it is probably because we have not yet learned to see the bitch for what she can be: a therapeutic and invigorating personality.

EVERYTHING YOU DO NOT WANT TO BE: PARKER POSEY

"It's fine. Just do the cones, make sundaes, stuff on them, burgers, ice cream, anything."

—Waiting for Guffman (1996)

If actresses such as Julia Roberts and Meg Ryan thrive in roles that invite identification, Parker Posey excels at portraying everything you do not want to be or ever become. Posey, who has been called the Katharine Hepburn of Generation X and the Queen of the Indies, intrigues her audience with her convincingly offbeat, quirky, neurotic, and disenfranchised characters. Posey's roles are designed to enact a return of the repressed, often focusing on types that our culture has chosen to ignore: the hysteric, the poor, the lonely. Her characters frequently inhabit the margins of society, both socially and psychologically. Whether they are white trash as in *Waiting for Guffman* (1996) and *A Mighty Wind* (2003), upper crust as in *The House of Yes* (1997) or *You've Got Mail* (1998), or bohemians as in *The Misadventures of Margaret* (1998), they are all trapped in unsatisfactory lives and driven by a desperate longing for an alternative. But for many of them, this unhappiness remains unspoken and even unrecognized.

In *Waiting for Guffman*, Christopher Guest's mock documentary about the planning, rehearsal, and premiere of a musical celebrating the 150th anniversary of Blaine, Missouri, Posey is cast as the feckless Dairy Queen employee Libby Mae Brown. The show, entitled *Red, White, and Blaine* and choreographed by Corky St. Clair (Christopher Guest), features a singularly untalented cast consisting of the town dentist Dr. Pearl (Eugene Levy), travel agents Sheila and Ron Albertson (Catherine O'Hara and Fred Willard), and Libby Mae herself. When Corky's invitations to several New York producers actually elicit one positive response, the entire cast has its hopes set on their future success in the Big Apple. Alas, like Godot, the producer Guffman never arrives, and all Broadway dreams turn to ashes.

Lampooning how an entire town has completely lost touch with reality accounts for the most hilarious and also most disturbing scenes of *Waiting for*

Guffman. At times, this communal dislocation finds expression in almost tragically overinflated visions of grandeur. When Corky still expects to make it on Broadway, for example, he requests $100,000 from a town council whose entire budget amounts to approximately $15,000. But Corky is not the only one who is completely deluded. In his attempt to assuage Corky's anger over the denial of said request, the mayor exhibits a similarly contorted view of his own importance: "Without your show, there is no Blaine; without Blaine, there is no Missouri; without Missouri, there is no United States."

Unsurprisingly, the disconnect between fantasy and reality is most blatant during the premiere of *Red, White, and Blaine*. During the rehearsal process, the urgent pleas of the music teacher Lloyd Miller (Bob Balaban), the only voice of reason, to devote some time to practicing the music meet with total incomprehension on Corky's part. But as it turns out, the fact that Blaine's enthusiastic amateurs can neither sing, nor dance, nor act is utterly irrelevant. Not only the actors themselves are carried away by their own spectacularly bad performances. The audience is equally entranced with the embarrassing antics onstage. The inhabitants of Blaine all partake of a shared fantasy world that is completely off-kilter. They may catch an occasional glimpse of the truth or experience a momentary sense of unease and displacement, but their attempts to escape both their fantasy worlds and their confined lives are destined to fail. It is in precisely such unbalanced realities poised between madness and desperation that the Parker Posey characters thrive.

Although all inhabitants of Blaine are trapped in their very own version of the Blaine Matrix, Libby Mae Brown's situation is more hopeless than that of anybody else. Whereas Dr. Pearl ends up as an entertainer in Florida nursing homes and the Albertsons resettle in California where they make a living as extras in commercials, Libby Mae's trip to New York terminates prematurely in a Dairy Queen in Alabama. Even more disheartening than her failed attempt to start over is Libby's inability to imagine a different life. When she still has her hopes set on Broadway and tries to envision what it would be like to live in New York, Libby's wildest fantasies amount to "meet guys and watch TV and stuff." In the end, with her Broadway dreams shattered, Libby Mae's ambition is again pared down to fit the Dairy Queen ambience: she now aspires to making a low-fat blizzard. Unlike all other characters who have (or pretend to have) family and friends, Libby Mae is completely isolated. She appears to be frozen in a gesture of semi-comprehension, signaled by her gaping mouth, continually hanging open, and a look that expresses both a tentative desire to understand and a muted memory of previous frustrations. Everything about Libby Mae spells deprivation. Even when she cries, her desperation is quiet and unsurprised. Although we may laugh at Libby Mae's exceptionally ungraceful performance of "Teacher's Pet," we also realize that she may never have experienced any affection or benefited from any instruction. Libby Mae, frying a puny chicken leg out in the cold in her trailer park, may well be one of the worst perversions of the American dream.

Whereas Libby Mae Brown inhabits the social fringe of society, Meg Swan (Parker Posey) in *Best in Show* (2000), Christopher Guest's faux documentary about a dog show, combines an upscale middle-class existence with grating neurotic edginess. Meg's troubles are rooted in her dysfunctional marital life, which consists of an endless chain of sexual frustration and verbal and emotional abuse. A shared dedication to consumer goods and semireligious adoration of brand names from J. Crew to L. L. Bean and Starbucks can barely veil the emotional wasteland of Meg's relationship to her husband Hamilton (Michael Hitchcock). In addition to their communally celebrated cult of consumption, the couple is also united in their determination to project all anger and frustration onto their dog Beatrice. Made irritable by her owners' constant bickering, Beatrice acts out their barely suppressed aggression: she barks, snaps, bites, and even attacks one of the judges at the dog show.

Meg's tendency to fly into a panic over the most unimportant trivia affords us a glimpse into the deep despair underneath this character's cashmere-enhanced

A girl and her dream: how to make a low-fat Blizzard. Parker Posey at a Dairy Queen in Waiting for Guffman *(1996). COLUMBIA TRISTAR/THE KOBAL COLLECTION.*

surface. Her frantic search for Beatrice's favorite toy, the busy bee, leaves the couple's hotel room in utter disarray and shows Meg viciously insulting everybody she encounters, from the maid and hotel manager to the clerk in the hotel gift shop. Meg and Hamilton's final attempt to exorcise their demons by getting rid of Beatrice only repeats the unhealthy pattern that has characterized the couple's interactions from the start. It is unlikely that their new dog Kipper will maintain his positive attitude for long once he acclimatizes to the Swan household.

Like poor Libby Mae Brown and yuppie Meg Swan, Jackie-O (Parker Posey) in *The House of Yes* (1997) also suffers from an unbearable existential emptiness. Unlike Libby Mae and Meg, however, Jackie-O is excessively talented and intellectually astute. Paradoxically, whereas Libby Mae's unhappiness appears to stem from her astounding lack of talent and imagination, Jackie-O's psychosis originates in the impossibility of finding a socially accepted outlet for her talents and her unusually vivid fantasy life. And whereas Libby Mae looks to show business as a substitute for an unsatisfactory reality, Jackie-O finds a perverted form of solace in her impersonation of Jackie Kennedy Onassis. Moreover, both Libby Mae's and Jackie-O's substitute realities are fueled by the deranged communities in which they live. But whereas the people of Blaine are blind to the ludicrous nature of their own delusions of grandeur, Jackie's family embraces the psychotic madness of its everyday life with great zest and clarity of vision.

Although Jackie lives in the House of Yes, where the word "no" is never spoken, her psychotic behavior appears to have been caused by perpetual frustration and denial. One senses Jackie's hunger for life and excitement when she refuses to take her medication because it keeps her from thinking clearly and when she burns her hands in a desperate attempt to boil flat seltzer water in order to restore its bubbles. Because Jackie-O is socially privileged and intellectually gifted, her unhappiness appears unmotivated. When Jackie claims that she is in a box and can't get out, we cannot help but wonder if she was victimized or if her misery is of her own making. Does Jackie suffer because she was never denied anything, as the fiancée of Jackie's brother Marty (Josh Hamilton) firmly believes, or because she was never given what she needed? Was she traumatized by the incestuous relationship with her brother and an early family tragedy (after all, Jackie claims that her mother murdered her father on the day of the Kennedy assassination)? Or is such recourse to familiar psychoanalytic narratives just "too bourgeois," as Jackie herself would object? Whatever the cause of her affliction, Jackie-O is deeply unhappy. And even though she enjoys all the privileges of wealth and status that Libby Mae Brown lacks, Jackie, just like Libby Mae, relies on a glamorous and yet pitiful fantasy as her only source of comfort.

Like Jackie-O, Margaret Nathan (Parker Posey), the heroine of *The Misadventures of Margaret* (1998), is socially privileged, exceptionally talented, impulsive, hungry for life, and thoroughly miserable. However, unlike Jackie-O, Libby Mae, and Meg Swan, Margaret is able to analyze her own situation and openly acknowledges her inner misery. Because of this awareness, Margaret manages to get to the bottom of her dissatisfaction and changes her life for the better.

To the casual observer, Margaret Nathan's life appears perfect. She is a Columbia-educated author of a best-seller and the wife of Edward (Jeremy Northam), a professor of literature who is not only handsome and charming but also utterly devoted to her. In spite of all these gifts and achievements, Margaret is deeply frustrated and dissatisfied. Both her success and her marriage came too easily and too early. Margaret feels stifled by her marriage and is desperate for genuine experiences. Her desire for the "real thing" expresses itself not only in her somewhat clumsy search for adventures but also in her visceral aversion to Edward's habit of quoting famous authors. Much as Margaret rejects substitutes and secondary experience, she herself is not immune to the allure of a fantasy life. A conversation about *The Wizard of Oz* shows Margaret as a lively advocate of the superiority of fiction over reality. She blames Dorothy for her decision to go back to Kansas when she could have stayed in Oz. When she is not dissatisfied with her real life, Margaret is absorbed in a fantasy world of her own making, namely, that of the book she is writing. For Margaret, the real challenge consists in combining the creativity of her career as a writer and the seductive beauty of her inner fantasy world with fulfillment in the real world.

The Misadventures of Margaret was inspired by the delightful screwball comedy *The Awful Truth* (1937) and exhibits many of the defining traits of this genre, including an unruly heroine.[1] Margaret's physical antics and social gaffes—she keeps falling off trees and ladders and spends most of her time hiding in somebody else's bathroom—place her in the tradition of classic screwball heroines such as Katharine Hepburn and Irene Dunne. She possesses the same spunk, independence, and sense of adventure that characterize the female protagonists of *Bringing Up Baby* (1938) and *Ball of Fire* (1941). But she also partakes of the almost neurotic nerviness typical of some Katharine Hepburn characters. At first glance, such mood swings and heightened sensitivity appear to play to stereotypes of conventional femininity. But a closer look reveals that all suggestions of female hysteria are undercut by the fact that Margaret is granted the license of the (male) creative genius. She is antisocial, cranky, and obsessed with her work, whereas Edward is patient, communicative, and supportive. Whereas Edward remains ever faithful, Margaret acts on her sexual fantasies and

embarks on a one-night stand with her dentist. Interestingly, Margaret's es-
capades are not followed by repentance and apologies. Rather, in the last scene,
it is Edward who apologizes and begs her to reconsider because he cannot live
without her. When Margaret finishes her book and reconciles with Edward, she
prevails where most Parker Posey characters fail. Margaret rejects vague dreams
and embraces the fulfilling reality of marriage and career. Of course, she can do
so only because her reality is near-immaculate to begin with. Unlike most other
Parker Posey characters, Margaret does not have to change the essentials of her
life; all she has to do is to own it. Margaret does not live in a trailer park like
Libby Mae but in a fancy Manhattan apartment; she is not married to sleazy
Hamilton Swan but to sexy Edward Nathan; and her immediate family consists
of a supportive sister, not an incestuous brother and a murderous mother. However, the fact that even such perfection can barely heal Margaret's misery only
serves to underline the urgency and ubiquity of the emotional angst, neurotic
off-centeredness, and social marginalization that Parker Posey portrays so well.

HIP-HOP IN THE HABIT: WHOOPI GOLDBERG

"By the power invested in me, I pronounce us ready to eat."

—*Sister Act* (1992)

When Whoopi Goldberg signed on for *Sister Act 2: Back in the Habit* (1993),
she received what was then the largest paycheck ever given to an actress in Hollywood. Goldberg's impressive clout in the business testifies to her extraordinary talent and star persona, but the roles on which her career is built tell a different story. In both *Ghost* (1990) and *Sister Act* (1992), which raked in a
spectacular $217,631,306 and $139,605,150, respectively, the Afro-American
actress portrays asexual characters who devote all their time and energy to making things right for white people. Goldberg's politically challenging role in *The
Associate* (1996), on the other hand, could not draw audiences to the cinema.
Still, the overall success of a black actress who was once described as "looking
like a covergirl for *Sharecropper's Monthly*" is a cause for celebration, even if it
comes at a price.[2]

   Ghost tells the story of a love that proves stronger than death itself. A young
couple, Sam (Patrick Swayze) and Molly (Demi Moore), has just moved in together when Sam is killed in what looks like a random mugging. Haunted by the
violence of the murder and his love for Molly, Sam's spirit refuses to enter the af-
terworld, choosing instead to linger on earth. As Sam's spirit follows Molly, he

learns that his death was not accidental but, in fact, engineered by his devious colleague Carl (Tony Goldwyn), whose financial misconduct Sam had unintentionally uncovered. With the help of the con artist Oda Mae Brown (Whoopi Goldberg), Sam manages to avenge his death and express his love for Molly one last time before he joins the heavenly hordes.

The character of the "spiritual adviser" Oda Mae is a composite of racist stereotypes enlivened only by Goldberg's masterful performance.[3] First presented as a small-time crook who capitalizes on the needs of grieving family members to communicate with deceased loved ones, Oda Mae is soon shown to possess the special connection to the spirit world often attributed to people of color. Because Oda Mae is the only living being who senses Sam's presence and understands his pleas, she is quickly enlisted as Sam's interpreter and helpmeet. Sam harasses her and keeps her from sleeping until Oda Mae consents to neglect her own job in order to pursue his agenda. Throughout her coerced cooperation with Sam, Oda Mae alternates between sassy resistance and grudging acquiescence. Although she initially refuses every single one of Sam's requests, she always obliges him in the end. When Sam wants to convey to Molly that she is in danger and insists that Oda repeat his instructions word for word, Oda responds, "I'll tell her in my own words: Molly, you in danger, girl." When Sam wants her to write his messages down, an indignant Oda fumes, "I'm no damn secretary," and then proceeds to do as she is told. Clearly, interactions of this kind simultaneously fulfill two purposes. Oda Mae's willingness to place Sam's interests above her own establishes her as a trustworthy, because subdued, black woman. Her spunk and feistiness, on the other hand, guarantee that this submission to white hegemony is not perceived as the tragic result of coercion and violence but, rather, as a willingly and ultimately joyously granted gift. Consequently, by the end of the movie, Oda Mae has not only effected Carl's punishment and enabled the final embrace of the lovers; she is also saddled with absolving the white man of all guilt for using her as his tool. Instead of complaining that she toiled for the happiness of others and was herself left empty-handed, Oda Mae assures Sam that he is all right before he walks off into the light.

And yet, there are also moments in which *Ghost* transcends its problematic portrayal of a black woman and offers space for transformative story lines and images. After all, the entire film is built on the idea of a white man who is condemned to invisibility and a black woman who has to speak for him if he is to be heard. Similarly, when Sam's spirit longs desperately to touch his beloved Molly, Oda Mae offers him her body. The ensuing close-up shows black hands tenderly caressing white hands. Although we are told that Sam has taken over Oda's body—and the film quickly moves on to images of Sam and Molly locked in an

In her biggest movie hits, Goldberg is forever taking care of white folks. Whoopi Goldberg and Demi Moore in Ghost *(1990).*
PARAMOUNT/THE KOBAL COLLECTION/PETER SOREL.

embrace—what we see in these initial shots is a black woman and a white woman making love to each other. Moreover, although the role of Oda Mae frequently conforms to stereotypes, she is also capable of manipulating racist assumptions for her own ends. When Oda Mae visits Sam's bank to move the funds that Carl has embezzled, her blithe and random chattiness distracts the attending clerk from the actual transaction and guarantees the success of her mission. Oda Mae is able to help Sam because she has developed an ability to "pass." She knows how to channel voices that are not her own and how to adopt disguises. Whereas Sam's white friends and even his lover remain deaf to his pleas, Oda Mae picks up Sam's signals because she has learned to listen closely to the words of those in power. Oda Mae's "special gift" results from her underprivileged position and as such is a reminder of oppression, but it also allows her to succeed where her white counterparts have failed.

In *Sister Act*, the Reno lounge singer and gangster's moll Deloris Van Cartier (Whoopi Goldberg) witnesses accidentally how minions of her underworld boyfriend Vince (Harvey Keitel) execute a limo driver. In order to protect her, the police place Deloris in a San Francisco convent where she is made to dress and live as a nun. As Sister Mary Clarence, the former nightclub singer is quickly put in charge of the convent choir. Her inspired leadership not only improves the choir but opens the convent to the community and ultimately transforms the entire neighborhood. During the final showdown, the sisters rally to Deloris's aid when Vince kidnaps her. Their courageous intervention leads to Vince's arrest, and Deloris can finally return to her life as a singer. Shots of magazine covers that celebrate Deloris's stunning adventure and her new and spectacularly successful career conclude the film.

Just like Oda Mae in *Ghost*, Sister Mary Clarence is placed under the authority of a white character who is herself in need of help. Like Sam in *Ghost*, the Mother Superior (Maggie Smith) is unable to communicate her message to the local congregation. Her convent is disconnected from its community, and her church remains deserted during services. Guided by Mary Clarence's example and instruction, the nuns learn to open up and reach out to their parish. But unlike Oda Mae in *Ghost*, Mary Clarence herself also benefits from this arrangement. Mary Clarence's positive energy effects a transformation of the white community, and she herself receives protection and help in return. Initially, she was an obscure performer in a sleazy club suffering under the abuse of her criminal boyfriend. By the end of the movie, she has achieved national fame as a singer and shares the cover of *People* magazine with the pope. Whereas Oda Mae has to make do with the satisfaction inherent in good deeds, Deloris draws tangible benefits from her association with the nuns. These benefits, however, do not extend to the realm of romance and love. Like Oda Mae, Deloris/Mary Clarence is denied any romantic, or even familial, attachments of her own. Her liaison with the major (and married) underworld figure Vince is over before the movie has barely begun. Throughout most of *Sister Act* Deloris is as asexual as the nuns.[4] Her relationship with the detective who is responsible for her safety contains subtle hints of mutual attraction but never blossoms into an actual romance. Utterly absorbed by their efforts to improve the lives of white people, Oda Mae and Mary Clarence are denied any romantic or sexual unions of their own.[5]

Just like Oda Mae's altercations with Sam, Mary Clarence's initial interactions with the Mother Superior are characterized by moments of spirited insurrection invariably followed by grudging acquiescence. Gradually, however, the balance of power shifts. Mary Clarence's methods prove vastly superior to those of the Reverend Mother and prompt the latter to announce her resignation. Mary Clarence's subsequent attempts to convince the Mother Superior not to leave her flock, accompanied by her refusal to take her place, are crucial prerequisites for the racial reconciliation enacted by *Sister Act*. Mary Clarence's disinterest in positions of power along with her commitment to return to her old life assure the viewer that the black intruder presents no threat. Rather, Mary Clarence functions as a catalyst designed to transform and, perhaps more important, validate the order of the convent. Mary Clarence's inspiring acts of resistance point to a need to reform ridiculous or unfair conditions. But they also convey to viewers that there is nothing fundamentally wrong with the convent because most of her complaints are directed at insignificant details. Given Mary Clarence's invincible spirit and her strong sense of self, we can be sure that she would not stand for it if any actual injustice were to occur.

A great deal of the humor of *Sister Act* arises from Mary Clarence's only partially successful attempts to conform to the norms of her new environment. When asked to say grace at the table, Mary Clarence rhapsodizes on "the valley of the shadow of no food" and finishes with "by the power invested in me, I pronounce us ready to eat." Although Mary Clarence wears the traditional nun's habit, she cannot mimic the sober demeanor that complements it. Underneath her frock, she still rocks and shakes her hips like a black lounge singer. Interestingly, it is Mary Clarence's inability to "perform" white Catholicism that sparks change in the convent and its neighborhood. In the fantasy world of *Sister Act*, Mary Clarence's racially coded difference is not denigrated but imitated by all the other nuns in the choir, who start to shake their hips and display some of that "deep shoulder action." We can read this either as an inspiring fantasy of racial reconciliation or as a blatantly ideological misrepresentation of the racism and injustice that mark contemporary U.S. society.

Whereas *Sister Act* imagines the redemptive potential of Otherness, *The Associate* offers a comical yet unrelenting critique of the continuing discrimination of women and racial minorities in the upper echelons of the business world. Laurel (Whoopi Goldberg) is a highly talented Wall Street broker who, in spite of her untiring and excellent work, has to watch helplessly as her mediocre male colleagues harvest all promotions. Frustrated by this injustice, Laurel decides to open her own firm. After numerous unsuccessful attempts to win clients, she invents a white male partner, whom she calls Cutty and to whom she attributes all her ideas while she herself claims to be his assistant. As Laurel's new business thrives, the phantasmagoria of her elusive male partner becomes increasingly difficult to maintain, and Laurel finds herself the victim of her own creation. After the failure of several "attacks" on Cutty's life, Laurel reveals publicly that she is the brain behind Cutty's success. Although Laurel, now without disguise, is admitted into the ranks of the exclusive Peabody Club, our hopes for her professional future remain rather dim.

In *The Associate*, Laurel's difference from white male culture is not employed as a catalyst that transforms a corrupt system; rather, it leads to her victimization. Similarly, Laurel's attempt to perform white masculinity when she cross-dresses as Cutty is not portrayed as a liberating experience but, rather, as the demeaning result of the societal injustice that threatens to ruin her career. Initially, Laurel profits from her invention of a white male boss. Gradually, however, the new situation proves to be an uncanny repetition of her old predicament, as Laurel does all the work while Cutty gets all the credit. Not one of Laurel's clients shows any interest in her other than as a conduit to Cutty. This condescending and unfair behavior culminates when a male business partner advises Cutty, that is, the cross-dressed Laurel, to put the blame for his subpoena on Laurel and then fire her. Clearly, in *The Associate*, cross-dressing is no solution. It can only perpetuate the injustice that it was meant to fight. Only by publicly exposing the mechanisms that exclude her, Laurel finally achieves a viable position.

In both *Ghost* and *Sister Act*, Goldberg's astounding success is predicated on her character's willingness to make things better for white folks and to be the only token black woman in a predominantly white environment. *The Associate*, on the other hand, which focuses on making things better for its black protagonist, failed at the box office. Interestingly, in all three movies, the ability to assume a disguise and pass as somebody else is crucial. In *Ghost* and *Sister Act*, passing is played for fun. Oda Mae's channeling of dead husbands' voices and Mary Clarence's hip-hop in the habit are meant to evoke laughter. Laurel's cross-dressing, on the other hand, although comical at times, is the precondition for success in corporate America and, as such, an uncomfortable reminder of the injustice that lies at the heart of our society. Whereas *Ghost* and *Sister Act* show the Goldberg character as fun loving and a good sport, *The Associate* depicts her as more edgy and even depressed. Given the box office performance of these three movies, one might wonder whether it is this crucial difference that accounts for what Andrea Stuart has called "Goldberg's solitary supremacy in the curious history of the black female in Hollywood."[6] Certainly, Goldberg's upbeat characters are attractive in and of themselves, but they are especially attractive when they maintain their positive attitude in the face of exploitation, thus absolving white viewers from any feelings of complicity or guilt.

Nonetheless, faulting Goldberg for the politics of her most successful films misses the point. It is not just Goldberg's success and visibility as an Afro-American actress in mainstream movies that make her unique. Even in films with problematic or reactionary plotlines, Goldberg's exuberant screen persona manages to control, mock, manipulate, and even transcend the stereotypes she is dealt. Neither sex symbol nor marginal sidekick, neither mammy nor tragic mulatto, Goldberg's characters truly represent alternatives to conventional (white and black) women's roles.

THE UNTOUCHABLES: FRANCES MCDORMAND

"There's more to life than a little money, you know."

—Fargo (1996)

Frances McDormand's career is evenly split between traditional Hollywood and independent films, including the extravaganzas produced and directed by the Coen brothers, her husband Joel and brother-in-law Ethan. Not pretty in the traditional sense, she rarely appears exclusively as a love interest. Instead, she is often cast as a professional woman, sometimes in roles that appear glamorous at first glance: she is a psychiatrist and expert witness in *Primal Fear* (1996), the chancellor of a university in *Wonder Boys* (2000), and a highly successful record producer in *Laurel Canyon* (2002). Her role as Chief Marge Gunderson in *Fargo* (1996) has become legendary. In traditional Hollywood films, her professional status is purely ornamental. Unlike her male colleague, *Primal Fear*'s Dr. Arrington is fooled by the criminal's ruse and predictably delivers the misdiagnosis that allows the murderer to escape. Chancellor Sara Gaskell in *Wonder Boys* also never displays her presumably formidable intellect and accomplishments. Instead, she spends much of the film chain-smoking, fearful that her lover Tripp will abandon her and their unborn baby and hoping against hope that he will divorce his spouse and start a happy family with her. In these movies her status as a professional is either compromised by bad judgment or entirely inconsequential to the film. But in independent films, including those produced and directed by the Coen brothers, McDormand has appeared in more memorable roles.

In *Fargo*, pregnant policewoman Marge Gunderson (Frances McDormand) embodies integrity and compassion in a world filled with petty and incompetent criminals, liars, and corrupt businessmen. The sleazy car salesman Jerry Lundegaard (William H. Macy) arranges for the abduction of his wife Jean (Kristin Rudrud). He plans to use the ransom to cover up the fact that he has embezzled money from his company. Jean's kidnappers and ultimately her murderers, the greedy Carl Showalter (Steve Buscemi) and the taciturn psychotic Grimsrud (Peter Stormare), are only marginally more heartless than her small-minded and thoughtless husband and her miserly father Wade (Harve Presnell). With very few exceptions, all characters in the film are defined by avarice, pettiness, and ineptitude; not one of them retains control over the course of events he or she has set in motion. Jerry arranges the abduction but is unable to manage either his hired criminals or his father-in-law, who haggles with the abductors over the ransom and refuses to pay up until his daughter is returned. We half expect Wade to demand a discount if his daughter sustains any damage in the transaction. To Jerry and

Wade, the negotiations with the criminals are a business deal; they act as if Jean were in no danger. The poor judgment and emotional dysfunction of most of these characters reach astounding depths: when Jerry finds Wade, who was shot by Carl, he puts the body in the trunk of his car to cover up his involvement in the abduction and drives home. On the other side of the equation, Carl and Grimsrud forget to put license plates on the getaway car and end up killing the cop who pulls them over as well as two drive-by witnesses to the murder. In the end, Carl blurts out their hiding place in a bar, thus putting Marge on their trail. Rather than absconding with the $1 million ransom, which his partner Grimsrud knows nothing about, Carl haggles with him over a $15,000 car and is killed in the altercation.

In the midst of all this incompetence, corruption, and brutality, we are invited into the idyllic home of Margie and Norm (John Carroll Lynch), defined by slow shots of Norm's down-home country paintings and the marital bed on which Margie and Norm talk, watch TV, and have junk food but never sex. From her comfy surroundings and supported by her sweetly sensitive husband, Margie emerges to deal with insanity and murder. In all her professional dealings, Margie is characterized by her effortless competence and her ineligibility as a sex symbol. She is sweetly persuasive with the most obstinate criminal, more perceptive than her colleagues, dedicated and thorough, and even heroic as she faces Grimsrud. Unlike many of her brother cops on celluloid, she does not kill the fleeing criminal, who would have been shot, stabbed, drowned, burned, or impaled had his pursuer been played by Clint Eastwood or Bruce Willis. Margie, on the other hand, is both humane and markswoman enough to shoot the criminal in the leg, pack him in the car, and deliver the film's moral—"There's more to life than a little money, you know"—as she calmly waits for the reinforcements she no longer needs.

In addition to her competence, Margie is also memorable because she is seven months pregnant and neither tries to hide the fact nor permits it to slow her down. Her pregnancy forms part of her loving and sweetly caring but fundamentally unerotic relationship with Norm. It also plays another role in the film. As Margie waddles slowly toward her ultimate triumph, maneuvering her belly very carefully, we do not think of her as someone who could pursue the criminal and overpower him single-handedly—an assumption that is corrected at the end of the film. As she gets nauseous while bending over a murder victim, we might suspect, as her colleague does, that she reacts to the brutality of the killing, but we are corrected again: it was just a bout of morning sickness, cured instantly by Margie's usual insatiable appetite. Margie at mealtimes is a recurring theme employed to take on stereotypes about pregnant women: it is always a joy to watch Margie put away five pounds of fried chicken with mashed potatoes and gravy. Margie with a loaded tray, Margie at McDonald's, Margie in bed with Norm, stuffing her face with junk

Chief Marge Gunderson, bundled up and ready to take on the world. Frances McDormand in Fargo (1996). WORKING TITLE/POLYGRAM/THE KOBAL COLLECTION/MICHAEL TACKETT.

food—these scenes are enough to make any weight-watching female viewer cringe, but perhaps that, too, is what Margie accomplishes for us. It would be inaccurate to interpret these scenes as the out-of-control appetites of the pregnant woman: with Margie, nothing is out of control. If she eats like a lumberjack, it is because she is hungry or enjoys it (her husband, incidentally, eats the same way). If she is content with the most bourgeois, boring, and pedestrian marriage ever to grace the silver screen, it is because she loves her husband and her life. Clearly, Margie gets enough excitement on the job.

It is a sign of Margie's emotional health that she confronts the horror and insanity of her professional life, but she does not bring it home with her. Her inner self is unaffected, untouchable. She is quite capable of companionably watching TV in bed with Norm after having witnessed a man being fed through a wood chipper. Nor does she need to unburden herself to her husband—on the contrary. She listens to Norm's comparatively unexciting news—his painting of a mallard will be on the three-cent stamp—and sums up their life together: "Heck, Norm, you know, we're doin' pretty good." But unlike most of the film's characters—psychotic Grimsrud, cold-blooded Carl, scheming Jerry, and greedy Wade—Margie is not callous. Her composure is not a sign of heartlessness. In her final scene with Grimsrud, she shows real empathy for the victims and tries, in vain, to understand why anyone would kill "for a little bit of money." The only person in the film not motivated by pettiness and greed, she goes home to a life untouched by the corruption that surrounds her. And we know that she will sleep soundly until she is rung out of bed to deal with another crime at three o'clock the next morning.

In *Laurel Canyon*, McDormand reappears as Jane, a highly successful record producer who, like Margie, insists on being in charge of her own life. She smokes dope with the band, engages in sex with a series of younger lovers (both male and female), drinks, swears, and generally lives like a teenager. Compared with her highly proper son, the medical resident Sam (Christian Bale), and his fiancée Alex (Kate Beckinsale), who is writing her dissertation about the genomics of the reproductive behavior of the fruit fly, Jane appears immature and irresponsible. Her son finds her embarrassing, accuses her of having a developmental disorder, and cringes when he informs Alex's wealthy high-society family that his mother is in the "entertainment industry." But contrary to her son's opinion of her, Jane turns out to be competent and successful: her house is crammed with gold and platinum records and photographs that show her with a number of rock 'n' roll greats, including Joni Mitchell, the Red Hot Chili Peppers, David Bowie, Iggy Pop, and Bruce Springsteen. Sam, who has withheld the extent of Jane's success from Alex, considers her obvious professional competence the "irony of all time," indicating that in private life—as a wife and, most important, as a mother—she is a failure.

Sam's judgment of Jane as a failed mother is rooted partly in his own inability to enjoy life in the same way she does, but it is also given credence at the end of the film, when Jane herself confesses to her personal failings as a mother. Initially, however, the contrast between Jane and Sam is the only basis for his judgment: Alex and Sam are lying in bed, next to each other but not touching, listening to the sounds of Jane's orgasm in the next room. What Sam finds so embarrassing about Jane is simply the fact that she refuses to behave like a middle-aged bore, a staid, bourgeois housewife and mother. But when both Sam and Alex get tangled up in illicit love and potentially sexual affairs of their own—Sam with his colleague Sara (Natascha McElhone), Alex with both Jane and Jane's current lover Ian (Alessandro Nivola)—their relationship with Jane undergoes a transformation. As Alex tells Sam, she was not so much attracted to Jane and Ian; her goal was simply to stop being Miss Perfect, to "learn how to fuck up." Conversely, Jane's admission of her failings as a mother leads to a cautious reconciliation with Sam.

Like Margie, Jane is another rarity among women's roles in Hollywood films: although she initially appears to be a reckless hippie mother, she emerges as the most responsible person in the film. She has the good sense to break off the dangerous liaison involving her son's fiancée when both Alex and Ian are swept off by temptation. Moreover, Jane's project—Ian's new record—is making considerably more progress than Alex's dissertation. Jane has everything—a younger lover, a soaring career, and a heart. Jane's emotional honesty is one of the great points of identification in the film precisely because it contrasts with Sam's coldness toward her, Alex's emotional confusion, and Sam's and Alex's inept handling of sexual temptation. Jane embodies the refutation of familiar clichés: bad mothers and sexually insatiable older women. In traditional Hollywood films, Jane would be cast as a siren, such as Mrs. Robinson (Anne Bancroft) of *The Graduate* (1967), who lures the young man from the straight path, stealing him from the much younger woman to whom he truly belongs. Not so here: "I've never met a braver woman, and I'm deeply, deeply attached to you," confesses her lover Ian, who is sixteen years younger than Jane. Ian's attraction to Alex pales in comparison with his attachment to Jane, who, unlike Mrs. Robinson, will not be abandoned for a younger woman.

Laurel Canyon is exceptional in two more ways: it does not villainize or ridicule other women to establish Jane as the heroine by contrast. And Jane does emerge as the heroine of the film even though both she herself and Sam consider her a bad mother. *Laurel Canyon* accomplishes what Hollywood products of our family values–infected era are unlikely to put on screen: it shows a multifaceted, middle-aged woman who is simultaneously a competent professional, a good person, and a bad mother. Interestingly, what makes Jane a good woman is also what makes her a bad mother: her inner-directedness, her insistence on living her life as she chooses, and her refusal to be hampered by the wishes and needs of others. She suffers greatly because of Sam's disapproval of her, but neither his rejection nor her sorrow causes her to change a single thing about her life. In this respect, she resembles *Fargo*'s Margie: her inner core is untouchable. Self-confident, always conscious of who she is and who she wants to be, the Frances McDormand character at her best personifies the exact opposite of Hollywood's prototypical romantic heroine: the Julia Robertses and Meg Ryans, the lovable but insecure honey bunnies in search of an identity.

NOTES

1. It is also significant that at the beginning of their love affair, Edward is likened to Cary Grant, the protagonist of *The Awful Truth*. Maria DiBattista has characterized Grant as "the most hypercivilized male in classic American film comedy. If any man ever

sported the manners of perfect freedom, it is the debonair Grant" (*Fast-Talking Dames* [New Haven: Yale University Press, 2001], 219). Edward, too, embodies this aura of "perfect freedom."

2. Andrea Stuart, "The Outsider: Whoopi Goldberg and Shopping Mall America," in *Women and Film: A Sight and Sound Reader*, ed. Pam Cook and Philip Dodd (Philadelphia: Temple University Press, 1993), 64.

3. Goldberg received an Oscar for her performance, "the first African-American woman so honored in fifty-one years" (Dawn B. Sova, *Women in Hollywood: From Vamp to Studio Head* [New York: Fromm International, 1998], 193).

4. See Stuart, who asks: "You take the black star out of the black community to make him more palatable, but then who does he date?" ("The Outsider," 66).

5. Yvonne Tasker makes a similar point in her analysis of *Fatal Beauty* (1987). She points out that "due to supposed audience hostility a love scene between the two [Goldberg's character and costar Sam Elliot] was cut from the film" (*Spectacular Bodies: Gender, Genre and the Action Cinema* [London: Routledge, 1993], 33).

6. Stuart, "The Outsider," 62.

☆ 7 ☆

Vamp(ire)s and Those Who Kill Them
Buffy the Vampire Slayer and Dana Scully

*"I would love to watch TV, but I have to save the world . . .
again."*

—*Buffy the Vampire Slayer*

Accounts of current developments in the media often highlight a trend that is
generally referred to as "the feminization of the television industry." Women
now play an increasingly important role in both the production and consumption of television programs. Women not only outnumber men in the television
audience, they also spend 16 percent more time watching TV. Audience research shows that female viewers now "make up over two-thirds of the adult
viewing audience on weekday afternoons. . . . Prime time evening audiences are
more evenly divided, but women viewers still outnumber men."[1] In addition, the
shows that this female audience watches are more likely to have been selected,
written, and produced by women. In 1997, women constituted 40.8 percent of
broadcast employees. As is to be expected, the television fare created by a growing female workforce and targeted at a predominantly female audience is more
likely to showcase strong women leads. From *Roseanne* to *Sex and the City*, from
Murphy Brown to *Ally McBeal*, shows with female protagonists have demon-
strated not only their entertainment value but also their financial viability. Even
more conventional shows that do not revolve around female characters now frequently include appealing female sidekicks.

Given these trends, it is reasonable to assume that television offers its women
audience the kind of female fantasies that most films withhold.[2] And indeed, although television has its share of ambiguous or even reactionary portrayals of

women, some programs grant us unalloyed pleasures. To be sure, television is no friendly haven for those who have suffered wreckage in the rough waters of the movie industry. The number of female network employees may have increased drastically, but the percentage of women in management positions is still exceedingly low. More important, men still own and control 98.1 percent of all television stations.[3]

And yet, whereas *Buffy the Vampire Slayer* the 1992 movie presented a forgettable female protagonist, *Buffy the Vampire Slayer* the series created one of the most enjoyable female omnipotence fantasies ever to have graced the tube. The difference in quality is not happenstance but, in fact, the result of the growing divide that separates television production and consumption from its movie equivalents. In the mainstream film industry, fewer movies attract larger resources. The pressure to recoup the initial investment discourages risk taking, such as the use of new talent. In the television industry, in contrast, the proliferation of cable channels has led to the atomization of the mass audience.[4] This manifests itself not only in the form of employment opportunities for a larger talent pool, including more women, but also in programs that appeal to a niche audience. Moreover, whereas movies are both short and short-lived, television is able to bank on its expanded time horizon. If a movie fails to cash in on its opening weekend, it is pulled very quickly. Quirky and unconventional television shows, on the other hand, occasionally benefit from (digital) word of mouth and are thus able to turn their initial popularity with a cult following into mainstream success. One might even argue that female characters are more likely to benefit from the long life span of the genre of TV series. Because female characters are frequently reduced to stereotypes and caricatures, they stand to gain from the complexity and nuances facilitated by a running time of several seasons.

In light of the superiority of the average television heroine over her movie counterpart, it is apt that this book conclude with a TV chapter. The following portraits of Buffy Summers, the plucky heroine of *Buffy the Vampire Slayer*, and Dana Scully, the courageous female agent from *The X Files*, are not so much interpretations as tributes to two of television's most admirable women characters.

BUFFY SUMMERS: *BUFFY THE VAMPIRE SLAYER*

In many horror movies, sexual intercourse carries violence in its wake.[5] Typically, some blond teenage girl sleeps with her boyfriend and is promptly killed by a bloodthirsty revenant. Not so Buffy Summers (Sarah Michelle Gellar), who died first and had plenty of sex thereafter.[6] Buffy, who sacrificed herself to save the life of her sister Dawn (Michelle Trachtenberg) in the season 5 finale of *Buffy the Vampire Slayer*, was resurrected by her friends and spent most of the remainder of season 6 engaged in sexual intercourse with her hot vampire lover Spike (James Marsters). But avid fans of *Buffy the Vampire Slayer* know well that Buffy's postmortem binge loving is only one of the many gender transgressions that make this series so much fun to watch.[7]

Buffy Summers is a superhero of the most impressive variety. Ditzy high school student in miniskirts by day and supernaturally strong vampire slayer by night, Buffy is humankind's most powerful weapon against the evil outgrowths of the demon world. One of the show's most notable attractions is the spectacle of the rather petite Buffy socking it to several opponents thrice her size. Whether she is dealing with five knights, emissaries of an ancient order wearing full body armor, with a seven-foot 300-pound biker, or with three especially virile warrior vampires, Buffy beats them all to a pulp in the end. Viewers relish vicariously the pleasure of uninhibited freedom as Buffy patrols lone alleyways by night without even a hint of fear. Although she has a Watcher, the Englishman Rupert Giles (Anthony Stewart Head), who is entrusted with her instruction and supervision, ultimately Buffy herself is in charge simply because she possesses superpowers. "How do you kill vampires?" asks Buffy's friend Xander (Nicholas Brendon). "You don't, I do," is Buffy's succinct reply ("The Harvest," 1.2). Chosen by destiny to stand against the forces of evil, Buffy is endowed with the kind of authority that derives from unquestionable competence. Neither her male friends nor male institutions such as the police or the military possess the skills, strength, or resilience to do Buffy's job: "Cops can't fight demons; I have to do it" ("Becoming Part II," 2.17). Buffy succeeds because she has both brain and brawn. Although she exhibits a "girly" interest in shopping, fashion, and the relative advantages and disadvantages of different brands of nail polish, Buffy is neither shallow nor stupid. Her quick-wittedness and ability to think outside the box are as crucial to her success as a slayer as her supernatural muscular strength. Even in season 1 when Buffy is arguably at her most bratty, she exhibits unusual insight. In "I Robot, You Jane" (1.8), Buffy alone realizes that the demon Moloch "went binary" and now hides in a computer; in "The Pack" (1.6), she recognizes that Xander was transformed into a hyena; and in "Teacher's Pet" (1.4), she alone understands that their sexy new teacher is a praying mantis in disguise. Buffy's impressive analytical skills are complemented by her resourcefulness. Numerous times, Buffy confounds and ultimately beats her opponents by employing unorthodox methods. It is little wonder that Sunnydale's demons live in fear of this prodigious fighter.

Although Buffy possesses many of the qualities of the traditional male hero, she also deviates from this model in several important respects. Like James Bond, she has a secret identity that she conceals from her fellow students and, initially, even from her own family. Like James Bond, Buffy accompanies her slaying activities with witty puns. When Buffy is missing at the beginning of season 3, her friends take care of the slaying for her but find that punning is the real challenge: "I've always been amazed with how Buffy fought, but I always took her punning for granted" ("Anne," 3.1). But unlike James Bond, who is one of many double-0 agents, Buffy Summers is the only one of her kind. More important, whereas James Bond works alone, Buffy Summers enjoys the support of the "Scooby gang," a motley crew consisting of Willow (Alyson Hannigan), a powerful witch and computer wizard; Xander, ever loyal and courageous but sadly lacking in superpowers or special skills; and, beginning in season 3, Anya (Emma Caulfield), an ex–vengeance demon who experiences some difficulties adjusting to the ways of humans.[8] The series is quite explicit in its rejection of the model of the lone hero. Rather, Buffy represents a mixture that combines the strength and determination of the male hero à la James Bond with a "female" vision of a community-centered team player. Viewers are told repeatedly that the support of her friends is essential for Buffy's survival. As Spike remarks, the only reason Buffy has lasted so long is because she has ties to this world in the form of a mother, a sister, and friends. This is exemplified in the season 4 episodes "The Yoko Factor" (4.20) and "Primeval" (4.21). The Frankensteinian monster-demon Adam (George Hertzberg) charges Spike to sow discord among the Scoobies because he knows that he cannot beat Buffy as long as she is with her friends. Although Spike succeeds initially, the Scoobies soon catch on to his schemes and reunite. During the final showdown, the friends join forces in a magical union to create a combo-Buffy who defeats Adam effortlessly. Conversely, in the season 3 episode "The Wish" (3.9), which depicts an alternate reality of a Sunnydale without the slayer—Buffy is stationed at the hellmouth in Cleveland—the alternate Buffy proclaims that she does not "play well with others." Unsurprisingly, Buffy, the loner, dies in a fight with the Master (Mark Metcalf), an Über-vampire.

Although Buffy possesses superpowers, it is easy to identify with her. Buffy is a multifaceted character who is both strong and insecure, both powerful and vulnerable. We witness her victories and her struggles. Buffy may be the Chosen One, but she is also a teenager who attends high school, makes friends, and goes on dates. Buffy's dual standing as a superheroine and as an adolescent with typically teenaged problems is beautifully expressed in the season 2 episode "When She Was Bad" (2.1), in which some minions of the Master attempt to resurrect the season 1 villain.[9] Buffy, who was almost killed by the Master and is still tormented by nightmares about him, first smashes the reassembled bones of her nemesis with a sledgehammer and then bursts into tears. We admire her triumphs all the more precisely because Buffy must confront her own anxieties and insecurities ("My life happens to, on occasion, suck beyond the telling of it" ["Earshot," 3.18]). Even when she is down and out, when her boyfriend turns into her mortal enemy, when her mother throws her out of the house, when the police are looking for her, she will eventually muster the strength to fight back, and her momentary weakness and hesitation will make her comeback all the more impressive. "No weapons, no friends, no hope, take all that away, what's left?" her ex-lover Angel (David Boreanaz) taunts her. "Me," Buffy replies and kicks his butt.

Frequently, Buffy's fights are exercises in self-assertion. In the season 3 episode "Anne" (3.1), for example, Buffy, who has run away from home after the cataclysmic season 2 finale, finds herself in hell. A demon warden tries to crush Buffy's and the other teenage slaves' sense of self by forcing them to answer, "I'm no one," to his question, "Who are you?" When Buffy's turn comes, she replies, "I'm Buffy," beats the crap out of the demon, and leads everybody out of hell. Buffy, who now feels ready to go back home, gives her apartment and job to her new friend Lily. When Lily confesses that she is not very good at taking care of herself, Buffy comforts her: "It takes practice."

Female viewers, in particular, might also identify with Buffy's efforts to combine family and career. After all, Buffy, who is continually torn between her commitment to her slaying job and her desire to have a life, reflects a typically female challenge. "I would love to watch TV, but I have to save the world . . . again" ("Becoming Part II," 2.17), an exasperated Buffy shouts in frustration when the demands of her duties overwhelm her. The fact that Buffy's relationships with men are fraught with disappointments—"I've had two boyfriends. Both left . . . left-town left" ("I Was Made to Love You," 5.15)—also brings the heroine closer to our own sphere. When Buffy's season 2 boyfriend Angel turns into a demon as a result of sleeping with Buffy, she, in stereotypically female fashion, feels responsible not only for her lover's plight but also for his subsequent crimes. The challenge of not blaming herself for her ex-lover's misdeeds proves far more difficult than that of physically killing the demon he has become. Once Buffy learns to refute Angel's accusation that "you made me the man I am today" ("Innocence," 2.13), defeating him in a fight is but an afterthought.

With the exception of Glory (Clare Kramer), a narcissistic goddess, silk- and leather-clad fashion victim, and the supervillain of season 5—she complains that there are "too many demons in Sunnydale, but not enough retail outlets"

("Checkpoint," 5.12)—most of Buffy's opponents are cut in the mold of the power-craving patriarch.[10] In season 1, Buffy must face the Master, a sort of Ur-vampire intent on ruling the world and killing everybody in it. In season 2, Buffy kills the Judge, "a demon brought forth to rid the earth of the plague of humanity" ("Surprise," 2.13). In season 3, Buffy prevents the ascension of the mayor of Sunnydale, who graces the high school graduation ceremony with his metamorphosis into a giant dragon. In season 4, Buffy saves the world by killing Adam, a Frankensteinian demon–machine hybrid who, in a reversal of the Frankenstein myth, was created by a power-hungry female scientist. Frequently, Buffy opposes not only individual male monsters but also large male-dominated organizations. In "Reptile Boy" (2.5), a fraternity turns out to be the front for a sect of demon-worshippers who offer the demon of their choice a yearly sacrifice of three young women to ensure their continued success and riches. In season 4, a secret military task force, in whose labs Adam was assembled, first attempts to co-opt Buffy and then turns against her when she proves less compliant than expected.

Eventually, Buffy's fight against destructive male authority figures and organizations must tackle the abuse of power by her own "employers," the Watchers. In a season 3 episode appropriately entitled "Graduation" (3.21), Buffy sends her new watcher Wesley (Alexis Denisof) packing: "I don't think I'm going to take any more orders. Go back to your council and tell them, until the next slayer comes along, they can close up shop. I'm not working for them anymore."[11] When Wesley calls her refusal to work with him mutiny, Buffy replies: "I like to think of it as graduation." By season 5, Buffy's self-assertion is no longer limited to telling off one Watcher but, in fact, culminates in the demotion of the entire council. In "Checkpoint" (5.12), the Watchers' Council, officially still Giles's employer and Buffy's superior, attempts to regain its hold over Buffy. Several Watchers descend on Sunnydale to test Buffy's strength and strategies. Initially, Buffy complies with their demands because they threaten to withhold vital information about Glory, Buffy's season 5 nemesis. But when they attempt to blackmail and bully her, Buffy realizes that she does not need them: they need her. She rejects their unreasonable demands and gives them a piece of her mind: "You are Watchers . . . but without a slayer you're pretty much just watching masterpiece theater" ("Checkpoint," 5.12). From now on, Buffy, who had always confined her obedience to orders that corresponded to her own ideas, is officially self-employed. Giles remains in his Watcher function, but his relationship with Buffy continues to be characterized by mutual respect and affection, not by differences in power or competence.

Although Buffy is by definition exceptional and the only one of her kind, *Buffy the Vampire Slayer* does not highlight the unusual and singular status of

Strong and competent, Buffy is the perfect omnipotence fantasy for women between fifteen and forty-five. Sarah Michelle Gellar in Buffy, the Vampire Slayer. 20TH CENTURY FOX TELEVISION/THE KOBAL COLLECTION/RICHARD CARTWRIGHT.

its lead character by surrounding her with a posse of weak female figures. Rather, the show presents an array of memorable women, all capable of holding our attention through a panoply of unusual skills and endearing personality traits. First and foremost among these female companions is Buffy's best friend Willow. In the first few seasons, Willow is most notable for her exceptional intelligence and computer skills. On numerous occasions, Willow hacks her way into school and community databases to access information that is essential to the success of the latest Scooby gang venture. Her talents are so great that, on her school's career day, one of the world's leading software companies comes to campus to recruit Willow ("What's My Line," 2.9). It hardly bears mentioning that she is also accepted by every prestigious university in the country. Beginning gradually in season 2, Willow also emerges as a powerful witch. By season 4, she works the most difficult spells with amazing ease and grace. In season 6, driven insane by the violent death of her girlfriend Tara (Amber Benson), Willow joins the dark side. By now, her power is so immense that nothing and nobody, not even Buffy, can stop her. It is only when her friend Xander reminds her of his love for her that she desists from destroying the world. In the series finale ("Chosen," 7.22), Willow, who, after her encounter with evil in season 6, had abstained from the use of magic, redeems herself by placing the full force of her power in the service of the good fight. With the help of Willow's magic, Buffy and her army of slayer potentials succeed in defeating the First, an unspeakable, shapeless source of evil. Buffy, who has realized that she and her allies are doomed to lose if all power is concentrated in one slayer, calls on Willow to change the rules: "In every generation, one slayer is born . . . because a bunch of men who died thousands of years ago made up that rule. They were powerful men. This woman (points to Willow) is more powerful than all of them combined. (Willow whimpers.) So I say we change the rule." During the final fight, a momentarily white-haired, transfigured Willow with an expression of supreme bliss on her face, effects the transfer of power from Buffy to all slayer potentials and thus makes victory possible.

Among Buffy's female friends and schoolmates, Willow is by far the most endearing and carefully drawn personality. But even characters who, at first glance, appear to be mere caricatures prove to be attractive and multilayered upon close inspection. Cordelia (Charisma Carpenter), for example, a fellow student at Sunnydale High in seasons 1 through 3, is not only a brand-conscious consumer of expensive fashion but also an A student ("I do well in standardized tests. What? I can't have layers?" ["Band Candy," 3.6]). Although, superficially, Cordelia conforms to the stereotype of the insensitive bitch, she is actually a gender bender in disguise. Unashamedly putting herself and her own interests first, Cordelia offers her viewers the clandestine pleasures of female self-assertion. It is refreshing to watch a character who gives the lie to woman's "natural" inclination toward self-sacrifice, even if her self-interest takes rather drastic forms at times. On one occasion, she convinces her grandmother to switch cars with her in order to protect herself from attack by the newly evil Angel, whom she had once invited for a ride and who now has access to her car. Moreover, Cordelia is also a truth teller who can be relied on to speak her mind.[12] In the season 3 episode "Earshot" (3.18), Buffy is subjected to demonic influence and acquires the ability to read other people's minds. Almost all her friends begin to avoid her in order to hide their embarrassing thoughts. In Cordelia's case, however, thought processes and actual utterances are completely identical. Clearly, Cordelia embodies not only the antithesis of female self-sacrifice but also the opposite of the kind of hypocrisy that is typically attributed to women.

Although *Buffy* frequently represents male-dominated organizations as evil, its portrayal of individual male characters is by no means one-dimensional. Rather, one might argue that *Buffy*'s depiction of the protagonist's male companions, in particular Xander, is crucial to its innovative approach to gender. From the very beginning, Xander is rendered as an average guy without any specific talents. Endowed with a great sense of humor and a modicum of courage, Xander lives by the motto: "I laugh in the face of danger, then I hide until it goes away" ("Witch," 1.3). He is neither particularly strong nor very smart, and yet, throughout all seven seasons, Xander is a crucial member of the Scooby gang. It is not male bravado but, rather, his unwavering loyalty and deep love for his friends that make Xander irreplaceable. Characteristically, when the friends create the combo Super-Buffy to defeat Adam, Xander is the heart of the group, while Buffy functions as its hand and Willow, as its brain. In the season 5 finale, Xander's commitment to his friends is celebrated as a very special kind of heroism. Xander turns out to be the only one who is able to stop a crazed Willow, who went off the deep end when her girlfriend Tara was killed. Succeeding where all superheroes have failed, Xander prevents Willow from destroying the world by appealing to their shared childhood memories and to his love for her. Thus, Xander, who would have been cast as "angry white man" potential in many other shows, saves the world—not through superpowers and derring-do but because he is a loyal and loving friend.

The character of Xander is not the only deviation from traditional representations of masculinity. Although Buffy is a snappy dresser, the series does not sexualize its female protagonist. Instead, there are numerous episodes that showcase the naked upper bodies of Buffy's first boyfriend Angel and her season 6 boy toy, Spike. Clearly, this too constitutes a gender reversal of sorts, but its emancipatory potential is somewhat questionable. Geared at raising the number of female spectators, the display of the sexualized male body merely replicates the exploitation of the female pinup. In this instance, market forces triumph over women's lib.

When it comes to portraying innovative gender roles, the show's celebration of male sex appeal is hardly as effective as its parodies of white male anger. In the season 3 episode "Lover's Walk" (3.8.), the vampire Spike, whom his lover Drusilla (Juliet Landau) abandoned for a chaos demon, comes back to Sunnydale, the site of the demonic lovers' past happiness. Spike returns to their former lair and reduces everything, including Drusilla's puppets, to smithereens. Engrossed in his orgy of destruction, Spike wails, "What have you done to me?" He gets senselessly drunk, is almost turned to ashes when he wakes up in plain sunlight, and finally sobers up enough to kidnap Willow, who is to perform a love spell for him. In the end, however, Spike rejects the love spell and adopts a method that is more to his liking: "I'll tie her up, torture her, until she likes me again." Having regained his sense of manhood, a newly invigorated Spike leaves town. Although we laugh about his antics, Spike's anger and violent rampages exemplify what it would mean to be allied with a "demonic" lover.

With its unconventional title and postmodern aesthetics, *Buffy the Vampire Slayer* has often invited ridicule. In early reviews, critics took umbrage at countless features of the show ranging from Buffy's cleavage to her bratty behavior. Gradually, however, *Buffy*'s cult followers have outnumbered its detractors. After seven successful seasons, numerous publications and websites testify to the show's continued appeal; an appeal that is largely based on *Buffy*'s innovative portrayal of gender roles. In a sea of sexist depictions of women, Buffy's competence, strength, and power are unique. She alone will stand against the patriarchs, the misogynists, and the forces of oppression. She is the Chosen One. She is the Slayer.

DANA SCULLY: *THE X FILES*

In many respects, *The X Files* is an odd choice if one wants to discuss the feminist potential of recent television series. Although this FBI drama created by Chris Carter features both a male and a female protagonist, Special Agents Fox Mulder (David Duchovny) and Dana Scully (Gillian Anderson), Fox Mulder is unquestionably the hero. Supremely reliable but not quite as brilliant as her partner, Scully is Watson to Mulder's Sherlock.[13] She goes everywhere Mulder goes, but she is usually a couple of steps behind him. Scholars have pointed out that Mulder frequently comes to Scully's aid whereas she rescues him but rarely.[14] This imbalance certainly compromises Scully's standing as a hero, but the real problem lies elsewhere. Paradoxically, it is the oft-celebrated gender reversal at the heart of the series that detracts most from its feminist potential. Critics generally remark that Mulder is associated with the realm of feeling and intuition whereas Scully is an adherent of science and hard facts.[15] This is certainly true. However, it is equally true that, in the world of *The X Files*, a series that takes delight in unexplained phenomena and supernatural occurrences, science is usually wrong; meanwhile Mulder's instincts, supported by his immense knowledge ranging from physics to the history of the occult, are generally proven right.[16] Scully plays doubting Thomas to Mulder's wunderkind. As the character who openly questions Mulder's bizarre theories, she represents common sense and thus provides a point of identification for viewers who share her disbelief in ghosts, miracles, and alien abductions. Scully is a sounding board for Mulder's flights of genius. Mulder saves the world, and Scully is dedicated to supporting his mission.

Scully's status as second fiddle suggests that she should not be included in a discussion of female role models on television. And yet it is hard to imagine that anyone watching *The X Files* could help feeling admiration for this courageous female agent.[17] Scully may not be a genius like Mulder, but she is highly educated, supremely intelligent, and unusually eloquent. She holds a medical degree and chose to rewrite Einstein for her senior thesis. Scully may be the only female character on prime-time television who habitually engages in lengthy discussions of physics and genomics, plastered with subordinate clauses and multisyllabic words of Greek origin. Because of her background in forensic medicine, Scully is frequently called on to conduct autopsies and routinely handles all kinds of bloody organs and intestines with competent poise and equanimity. Her dedication to her work is such that, in one episode, she immerses herself completely in elephant guts to get to the root of the problem. When the situation calls for it, Scully also knows how to make her authority felt. She issues commands with great confidence and expects her colleagues to treat her with the same kind of respect and commitment that she accords others.

Although Scully's academic record and professional accomplishments are outstanding, they pale in comparison with her merits as a colleague and friend. Scully is a person of unusual integrity. Mulder's theories may point the way to salvation, but Scully's unshakable sense of right and wrong, her steadfastness

Dana Scully is never afraid to get to the bottom of things. Gillian Anderson in The X-Files. *20TH CENTURY FOX TELEVISION/THE KOBAL COLLECTION/JACK ROWAND.*

and loyalty, her professionalism, and her commitment to her work and to finding the truth possess a redeeming quality in and of themselves. More than once,
she puts her own life on the line in order to save others. In "Kill Switch" (5.11),
for example, a computer system gone haywire has tracked down Scully's car and
is targeting it with an armed satellite. Although her car, followed by a truck car-
rying flammable material, is about to blow up, Scully does not leave until she has
warned the truck's driver. Faithfully guided by her unerring sense of duty, Scully
is a rock in a sea of corruption and lies. Neither Mulder's nor the viewers' trust
in her is ever disappointed.

Whereas Buffy represents a youthful omnipotence fantasy in a supernatural
world of monsters and demons, Dana Scully is a grown-up heroine in the very
real world of government bureaucracy—alien infiltration, vampires, and acts of
witchcraft notwithstanding. Buffy Summers enjoys the relative freedom of ado-
lescence. Dana Scully, on the other hand, must deal with the daily grind and
frustrations of being among the few women who have made their way in the FBI,
arguably one of the most tenacious strongholds of male dominance. Clearly,
Mulder's freedom to indulge in unorthodox beliefs and Scully's insistence on
the virtues of protocol are functions of gender and of the institutional power that
gender affords. As a woman in a male organization, Scully has learned to tread
carefully. If Mulder's position in the FBI is precarious, it is a consequence of his
actions; but if Scully is in danger of being demoted, it is because her gender will
always leave her vulnerable. Indeed, Scully's initial assignment to the X Files in
the very first episode of the series is a setup, intended not only to debunk Mulder's work but also to throw a wedge in the spikes of Scully's own promising career. Through her association with "spooky Mulder," Scully herself is likely to
become an object of ridicule to her more conventional colleagues. Scully's male
superiors appear to be well aware that her excellent record as a scientist and her
exposed position as a woman in a male profession make her an ideal fall "girl"
for this dead-end job. What they had not counted on is that Scully, just like Mulder, is more committed to the truth than to her own ambition. But unlike her fire-
brand colleague who stops at nothing if it serves his cause, Scully combines her
dedication to the truth with respect for rules and proper procedure. Interestingly, Scully's attentiveness to the FBI code does not mark her as the more conventional and pedestrian character. Rather, it singles her out in an agency whose
surface of correctness barely suffices to conceal a seedy underbelly of intrigues
and corruption. In *The X Files*, patriarchy truly is the source of all evil.[18] If the
world is in peril, it is not so much because of alien invasion as of the selfish cynicism of a group of power-hungry, destructive old men. Engineers of a conspiracy of immense proportions, they collude in concealing the truth from the pub-

lic and are responsible for every abomination in recent history, including the assassination of John F. Kennedy, the war in Yugoslavia, and Oscar nominations ("Musings of a Cigarette-Smoking Man," 4.7). In light of such formidable enemies, Scully's courage and persistence are all the more remarkable. Whether she protects the mind-reading miracle boy Gibson (Jeff Gulka) against alien bounty hunters ("Within," 8.1) or works as a bodyguard charged to protect a scientist from the fangs of the Nazis, as is the case in the time-traveling episode "Triangle" (6.3), we can always rely on Scully to fight the good fight and to speak up in the face of cruelty and injustice.[19]

Scully's resistance to the forces of evil inspires our awe, but it is her ability to withstand Mulder's dissatisfaction with her that leaves a lasting impression on the viewer. After all, in the realm of female identity and emotions, risking one's life ranks a distant second to incurring the displeasure of loved ones. Although Scully is drawn to her partner—the unresolved sexual tension between the two agents is one of the hallmarks of the show—she is able to forgo his love and approval for what she believes is right. Even in season 6, when Mulder grows increasingly impatient with Scully's insistence on science and hard facts, she still stands by her convictions. Under pressure from Mulder and threatened by the presence of Agent Diana Fowley (Mimi Rogers), who is Mulder's old flame and, unlike Scully, in tune with Mulder's beliefs, Scully is able to hold her own: "I'm willing to believe, but not in a lie and not in the opposite of what I can prove. . . . It comes down to a matter of trust. . . . I'm asking you to trust my judgment. To trust me" ("The Beginning," 6.1). One might feel that Scully's stubborn refusal to acknowledge the existence of extraterrestrial life, in spite of constant proof to the contrary, turns her into a stock character of flawed design. But one might also claim that Scully's ability to remain true to herself is equally heroic, if not more so, as her willingness to stand up to the Cigarette-Smoking Man (William B. Davis), the show's arch villain, and his minions.

In the course of several seasons, Scully undergoes numerous trials and suffers from various illnesses. She is held hostage by serial killers, infected with a deadly virus, almost defeated by cancer, abducted by aliens, and subjected to inhuman and cruel experiments. At times, her body appears to be the battleground on which the X Files win their most important victories or incur their most painful losses. But if *The X Files* victimizes its female agent by highlighting the vulnerability of her body, it also shows that bodily appearances can be misleading. One of the most frequently recurring images of *The X Files* is the alien bounty hunter who can assume the looks—body, face, and voice—of every living person, including Mulder and Scully. Thus, the famous motto of *The X Files*, its much touted "Trust no one," might also be read as a warning not to judge a book by its cover, particularly if the cover is that of gender or race. Scully may be the smallest, most delicate-looking agent in the entire force, but her endurance, courage, and skills exceed those of her burlier colleagues by far.

In her professional life, Scully is confronted with every variety of criminal and monster that walks this planet (and others), ranging from alien shape-shifters to devil-worshipers, from vampires to serial killers, from killer bees to employees of fast food restaurants whose diet consists of human brain. In addition to all these aberrations of nature, Scully must defend herself against the most annoying of all plagues: the everyday sexism of her male colleagues at the FBI. The episodes that illustrate this most poignantly are "Dreamland I" and "Dreamland II" (6.4 and 6.5). Because of a tear in the space-time continuum, Mulder switches bodies with Morris Fletcher (Michael McKean), a quintessential Man in Black who works at a secret military compound. Unlike Mulder, Morris is a coward and conformist who does not give a hoot about any purpose grander than his own self-interest. A smug and less-than-smooth womanizer, he pats Scully on the behind, calls her "baby," and patronizes her in every way imaginable. Morris expects to be waited on hand and foot, sends Scully to buy cigarettes for him, and watches complacently as Scully does all the work while he plays golf on his office computer. When Scully reproaches him for his lack of ethics, he dismisses her with a flippant comment: "Look, little lady, it's time you got your panties straight." Needless to say that Scully gets the better of him in the end. Once Morris's unethical and disrespectful behavior arouses her suspicion, Scully quickly realizes that she is dealing with a fake. When Morris invites Scully to his, that is, Mulder's, apartment and attempts to seduce her with a bottle of champagne, he ends up handcuffed to the post of his newly acquired waterbed. When he tries to placate Scully and again calls her "baby," she responds with the pithy threat: "Baby me and you'll be peeing through a catheter." Although Scully defeats many a villain in the course of her professional life, her triumph over Morris Fletcher must be counted among her most memorable achievements.

In "Dreamland I" and "Dreamland II," Scully is able to see through the deception because Mulder is strikingly different from Morris Fletcher. But the humor of these two episodes hinges on the assumption that Mulder and Morris have more in common than one would like to think. Indeed, two of the funniest and most entertaining episodes of *The X Files*, "Bad Blood" (5.12) and "Arcadia" (6.13), develop the dysfunctional potential of Scully and Mulder's routine interactions. In "Bad Blood," Mulder and Scully's recent course of action in a murder case is the object of an investigation. In order to compare notes, Scully and Mulder both report their personal recollection of the events in question. Thus, viewers are presented with two different versions. In Scully's version,

Mulder is rash, overly dramatic, and prone to outbursts of anger. He orders Scully around ("Get those little legs moving") and shows no respect for her person or ideas. He almost forgets to introduce Scully to the local officer, makes quotation marks with his fingers when he refers to Scully's "theories," and violates her personal space with glee. His clothes covered in mud, Mulder storms Scully's motel room, makes himself comfortable on her bed, and prepares for a good night's rest as he sends Scully off to do the second autopsy in a row. Naturally, in his own version, Mulder is shy, submissive, and always eager to hear Scully's opinion, whereas Scully is impatient, passive-aggressive, and unmotivated. Although both stories are exaggerations and the truth lies somewhere in between, Scully and Mulder's interaction as they respond to each other's stories provides a framework that helps us separate the wheat from the chaff. Scully's repeated admonishments to get to the point prove that she does indeed get impatient with Mulder. On the other hand, the fact that Mulder cuts her off when she objects, interrupts her telling of the story, and puts pressure on her to support his version illustrate his lack of respect for his partner. Scully's defense mechanisms may be less than ideal, but so is Mulder's machismo. Clearly, not even this most intimate and unconventional of relationships is free of the calcified power games associated with traditional gender roles.

Whereas "Bad Blood" pokes fun at the dysfunctional aspects of Scully and Mulder's actual partnership, "Arcadia" imagines what their relationship might be like if it were less unconventional. In this hilarious season 6 episode, Mulder and Scully go undercover in an upscale gated community. As Rob and Laura Petrie, a married upper-middle-class couple, Scully and Mulder hobnob with their neighbors to get to the bottom of several mysterious deaths. Calling each other "honeybunch" and "poopyhead," they move and act like a single entity, constantly putting their arms around each other's shoulders and completing each other's sentences. In this brave new world, Scully must bear the humiliation of being introduced as a New Ager who is fond of crystals, mood rings, and magnetic bracelets. She also has to put up with Mulder's imitation of a domestic tyrant who orders her to make food for him ("Woman, get back in here and make me a sandwich"), distributes his dirty laundry all over the house, and always forgets to put the toilet lid down. Small wonder that during ten years of *The X Files* Scully, although she occasionally expresses a desire to settle down, does not once complain about being single. We are left with the distinct impression that Scully is far better off as Mulder's professional partner than she ever could be as his wife.

This impression is confirmed by the season 7 episode "Chimera" (7.16). In "Chimera," Mulder is sent to investigate the disappearance of Martha Crittendon

(Wendy Schaal), a perfect housewife and pillar of the community in Bethany, Vermont. This time he has to work and travel solo while Scully remains in Washington to continue surveillance of a strip club and its unsavory clients. Once on location, Ellen Adderly (Michelle Joyner), the local sheriff's wife, urges Mulder to stay at their house, a Martha Stewart fantasy come to life. Ellen keeps her house immaculately clean and routinely serves elaborate meals in elegant china and crystal dishes. On an average day, Ellen prepares roast for dinner and whips up eggs Benedict for breakfast. She lives only for her husband and child and advises Mulder not to miss out on the comforts of marriage, home, and family. Needless to add that Ellen is also the killer responsible for the murder of Martha Crittendon. When Ellen found out that her best friend Martha had an affair with her husband, she swallowed her anger. The repression of such powerful feelings caused a dissociative disorder that manifested itself in the form of a vicious and violent alter ego. Ellen's double, a wild creature with long hair and black eyes, attacked everything that constituted a threat to the stability of her home and family. Compared with such small-town mayhem and family feuds, Scully's surveillance of transvestites and prostitutes looks like a rather wholesome occupation.

In many ways, Mulder and Scully represent an alternative to and improvement on the traditional variety of male–female romance.[20] There is a good deal of erotic tension, but the glue that binds them together is a shared commitment to work toward a common goal. They may get annoyed with each other, may even mistreat each other occasionally, but the trust and respect that form the foundation of their partnership always win out in the end. In this they differ radically from almost all other heterosexual couples portrayed in *The X Files* and quite possibly on celluloid in general. It is not until the end of season 8 that Mulder and Scully begin to engage in activities that define most other relationships from the start. They kiss, they have a child—probably fathered by Mulder although we cannot ever be sure—and, most important, they begin to realize that the truth they have been looking for cannot be found by uncovering some government conspiracy but, in fact, consists in the love that they have grown to share. Eight years might seem like an unusually long period of courtship. But really, the truly unusual fact is not that it took Mulder and Scully eight years (or nine if we count the season finale) to feel comfortable with intimacy but, rather, that they got there at all. Moreover, in all these years, Scully never has to make a choice between her man and her mission. For as long as Mulder and Scully are together, they will battle evil and uncover the truth. When Scully declares in the final episode that she has no regrets—"Why, I'd do it all over again" ("The Truth," 9.19)—she has every right to be proud of her choices. Scully is what very few women in film can boast to be: she is an agent in every sense of the word.

NOTES

1. Steve Craig, "Selling Masculinities, Selling Femininities: Multiple Genders and the Economics of Television," *The Mid-Atlantic Almanack* 2 (1993), 16–17. Craig also points out that, because women do most of the shopping and still make the brand decisions for the household, most television advertisers consider women to be their primary target audience when they place commercials and consequently purchase time during those programs watched by women. See also Rhonda Wilcox and J. P. Williams, who write: "Television is a medium in which large blocks of programming have been conceived with the express purpose of attracting a female audience that can then be delivered to advertisers" ("What Do You Think: *The X-Files*, Liminality and Gender Pleasure," in *Deny All Knowledge: Reading* The X-Files, ed. David Lavery, Angela Hague, and Marla Cartwright [Syracuse: Syracuse University Press, 1996], 101).

2. See Kathleen Rowe, who claims that "television provides a more hospitable medium for female unruliness" (*The Unruly Woman: Gender and the Genres of Laughter* [Austin: University of Texas Press, 1995], 115).

3. This statistic is from a speech by William E. Kennard, the chairman of the Federal Communications Commission, to American Women in Radio and Television, 1998.

4. See Steven D. Stark, *Glued to the Set: The 60 Television Shows and Events That Made Us Who We Are Today* (New York: Delta, 1997). Jimmie L. Reeves, Mark C. Rodgers, and Michael Epstein ("Rewriting Popularity: The Cult Files," in *Deny All Knowledge: Reading* The X-Files, ed. David Lavery, Angela Hague, and Marla Cartwright [Syracuse: Syracuse University Press, 1996], 30) speak of *The X Files* as a show that is targeted at a niche audience.

5. Yvonne Tasker speaks of the "thriller cliché that sexual encounters bring dangers" (*Working Girls: Gender and Sexuality in Popular Cinema* [London: Routledge, 1998], 129).

6. For an analysis of the nexus of death and sex in *Buffy*, see Elisabeth Krimmer and Shilpa Raval, who claim that the series redefines traditional concepts of femininity "since woman's death does not restore order, nor does her desire corrupt it" ("Digging the Undead: Death and Desire in *Buffy*," in *Fighting the Forces: What's at Stake in* Buffy the Vampire Slayer, ed. Rhonda V. Wilcox and David Lavery [Lanham, Md.: Rowman & Littlefield, 2002], 158).

7. Sadly, *Buffy*'s innovative gender roles are not complemented by an equally progressive portrayal of race. See, for example, Elyce Rae Helford, who draws attention to the fact that "the series denies people of color access to insider status or heroic power" ("My Emotions Give Me Power: The Containment of Girls' Anger in *Buffy*," in *Fighting the Forces: What's at Stake in* Buffy the Vampire Slayer, ed. Rhonda V. Wilcox and David Lavery [Lanham, Md.: Rowman & Littlefield, 2002], 21). See also Lynne Edwards, "Slaying in Black and White: Kendra as Tragic Mulatta in *Buffy*," in *Fighting the Forces: What's at Stake in* Buffy the Vampire Slayer, ed. Rhonda V. Wilcox and David Lavery (Lanham, Md.: Rowman & Littlefield, 2002), 85–97.

8. See Rhonda V. Wilcox, who points out that "the series counterbalances the idea of the lonely hero with the presentation of a community of friends" ("Who Died and Made Her the Boss: Patterns of Mortality in *Buffy*," in *Fighting the Forces: What's at Stake in* Buffy the Vampire Slayer, ed. Rhonda V. Wilcox and David Lavery [Lanham, Md.: Rowman & Littlefield, 2002], 4).

9. See Catherine Siemann, who claims that Buffy is a feminist icon "because she is an empowered yet ordinary woman with ordinary problems" ("Darkness Falls on the Endless Summer: Buffy as Gidget for the Fin de Siècle," in *Fighting the Forces: What's at Stake in* Buffy the Vampire Slayer, ed. Rhonda V. Wilcox and David Lavery [Lanham, Md.: Rowman & Littlefield, 2002], 124).

10. Rhonda V. Wilcox and David Lavery point out that there is a website entitled "Buffy the Patriarchy Slayer" ("Introduction," in *Fighting the Forces: What's at Stake in* Buffy the Vampire Slayer, ed. Rhonda V. Wilcox and David Lavery [Lanham, Md.: Rowman & Littlefield, 2002], xviii).

11. This and many similar scenes disprove Helford's claim that in *Buffy* female aggression is always assuaged by humor and that Buffy is not "an assertive adult, directly expressing her anger to create empowering change in her life" ("My Emotions Give Me Power," 26).

12. See Mary Alice Money, who points out that Cordelia is "so forthright—or self-centered—that her words express exactly what she thinks no matter whom she might offend or hurt" ("The Undemonization of Supporting Characters in *Buffy*," in *Fighting the Forces: What's at Stake in* Buffy the Vampire Slayer, ed. Rhonda V. Wilcox and David Lavery [Lanham, Md.: Rowman & Littlefield, 2002], 103).

13. For an analysis of the similarities between Mulder and Sherlock, see Wilcox and Williams, "What Do You Think," 106.

14. See Michele Malach, "I Want to Believe . . . in the FBI: The Special Agent and *The X Files*," in *Deny All Knowledge: Reading* The X-Files, ed. David Lavery, Angela Hague, and Marla Cartwright (Syracuse: Syracuse University Press, 1996), 74.

15. It has often been claimed that "Scully—as a doctor, an officer of the law, and a skeptic—is a 'masculine' woman" (Leslie Jones, "Last Week We Had an Omen: The Mythological X-Files," in *Deny All Knowledge: Reading* The X-Files, ed. David Lavery, Angela Hague, and Marla Cartwright [Syracuse: Syracuse University Press, 1996], 88).

16. See David Lavery, Angela Hague, and Marla Cartwright, who point out that the series tends to "validate Mulder's state of 'ontological shock' more frequently than Scully's scientific-reductionist theories" ("Introduction: Generation X—*The X-Files* and the Cultural Moment," in *Deny All Knowledge: Reading* The X-Files, ed. David Lavery, Angela Hague, and Marla Cartwright [Syracuse: Syracuse University Press, 1996], 12). See also Wilcox and Williams, who draw attention to the fact that, ironically, the "frequent sex role reversals result in Scully's investigative gaze being disempowered" ("What Do You Think," 99).

17. Several scholars have pointed out that the character Scully is inspired by the female agent Clarice Starling in *The Silence of the Lambs* (1991); see, for example, Wilcox

and Williams, "What Do You Think," 102. In turn, Mulder resembles Dale Cooper of *Twin Peaks*.

18. Elizabeth Kubek ("You Only Expose Your Father: The Imaginary, Voyeurism, and the Symbolic Order in *The X-Files*," in *Deny All Knowledge: Reading* The X-Files, ed. David Lavery, Angela Hague, and Marla Cartwright [Syracuse: Syracuse University Press, 1996], 168–204) points out that *The X Files* frequently exposes the guilt of fathers and thus represents an attack on patriarchal structures. For example, the ur-experience that inspires Mulder's (and the show's) quest revolves around the complicity of Mulder's father in the abduction of his daughter, Mulder's younger sister: "The revelation that Mulder's father is implicated in Samantha's loss thus exposes one key secret of patriarchy: its repression of the feminine and the cost that that sacrifice exacts on all subjects" (Kubek, "You Only Expose Your Father," 171).

19. Wilcox and Williams maintain that Scully's resistance to the evil machinations of the old boys' club is crucial for her survival, whereas "a woman who is co-opted by the patriarchal order gets turned into a puddle of goo" ("What Do You Think," 119), as is evident in the episode "Soft Light" (2.23).

20. See Martha P. Nochimson, who claims that *The X Files* "provide[s] the ideal context for the representation of the modern, troubled path to intimacy" (*Screen Couple Chemistry: The Power of 2* [Austin: University of Texas Press, 2002], 246).

Conclusion
Is This as Good as It Gets?

Our survey of movies for and about women from 1990 to 2004 includes vastly diverse material ranging from box office hits such as *Charlie's Angels* to indie gems such as *The House of Yes*. In spite of this diversity, the conception and reception of these films follow certain unwritten laws. When it comes to women in the movies, the rule that trumps all others might be summarized as: You can tell any story you like, but can you sell it? To call this a paradox inherent in the much-vaunted freedom of capitalism captures only one part of the truth. The recent explosion of the costs of advertising and distribution demonstrates quite clearly that the freedom to listen is substantially hampered by the inequality of the resources that back certain stories but not others. Consequently, unconventional stories about women who are neither Miss Hollywood nor Mother Teresa are invariably relegated to the sidelines. Actresses who do not conform to the dominant body or character types either work for independent productions or appear in minor roles in mainstream movies. On the other hand, conventional Hollywood fare has perfected the art of forging contradictory messages into a (more or less) unified whole. The formula for success rests on the combination of emancipatory exhortations with reactionary content. And it is unlikely that this is going to change in the next decade.

If the movies that were released in the first four years of the new millennium are any indication of what is to come, we can look forward to years of stagnation interrupted by occasional leaps and jumps. Two sequels to movies discussed in a previous chapter, *Charlie's Angels: Full Throttle* and *Lara Croft Tomb Raider: The Cradle of Life* (both 2003), suggest that the trend to mix messages is certain to remain with us. Only now there is a new form of stagnation, which proceeds in the manner of the crab walk: one step forward, two steps back.

If we are not crab walking, we are progressing in huge leaps backward. Paradoxically, films that deliver convincing portrayals of female independence, such as *Cold Mountain*, *Mona Lisa Smile*, or *Down with Love* (all 2003), are set in the distant (Civil War era) and not-so-distant (1950s–1960s) past. Unable to change the present, these films feel inspired to rewrite the past. Moreover, because there is nothing as old as yesterday's news, they not only wrongly project women's liberation into the past—the 1950s, for crying out loud!—but also imply that we need no longer have any commerce with women's lib today. After all, it has all been taken care of centuries ago.

Nonetheless, the picture is not entirely bleak. First, there are some signs that the industry may be changing—yet again. In an article in the *New York Times*, Frank Rich recently discussed the miserable box office failure of the latest crop of blockbuster potentials.[1] Rich believes that the initial investment needed to make and market megahits has grown to such dimensions that this mode of production has outlived its own viability. Instead, he perceives a renewed effort to pursue niche markets, that is, to produce movies targeted not at the entire population of the United States but, rather, at narrowly defined audience groups. If this trend comes to fruition, it might result in a greater variety of women's roles portrayed in film. As women are particularly vulnerable to *reductio ad stereotypicum*, they stand to gain from such diversification.

But what if Rich is wrong? Well, there are always some intriguing, albeit rare, highlights: films that not only portray unconventional story lines and characters but also manage to be successful at the box office. Thus, it is only apt that our book conclude with a tribute to *Something's Gotta Give* (2003), a delightful romantic comedy in which a sixty-plus-year-old woman achieves something that rarely forms the subject of a successful film—she finds a lover half her age—and something that is almost never shown in a mainstream film—she actually has a lover who is as old as she is.

ONE STEP FORWARD, TWO STEPS BACK: THE CRAB WALK

If there is one overriding tendency that characterizes the portrayal of women in movies from the early 1990s to the first years of the new millennium, it is that progress is meted out in the form of the crab walk: For every step forward, there are two steps back. In mainstream movies, emancipatory statements and images are invariably accompanied and countermanded by a plethora of reactionary messages. In order to illustrate this point, let us take a quick look at two sequels to movies discussed in chapter 5: *Charlie's Angels: Full Throttle* (2003) and *Lara Croft Tomb Raider: The Cradle of Life* (2003).

In *Charlie's Angels: Full Throttle*, the three protagonists are again degraded, ridiculed, sexualized, and objectified, all in the spirit of campy humor and to an even higher degree than in *Charlie's Angels*. Again, we are dealing with ditzy caricatures of the superheroines they are supposed to be. Natalie (Cameron Diaz) is even clumsier than before; Alex (Lucy Liu) no longer pretends to be a bikini waxer but is now mistaken for a prostitute; the décolletage of the Angels' various evening gowns is even lower, and the inevitable dirndls are even cheesier. When the Angels visit a crime scene, their expertise is so ridiculously exaggerated, and the room is lit in such surreal colors, that the three are stripped of the last lingering shadow of credibility. Their outrageous stunts on motorbikes, trucks, and airplanes are still splattered throughout the movie, but they are now shown in slow motion and freeze-frame to remind us of their artificiality. In short, the movie has abandoned all pretense that we are dealing with superwomen and instead flaunts self-referential delight about its own campy fakeness.

But just when we are ready to give up on it entirely, *Charlie's Angels 2* introduces the intriguing character of Madison Lee (Demi Moore), a renegade Angel who has left the Angels' patriarchal work environment and now goes solo: "I don't take orders from a speaker box anymore." Madison, an invincible fighter and the recipient of a Noble Prize in astrophysics, is an "Ur"-omnipotence fantasy, but unlike her three ditzy avatars, she plays it straight. Neither clumsy nor silly, Madison exudes self-confidence and commands respect. She is the Angel we have been waiting for, and it is needless to add that she is also a femme fatale who will not live to see the end of the movie. Like all fallen angels, Madison has joined the forces of evil. She is punished for her hubris—"Why be an Angel when I can play God?"—and, in the final showdown, which takes place in a theater, she quite literally ends up in hell. *Charlie's Angels 2* destroys its own fantasy of a strong Angel who is her own boss and features three heroines who are even more inane and vacuous than previously deemed possible: one step forward, three steps back.

Like *Charlie's Angels: Full Throttle*, *Lara Croft Tomb Raider: The Cradle of Life* (2003) graduates beyond some of the problems that plagued the first installment only to introduce new tribulations. Although Lara still performs some of her feats in a bikini, the sexualization of her body is not as relentless and pervasive as in the previous feature. Whereas the first *Lara Croft: Tomb Raider* (2001) showcases a lifeless cartoon character who is completely invincible and self-sufficient, the new Lara has friends and a past. She shows signs of emotional and physical vulnerability; at times, she even needs the help of her friends to survive. Clearly, *Lara Croft Tomb Raider: The Cradle of Life* has learned from the mistakes of *Lara Croft: Tomb Raider*. And yet the specific nature of these improvements threatens to eclipse the minor progress they represent. For example, although the new Lara is no longer daddy's girl, she is still one of the guys. With her dad safely deceased in the first installment, the new Lara is no longer beholden to her father but, instead, chooses to place her skills at the service of the fatherland. At the beginning of the movie, she agrees, albeit grudgingly, to complete a mission for MI6. Furthermore, the new Lara admittedly has a female friend and even a partner and boyfriend, whereas the old Lara reveled in splendid isolation. But her friend, a Chinese woman who provides Lara and her partner with guns, clothing, and motorbikes, remains relegated to a three-minute cameo appearance. Similarly, Lara now shares intimacy with a man, but her boyfriend is a criminal and traitor, and she is forced to kill him in the end. Curiously, his dead body concludes a plot that was set in motion by two male corpses. One of the first scenes shows Lara exploring an underwater cave. She is accompanied by two young Greek helpers who fall victim to the evil schemes of Lara's opponent. Thus, Lara undergoes a development from having no partners at all (in the first movie) to watching how her partners are killed and finally killing them herself. Paradoxically, *Tomb Raider 2*, which begins and ends with a wedding—a joyous celebration in a Greek village and an African ritual—still shows a heroine who forms no lasting human attachments. Whereas James Bond, Superman, and Indiana Jones always get their girl in the end, Lara Croft not only does not get the guy; she has to finish him off herself. In this way, the splendid isolation that makes Lara so difficult to identify with in the first movie is temporarily suspended in the second, only to be reinstated with a vengeance. Lara too is a crab walker: one step forward, three bodies back.

TWO GREAT LEAPS BACKWARD: BACK TO THE FUTURE, OR, FORWARD TO THE PAST

If the most recent crop of action films hardly succeeds in offering us progressive female role models, we may want to consider the latest products featuring the most successful screen divas of the past decade. Both Julia Roberts, in *Mona Lisa Smile* (2003), and Meg Ryan, in *In the Cut* (2003), have tried to overcome the image of the romantic comedy heroine. If Renée Zellweger films of the past have, again and again, shown us her character's flight from reality, 2003 brought us two Zellweger films that represent different takes on real life: whereas *Down with Love* reprises the attitude of earlier films, *Cold Mountain*'s Ruby personifies the exact opposite of the refusal to deal with real life on its own terms. All of these films present women viewers, finally, with gutsy, smart, and independent screen heroines who insist on their own independence and, in some cases (*Mona Lisa Smile, Down with Love, Cold Mountain*), they encourage other women to do the same. *Down with Love* shows a world-famous and best-selling woman writer who propagates women's independence from men and their right to a career. Best of all, at the end the heroine gets to practice what she preaches: she is on top of the world and at the head of her firm, with her superhandsome boyfriend at her feet. In *Cold Mountain*, Zellweger plays down-to-earth Ruby, an impressively self-confident and no-nonsense country lass who seems to respect neither gender nor class boundaries. She rescues hapless Ada (Nicole Kidman) from aesthetically pleasing starvation by managing the farm and teaching her to work. Ruby is a hard worker but no servant; she is a kind soul but immune to emotional manipulation or masculine oppression ("Ain't no man better than me," she states confidently). And finally, 2003 also brought us *Mona Lisa Smile*, in which college teacher Katherine Ann Watson (Julia Roberts) tries to teach her female students the value of self-worth and independence as well as art history. Watson spends most of the film attempting to impress upon her students that marriage and motherhood are no longer the only options in a woman's life and that further education—one of her students is accepted at Yale law school but gives it all up for marriage—can present both productive and satisfying alternatives. At the end of the film, Watson resigns under conservative pressure, but still, she must be credited with forcing her female students—and that includes us in the audience—to consider the terrible price exacted by conformity. The film lands viewers in a quandary—but in a highly productive one: while we mourn Katherine Watson's defeat, we think about the difference between appearing happy, Mona Lisa smiles firmly plastered on our faces, and actually being happy and about the possibilities we have of making ourselves happy.

So what is wrong with these pictures? Part of what is wrong with these pictures is that at the same time, the *first* time, that they show us a lead woman endowed with authority who is neither condemned nor killed for this, they define this refreshing sight as a thing of the past. *Cold Mountain* is set in the 1860s; both *Down with Love* and *Mona Lisa Smile* are set in the 1950s–1960s. To the extent that these films portray the struggle for female independence (*Down with Love, Mona Lisa Smile*) or simply a woman's fight to survive in a world defined by male violence (*Cold Mountain*), they implicitly define these battles as no longer necessary. To today's women viewers, who still struggle to combine career and family (like Barbara Novak in *Down with Love*), or who face tremendous inequalities in terms of education or job opportunities (like the young women in *Mona Lisa Smile*), or who are still trying to fight their way out of poverty (like *Cold Mountain*'s Ruby), it may well seem somewhat disingenuous to portray the 1860s or—for Pete's sake—the 1950s as a time of burgeoning female emancipation.

If Hollywood movies of the 1990s can be accused of indulging in "feminism lite," as we have claimed in the introduction, perhaps Hollywood finally entered its "postfeminist" age in 2003. Today's feminist struggles transported back in time are made to appear passé and outdated. If the message of these films is to be credited, it seems that we have known for decades, since at least the 1950s, that women are entitled to a career and a family—so why waste any more time on the subject? Perhaps this women's libber stuff was necessary in the distant past, these films seem to say, but haven't we gone beyond that today? Hollywood's attempts to rewrite women's history are the surest sign of how far we have not come. The great leap backward that these films represent is not only a leap backward in time, into the 1860s or 1950s, but also a leap backward in the development of social ideas about women. For in inviting us to identify with female role models of our grandmother's (or, as the case may be, our great-great-great-great-great-grandmother's) generation, the film industry refuses to admit that there is still a need for such role models in the present. Progressive intentions aside, the films' discovery of forward female thinkers of the past seems, above all, to acknowledge one thing: if set in the present day, movies celebrating female independence and survival skills or advocating women's right to a career and an education would appear shrill and demanding—in short, "feminist." And in a context in which commercial viability is everything, that appearance has to be avoided at any cost.

GOING NOWHERE FAST: STAGNATION

The year 2003 witnessed several attempts of actresses to redefine their screen personae and saw the release of movies with unusually plucky and innovative heroines. Some were greeted enthusiastically by the critics and rewarded with box office success; others were ignored and reviled. Renée Zellweger got an Oscar for her role in *Cold Mountain*; *Mona Lisa Smile* tanked; *Something's Gotta Give* was number one at the box office during its opening weekend; *In the Cut* flopped. Clearly, it is difficult to predict how an audience will respond to Meg Ryan or Julia Roberts in any role different from that of a romantic heroine or to a sixty-something woman as a romantic heroine. In an industry that has its eyes firmly on the prize, such unpredictability poses a serious financial risk. It stands to reason that innovative or unusual women's roles might fall victim to censorship or self-censorship before they ever see the light of preproduction. Absence of risk entails stagnation. Any given year, we are faced with a barrage of images of women in film, but all too often this is tantamount to going nowhere fast. This sentiment was expressed by Diane Keaton when, after reading the script of what was to become the hit movie *Something's Gotta Give*, she speculated that this movie would never be made because Hollywood would never accept a love story involving a woman her age.[2] The fact that *Something's Gotta Give* was not only produced but extremely popular with the general public shows that something may be moving after all.

SOMETHING'S GOTTA MOVE

In *Something's Gotta Give* (2003), directed by Nancy Meyers, Harry Sanborn (Jack Nicholson), a famous bachelor who specializes in dating women less than half his age, suffers a heart attack during one of his amorous sprees. Unable to travel, Harry finds that his love nest in the Hamptons, owned by the mother of his twenty-something sweetheart Marin (Amanda Peet), becomes his makeshift nursing home. Instead of tumbling in bed with Marin, Harry now engages in feuds with Marin's mother Erica Barry (Diane Keaton), a successful playwright and divorcée. Soon enough Harry tames the shrew, and he and Erica get it on. During the rest of the movie, Erica waits patiently—the audience somewhat less patiently—until Harry acknowledges that he too is in love with Erica and that his life must change.

Something's Gotta Give is not a stellar accomplishment. The dialogues are not as snappy as one might wish; the plot is predictable; the cinematography is mediocre; the ambience of the Hamptons and Erica's Crate-and-Barrel-perfect house is clichéd; and it really *is* much too long for its own good. In short, although the basic idea of *Something's Gotta Give* is wonderful, its execution is not. And yet there is something about *Something's Gotta Give*: Nancy Meyers's movie centers on an omnipotence fantasy for a sixty-year-old woman, and there sure aren't many of those.[3] The audience is treated to the sight of a quintessential hunk falling for the aging Erica. When Erica takes the ailing Harry to the hospital, she meets the handsome and unmarried doctor Julian Mercer, played by *Matrix* star Keanu Reeves. Julian, a God in White with a taste for literature, is a huge fan of Erica and has seen every play she has ever written. But it is not just Erica's artistic brilliancy that has Julian spellbound. He also finds Erica incredibly sexy and professes to have feelings for her that he has never experienced. Although in the end Julian is rejected for the age-appropriate and newly reformed rake Harry, his preference for personality over looks—looks here defined by Hollywood standards (in any other universe, Diane Keaton's slender Erica would be beautiful)—is gratifying to both Erica and the audience. Although impressive, Erica's liaison with the young hunk pales in comparison with her conquest of Harry Sanborn, who, because he managed to live to the ripe age of sixty-three without tying the marital noose, is also known as the "Escape Artist." In his own way, Harry is quite a catch. He is a fabulously rich businessman with a cohort of personal assistants and a legion of ex- and current girlfriends. When pressed, Harry, who once dated Diane Sawyer, even knows how to be charming. His charm, however, is usually directed exclusively at women under thirty. The irony of *Something's Gotta Give* consists in the fact that a young man's love for an older woman is presented as rare but an older man's attraction to a woman his own age is earth-shattering. Erica truly gets to have it all: a hit play, a younger lover, and, finally, even a husband her own age.

Still, *Something's Gotta Give* is not all we want it to be. Sometimes the movie shifts gears, and instead of a female omnipotence fantasy we are dealt yet another reworking of a male midlife crisis. One might even claim that the movie's real accomplishment lies not in its theme but in its box office performance. *Something's Gotta Give* raked in $112,904,000 during its first two months and proved that there is a market both for older actresses and for movies that tell less conventional stories. It may not be perfect, but at the moment, it is as good as it gets.

NOTES

1. Frank Rich, "Bullies Are Not What Ails Hollywood," *The New York Times* (Late Edition–Final), January 11, 2004, 2-1.

2. Diane Keaton's comment was reported by host Mark Eccleston on *The Preview Show*, aired on BBC, March 10, 2004.

3. David Denby's review in the *New Yorker* proves that there is a dire need for such fantasies. His utterly gender-blind reading fails to perceive the central premise of the movie. Denby, who believes that *Something's Gotta Give* is about "the national habit of youth worship" and who speaks of the "allegedly unlikely love affair between the goat and the turtleneck" ("Star Season: *Cold Mountain, Something's Gotta Give, Mona Lisa Smile*," *The New Yorker*, December 22 and 29, 2003, 167), fails to acknowledge that there is any validity to the movie's representation of gendered relations.

Bibliography

Abramovitz, Rachel. *Is That a Gun in Your Pocket: The Truth about Female Power in Hollywood*. New York: Random House, 2000.

Acker, Ally. *Reel Women: Pioneers of the Cinema, 1896 to the Present*. New York: Continuum, 1991.

Basinger, Jeanine. *A Woman's View: How Hollywood Spoke to Women, 1930–1960*. New York: Alfred A. Knopf, 1993.

Bennett, Tony. "The Bond Phenomenon: Theorizing a Popular Hero." *Southern Review* 6, no. 2 (1983): 195–225.

Bennett, Tony, Susan Boyd-Bowman, Colin Mercer, and Janet Woollacott, eds. *Popular Television and Film: A Reader*. London: British Film Institute, 1981.

Bordo, Susan. *The Male Body: A New Look at Men in Public and in Private*. New York: Farrar Strauss Giroux, 2000.

Brooker, Will. "Rescuing *Strange Days*: Fan Reaction to a Critical and Commercial Failure." In *The Cinema of Kathryn Bigelow: Hollywood Transgressor*, ed. Deborah Jermyn and Sean Redmond, 198–219. London: Wallflower Press, 2003.

Bruzzi, Stella. *Undressing Cinema: Clothing and Identity in the Movies*. New York: Routledge, 1997.

Buhle, Paul, and Dave Wagner. *Radical Hollywood: The Untold Story behind America's Favorite Movies*. New York: The New Press, 2002.

Cavell, Stanley. *Pursuits of Happiness: The Hollywood Comedy of Remarriage*. Cambridge: Harvard University Press, 1981.

Conley, Tom. "Noir in the Red and the Nineties in the Black." In *Film Genre 2000: New Critical Essays*, ed. Wheeler Winston Dixon, 193–210. Albany: State University of New York Press, 2000.

Craig, Steve. "Selling Masculinities, Selling Femininities: Multiple Genders and the Economics of Television." *The Mid-Atlantic Almanack* 2 (1993): 16–17.

Denby, David. "Star Season: *Cold Mountain, Something's Gotta Give, Mona Lisa Smile*." *The New Yorker*, December 22 and 29, 2003: 166–69.

Desser, David. "The Martial Arts Film in the 1990s." In *Film Genre 2000: New Critical Essays*, ed. Wheeler Winston Dixon, 77–109. Albany: State University of New York Press, 2000.

DiBattista, Maria. *Fast-Talking Dames*. New Haven: Yale University Press, 2001.

Dixon, Wheeler Winston. "Introduction: The New Genre Cinema." In *Film Genre 2000: New Critical Essays*, ed. Wheeler Winston Dixon, 1–12. Albany: State University of New York Press, 2000.

——. "Twenty-five Reasons Why It's All Over." In *The End of Cinema as We Know It: American Film in the Nineties*, ed. Jon Lewis, 356–66. New York: New York University Press, 2001.

Dixon, Wheeler Winston, ed. *Film Genre 2000: New Critical Essays*. Albany: State University of New York Press, 2000.

Doherty, Thomas. *Pre-Code Hollywood: Sex, Immorality, and Insurrection in American Cinema 1930–1934*. New York: Columbia University Press, 1999.

Drew, William M. *At the Center of the Frame: Leading Ladies of the Twenties and Thirties*. Lanham, Md.: Vestal Press, 1999.

Dyer, Richard. *Only Entertainment*. New York: Routledge, 2002.

Edwards, Lynne. "Slaying in Black and White: Kendra as Tragic Mulatta in *Buffy*." In *Fighting the Forces: What's at Stake in Buffy the Vampire Slayer*, ed. Rhonda V. Wilcox and David Lavery, 85–97. Lanham, Md.: Rowman & Littlefield, 2002.

Ehrenreich, Barbara. *Nickel and Dimed: On (Not) Getting by in America*. New York: Henry Holt and Co., 2001.

Elsaesser, Thomas. "The Blockbuster: Everything Connects, but Not Everything Goes." In *The End of Cinema as We Know It: American Film in the Nineties*, ed. Jon Lewis, 1–22. New York: New York University Press, 2001.

Evans, Peter William. "Meg Ryan, Megastar." In *Terms of Endearment: Hollywood Romantic Comedy of the 1980s and 1990s*, ed. Peter William Evans and Celestino Deleyto, 188–208. Edinburgh: Edinburgh University Press, 1998.

Evans, Peter William, and Celestino Deleyto, eds. *Terms of Endearment: Hollywood Romantic Comedy of the 1980s and 1990s*. Edinburgh: Edinburgh University Press, 1998.

Faludi, Susan. *Backlash: The Undeclared War against American Women*. New York: Doubleday, 1991.

——. *Stiffed: The Betrayal of the American Man*. New York: Perennial, 2000.

Fiske, John. "British Cultural Studies and Television." In *What Is Cultural Studies? A Reader*, ed. John Storey, 115–46. London: St. Martin's Press, 1997.

——. *Television Culture*. New York: Routledge, 1987.

Flanders, Laura. *Bushwomen: Tales of a Cynical Species*. London: Verso, 2004.

Gabbard, Krin. "Saving Private Ryan Too Late." In *The End of Cinema as We Know It: American Film in the Nineties*, ed. Jon Lewis, 131–38. New York: New York University Press, 2001.

Giroux, Henry A., and Imre Szeman. "Ikea Boy Fights Back: *Fight Club*, Consumerism, and the Political Limits of Nineties Cinema." In *The End of Cinema as We Know It: American Film in the Nineties*, ed. Jon Lewis, 95–104. New York: New York University Press, 2001.

Green, Philip. *Cracks in the Pedestal: Ideology and Gender in Hollywood*. Amherst: University of Massachusetts Press, 1998.

Grossberg, Lawrence, and Ellen Wartella, eds. *Toward a Comprehensive Theory of the Audience*. Champaign: University of Illinois Press, 1992.

Hall, Stuart. "Encoding/Decoding." In *Culture, Media, Language*, ed. Stuart Hall, Dorothy Hobson, Andrew Lowe, and Paul Willis, 128–39. London: Hutchinson, 1980.

Haskell, Molly. *From Reverence to Rape: The Treatment of Women in the Movies*. New York: Holt, Rinehart and Winston, 1974.

Helford, Elyce Rae. "My Emotions Give Me Power: The Containment of Girls' Anger in *Buffy*." In *Fighting the Forces: What's at Stake in* Buffy the Vampire Slayer, ed. Rhonda V. Wilcox and David Lavery, 18–34. Lanham, Md.: Rowman & Littlefield, 2002.

"Here Comes the Bride, Again." *The Washington Post Express*, June 22, 2004: 19.

Jones, Leslie. "Last Week We Had an Omen: The Mythological X-Files." In *Deny All Knowledge: Reading* The X-Files, ed. David Lavery, Angela Hague, and Marla Cartwright, 77–98. Syracuse: Syracuse University Press, 1996.

Juhasz, Alexandra. "The Phallus Unfetishized: The End of Masculinity as We Know It in Late-1990s 'Feminist' Cinema." In *The End of Cinema as We Know It: American Film in the Nineties*, ed. Jon Lewis, 210–21. New York: New York University Press, 2001.

King, Geoff. *Film Comedy*. London: Wallflower Press, 2002.

——. *New Hollywood Cinema: An Introduction*. New York: Columbia University Press, 2002.

Klein, Christina. "The Hollowing-Out of Hollywood: 'Runaway Productions' Boost Profits but Also Take Jobs Abroad." *YaleGlobal*, April 30, 2004. Available at www.yaleglobal.yale.edu.

Krimmer, Elisabeth. "Nobody Wants to Be a Man Anymore? Cross-Dressing in American Movies of the 90s." In *Subverting Masculinity: Hegemony and Alternative Versions of Masculinity in Contemporary Culture*, ed. Russell West and Frank Lay, 29–53. Amsterdam: Rodopi, 2001.

Krimmer, Elisabeth, and Shilpa Raval. "Digging the Undead: Death and Desire in *Buffy*." In *Fighting the Forces: What's at Stake in* Buffy the Vampire Slayer, ed. Rhonda V. Wilcox and David Lavery, 153–64. Lanham, Md.: Rowman & Littlefield, 2002.

Kubek, Elizabeth. "You Only Expose Your Father: The Imaginary, Voyeurism, and the Symbolic Order in *The X-Files*." In *Deny All Knowledge: Reading* The X-Files, ed. David Lavery, Angela Hague, and Marla Cartwright, 168–204. Syracuse: Syracuse University Press, 1996.

Lane, Anthony. *Nobody's Perfect: Writings from the* New Yorker. New York: Alfred A. Knopf, 2002.

Lane, Christina. *Feminist Hollywood: From* Born in Flames *to* Point Break. Detroit: Wayne State University Press, 2000.

———. "The Strange Days of Kathryn Bigelow and James Cameron." In *The Cinema of Kathryn Bigelow: Hollywood Transgressor*, ed. Deborah Jermyn and Sean Redmond, 178–97. London: Wallflower Press, 2003.

Lasalle, Mick. *Complicated Women: Sex and Power in Pre-Code Hollywood*. New York: St. Martin's Press, 2000.

Lavery, David, Angela Hague, and Marla Cartwright. "Introduction: Generation X—*The X-Files* and the Cultural Moment." In *Deny All Knowledge: Reading* The X-Files, ed. David Lavery, Angela Hague, and Marla Cartwright, 1–21. Syracuse: Syracuse University Press, 1996.

Lavery, David, Angela Hague, and Marla Cartwright, eds. *Deny All Knowledge: Reading* The X-Files. Syracuse: Syracuse University Press, 1996.

Lawrence, Amy. *Echo and Narcissus: Women's Voices in Classical Hollywood Cinema*. Berkeley: University of California Press, 1991.

Lewis, Jon. "The End of Cinema as We Know It and I Feel. . . : An Introduction to a Book on Nineties American Film." In *The End of Cinema as We Know It: American Film in the Nineties*, ed. Jon Lewis, 1–8. New York: New York University Press, 2001.

Lewis, Jon, ed. *The End of Cinema as We Know It: American Film in the Nineties*. New York: New York University Press, 2001.

Livingstone, Sonia. *Making Sense of Television: The Psychology of Audience Interpretation*. London: Routledge, 1990.

Malach, Michele. "I Want to Believe . . . in the FBI: The Special Agent and *The X Files*." In *Deny All Knowledge: Reading* The X-Files, ed. David Lavery, Angela Hague, and Marla Cartwright, 63–76. Syracuse: Syracuse University Press, 1996.

McLellan, Diana. *The Girls: Sappho Goes to Hollywood*. New York: St. Martin's Press, 2000.

McQuail, Denis, J. Blumler, and R. Brown. "The Television Audience: A Revised Perspective." In *The Sociology of Mass Communications*, ed. Denis McQuail, 135–65. Harmondsworth, England: Penguin, 1972.

Mellencamp, Pat. "The Zen of Masculinity—Rituals of Heroism in *The Matrix*." In *The End of Cinema as We Know It: American Film in the Nineties*, ed. Jon Lewis, 83–94. New York: New York University Press, 2001.

Money, Mary Alice. "The Undemonization of Supporting Characters in *Buffy*." In *Fighting the Forces: What's at Stake in* Buffy the Vampire Slayer, ed. Rhonda V. Wilcox and David Lavery, 98–107. Lanham, Md.: Rowman & Littlefield, 2002.

Morley, David. *Family Television: Cultural Power and Domestic Leisure*. London: Comedia, 1986.

Mosher, Jerry. "Having Their Cake and Eating It Too: Fat Acceptance Films and the Production of Meaning." In *The End of Cinema as We Know It: American Film in the Nineties*, ed. Jon Lewis, 237–49. New York: New York University Press, 2001.

Muller, Eddie. *Dark City Dames: The Wicked Women of Film Noir.* New York: Harper-Collins, 2001.

Mulvey, Laura. *Fetishism and Curiosity.* Bloomington: Indiana University Press, 1996.

———. *Visual and Other Pleasures.* Bloomington: Indiana University Press, 1989.

———. "Visual Pleasure and Narrative Cinema." In *Film Theory and Criticism: Introductory Readings*, ed. Leo Braudy and Marshall Cohen, 833–44. Oxford: Oxford University Press, 1999.

Nadel, Alan. *Flatlining on the Field of Dreams: Cultural Narratives in the Films of President Reagan's America.* New Brunswick, N.J.: Rutgers University Press, 1997.

Nochimson, Martha P. *Screen Couple Chemistry: The Power of 2.* Austin: University of Texas Press, 2002.

Parks, Lisa. "Special Agent or Monstrosity? Finding the Feminine in *The X-Files.*" In *Deny All Knowledge: Reading* The X-Files, ed. David Lavery, Angela Hague, and Marla Cartwright, 121–34. Syracuse: Syracuse University Press, 1996.

Pomerance, Murray, ed. *Ladies and Gentlemen, Boys and Girls: Gender in Film at the End of the Twentieth Century.* Albany: State University of New York Press, 2001.

Preston, Catherine L. "Hanging on a Star: The Resurrection of the Romance Film in the 1990s." In *Film Genre 2000: New Critical Essays*, ed. Wheeler Winston Dixon, 227–43. Albany: State University of New York Press, 2000.

Reeves, Jimmie L., Mark C. Rodgers, and Michael Epstein. "Rewriting Popularity: The Cult Files." In *Deny All Knowledge: Reading* The X-Files, ed. David Lavery, Angela Hague, and Marla Cartwright, 22–35. Syracuse: Syracuse University Press, 1996.

Rich, Frank. "Bullies Are Not What Ails Hollywood." *The New York Times* (Late Edition-Final), January 11, 2004: 2-1.

Rowe, Kathleen. *The Unruly Woman: Gender and the Genres of Laughter.* Austin: University of Texas Press, 1995.

Rutsky, R. L. "Being Keanu." In *The End of Cinema as We Know It: American Film in the Nineties*, ed. Jon Lewis, 185–94. New York: New York University Press, 2001.

Sanjek, David. "Same as It Ever Was: Innovation and Exhaustion in the Horror and Science Fiction Films of the 1990s." In *Film Genre 2000: New Critical Essays*, ed. Wheeler Winston Dixon, 111–23. Albany: State University of New York Press, 2000.

Shaviro, Steven. "Straight from the Cerebral Cortex: Vision and Affect in *Strange Days.*" In *The Cinema of Kathryn Bigelow: Hollywood Transgressor*, ed. Deborah Jermyn and Sean Redmond, 159–77. London: Wallflower Press, 2003.

Shumway, David R. "Woody Allen, 'the Artist,' and 'the Little Girl.'" In *The End of Cinema as We Know It: American Film in the Nineties*, ed. Jon Lewis, 195–202. New York: New York University Press, 2001.

Siemann, Catherine. "Darkness Falls on the Endless Summer: Buffy as Gidget for the Fin de Siècle." In *Fighting the Forces: What's at Stake in* Buffy the Vampire Slayer, ed. Rhonda V. Wilcox and David Lavery, 120–29. Lanham, Md.: Rowman & Littlefield, 2002.

Sova, Dawn B. *Women in Hollywood: From Vamp to Studio Head.* New York: Fromm International, 1998.

Stark, Steven D. *Glued to the Set: The 60 Television Shows and Events That Made Us Who We Are Today*. New York: Delta, 1997.

Stepovich, Romi. "*Strange Days*: A Case History of Production and Distribution Practices in Hollywood." In *The Cinema of Kathryn Bigelow: Hollywood Transgressor*, ed. Deborah Jermyn and Sean Redmond, 144–58. London: Wallflower Press, 2003.

Strick, Philip. *Great Movie Actresses*. New York: Beech Tree Books/William Morrow 1985.

Stuart, Andrea. "The Outsider: Whoopi Goldberg and Shopping Mall America." In *Women and Film: A Sight and Sound Reader*, ed. Pam Cook and Philip Dodd, 62–67. Philadelphia: Temple University Press, 1993.

Sturken, Marita. "*Affliction*: When Paranoid Male Narratives Fail." In *The End of Cinema as We Know It: American Film in the Nineties*, ed. Jon Lewis, 203–9. New York: New York University Press, 2001.

Tasker, Yvonne. *Spectacular Bodies: Gender, Genre and the Action Cinema*. London: Routledge, 1993.

———. *Working Girls: Gender and Sexuality in Popular Cinema*. London: Routledge, 1998.

Tibbetts, John C. "So Much Is Lost in Translation: Literary Adaptations in the 1990s." In *Film Genre 2000: New Critical Essays*, ed. Wheeler Winston Dixon, 29–44. Albany: State University of New York Press, 2000.

Tomasulo, Frank P. "Empire of the Gun: Steven Spielberg's *Saving Private Ryan* and American Chauvinism." In *The End of Cinema as We Know It: American Film in the Nineties*, ed. Jon Lewis, 115–30. New York: New York University Press, 2001.

Wanamaker, Marc. "Afterword." In *Reel Women: Pioneers of the Cinema, 1896 to the Present*, Ally Acker, 335–36. New York: Continuum, 1991.

Wayne, Jane Ellen. *The Golden Girls of MGM: Greta Garbo, Joan Crawford, Lana Turner, Judy Garland, Ava Gardner, Grace Kelly and Others*. New York: Carroll and Graf Publishers, 2002.

Welsh, James M. "Action Films: The Serious, the Ironic, the Postmodern." In *Film Genre 2000: New Critical Essays*, ed. Wheeler Winston Dixon, 161–76. Albany: State University of New York Press, 2000.

Wilcox, Rhonda V. "Who Died and Made Her the Boss: Patterns of Mortality in *Buffy*." In *Fighting the Forces: What's at Stake in* Buffy the Vampire Slayer, ed. Rhonda V. Wilcox and David Lavery, 3–17. Lanham, Md.: Rowman & Littlefield, 2002.

Wilcox, Rhonda V., and David Lavery. "Introduction." In *Fighting the Forces: What's at Stake in* Buffy the Vampire Slayer, ed. Rhonda V. Wilcox and David Lavery, xvii–xxix. Lanham, Md.: Rowman & Littlefield, 2002.

Wilcox, Rhonda V., and David Lavery, eds. *Fighting the Forces: What's at Stake in* Buffy the Vampire Slayer. Lanham, Md.: Rowman & Littlefield, 2002.

Wilcox, Rhonda, and J. P. Williams. "What Do You Think: *The X-Files*, Liminality and Gender Pleasure." In *Deny All Knowledge: Reading* The X-Files, ed. David Lavery, Angela Hague, and Marla Cartwright, 99–120. Syracuse: Syracuse University Press, 1996.

Williams, Raymond. *Television: Technology and Cultural Form*. London: Fontana, 1974.

Wilson, Ron. "The Left-Handed Form of Human Endeavor: Crime Films during the 1990s." In *Film Genre 2000: New Critical Essays*, ed. Wheeler Winston Dixon, 143–59. Albany: State University of New York Press, 2000.

Wollstein, Hans J. *Vixens, Floozies and Molls: 28 Actresses of Late 1920s and 1930s Hollywood*. Jefferson, N.C.: MacFarland and Co., 1999.

Wood, Robin. *Hollywood from Vietnam to Reagan . . . and Beyond*. New York: Columbia University Press, 2003.

Young, Elizabeth. "Bods and Monsters: The Return of the Bride of Frankenstein." In *The End of Cinema as We Know It: American Film in the Nineties*, ed. Jon Lewis, 225–36. New York: New York University Press, 2001.

Young, Kay. *Ordinary Pleasures: Couples, Conversations, and Comedy*. Columbus: Ohio State University Press, 2001.

Index

About the Authors

Susanne Kord is a professor at the University College London. She has published extensively on women's cultural history and performance studies and is the author of many literary translations, some of which have been performed. Her translation of Elsa Bernstein's *Maria Arndt* saw a six-week run to sold-out houses at the Steppenwolf Theater in Chicago, February–March 2002.

Elisabeth Krimmer is an assistant professor at the University of California, Davis. She has published a book on cross-dressing and numerous articles on literature and film. Her works include analyses of gender in Hollywood movies of the 1990s and *Buffy the Vampire Slayer*.

Both authors are recovering Hollywood addicts.